The Strategy of Truth

THE STORY OF THE U. S. INFORMATION SERVICE

By Wilson P. Dizard

PUBLIC AFFAIRS PRESS, WASHINGTON, D. C.

FOR MY FATHER AND MOTHER

419 New Jersey Avenue, S.E., Washington 3, D. C.

Printed in the United States of America
Library of Congress Catalog Card No. 61-84-41

FOREWORD

For a nation whose founding statesmen affirmed the importance of public opinion in their very Declaration of Independence, a nation which always has been inordinately sensitive to the good opinion of others, the United States has been singularly irresponsible in its international information programs.

Only in the last three or four years, since the United States Information Agency took the stable and mature form it now enjoys, has anything resembling an adequate official voice been in existence. During the two world wars, ad hoc agencies coped as best they could with complex problems of world opinion. When the present cold war was declared, say in 1947, it took a year for Congress to see the need for an official information program, and a decade for that program to reach reasonable competence.

Meantime, and to this hour, Americans have tended to expect far too much from their propaganda. Conscious as they were of their own virtue, they thought all that was necessary to persuade others was a selling campaign. Over and over again, the presumed skills and strengths of Madison Avenue were proclaimed, and it was asked —with pathetic vanity—why these private magics were not used to produce public persuasion throughout the world. When the winds of confusion and demagoguery blew, as during the McCarthy period, the information program was a prime target for attack.

Ultimately it came to be seen that, as George V. Allen, the U.S.I.A.'s most succesful director to date put it, our "Ninety percent of the impression which the United States makes abroad depends on our policies and . . . not more than ten percent . . . is how we explain it . . . We can work our hearts out for years building up goodwill for the United States in a given country when suddenly one little policy action is taken which does more to destroy our position than the USIA can rebuild in a very long time." Mr. Allen might have added that some quite unofficial action from a private source, an irresponsible legislator, a business or intellectual leader, may also suddenly make a greater impact for good or ill than months of conscious propaganda. And as Edward R. Murrow, the Agency's latest and most noted Director, said before the Senate Foreign Relations Committee: "In the end of the day it may well be that the example of this nation will be more important than its dollars or its words."

Mr. Dizard presents in this book an extremely competent history and survey of the information program since 1948. He writes from the perspective of an employee of the Agency, which gives him a good deal of insight but inhibits the kind of sharp criticism which would also be beneficial. On the whole, however, his study is remarkably objective, even if it does not look closely at the rough spots which have existed down through the years. He gives an excellent picture of the instrument which can now be used by the Kennedy Administration.

It would seem, therefore, that with this relatively efficient tool at hand, and the extraordinary policy dynamism of the Administration, that the image of America in the eyes of the world ought to be clearer and more impelling than it has been for many years. The executive branch of government is bristling with men of ideas. Unless they get in one another's way, they should produce a fertile flow of policies and prospects for the USIA to publicize. Ed Murrow himself is perhaps the nation's leading professional communicator on the global scale. The President has already established, during the campaign and in his early months in office, the spirit of youth, vigor, change, imagination, and shrewd, hard-hitting, well-informed political action. With him in the White House itself are some of the nation's brightest intellectuals with world experience: the Bundys, Rostows, and Schlesingers, while to missons overseas have gone men like Professors Galbraith and Reischauer, and that formidable formulator, Adlai Stevenson, holds the fort at the U.N.

In short, the policy-makers are more vigorous and inventive than ever before, and more conscious of the importance of public opinion. They will by no means please everyone, as G. Mennen Williams learned in Africa. The American image is not very glowing in Portugal. There will be plenty of other places where policies will rub convictions the wrong way. Nevertheless, candor and honesty will in the end be better than a transparent effort to be all things to all men.

Thus, as a hopeful new period in American world relations begins, it is most appropriate that a careful study of the governmental means of informing the world should appear. It would be equally useful if a comparable study of the various private ways by which Americans hold up an image to the world could be analyzed. For the private voice is not second to the public.

It is quite clear that an official information program will be required for as far as we can see into the future. "No man," testified

Mr. Murrow, "can set either a time or dollar limit upon this contest between the forces of freedom and those who would demean and brutalize mankind . . . We live in a world we didn't make. We are honored by an awesome responsibility of leadership we did not seek . . . Our task is formidable and difficult but difficulty is one excuse history has never accepted."

Such words have given heart-warming encouragement to the men and women who have operated the information program through thick and thin. They were praised by the Senators to whom they were addressed. They epitomize the task of communcating the meaning of America and its policies to a world in which the role of the great power is usually thankless and often misunderstood. But it is a world in which the war will surely at last be won in the minds of men.

ERWIN D. CANHAM

Editor, *The Christian Science Montor*

PREFACE

Never was it more important for our national interests that the rest of the world have a clear idea of America and Americans. What we are and what we stand for must be unequivocally understood if we are to meet the challenges of our time.

Even if there were no threat of Communist imperialism, we would need to state our case before the world. Every great civilization has appealed beyond its own borders for support of what it considers to be a new order of ideas and ideals. This is our hour to do so. One of the premises of our society is the desirability of extending to all mankind the benefits of our own social and political revolution. This concept was implicit in the ideas of the men who founded the Republic; our national purpose cannot be fully served until it is fulfilled. As Woodrow Wilson once said: "There have been other nations as rich as we; there have been other nations as powerful; there have been other nations as spirited; but I hope we shall never forget that we created this nation not to serve ourselves but to serve mankind. No other nation was ever born into the world with the purpose of serving the rest of the world just as much as it served itself."

This is the most compelling reason why we need a strategy of truth to strengthen the faith of peoples everywhere in America as a vigorous democratic society whose aspirations and actions include their own interests. In 1961 we are carrying out this strategy under the leadership of a new President who has stressed the urgency of presenting a clear image of America to a world that is now swept up in what he has called "the revolution of hope".

There are powerful counterappeals to the American message. One third of the human race under Soviet and Chinese Communist control is being told, day in and out, that the United States is the enemy which must be destroyed. A massive Red campaign of military, political, economic and psychological pressures is assaulting the free world with the slogan that the future belongs to Communism. We need not look any further than Cuba, ninety miles from our own shores, to see the consequences and implications of this Communist campaign.

This book describes how the American story is being told to the world. Despite the growing importance of the subject, there is surprisingly little material readily available on the nature and extent of our overseas strategy of truth. What does exist is in bits and pieces. A definitive study of America's impact on the rest of the world cannot, of course, be written for many years. All that can be written now is an interim report, outlining what has been done in the past and what is presently being done.

My purpose has been to tell the story of our overseas information efforts, both government and private, so that my fellow citizens may judge whether or not we as a nation are adequately fulfilling our duty in this field. The decision is left to the reader; here he will find most of the facts for his judgment. For those who want to pursue the subject further, I have appended a bibliography on public opinion and information activities.

The book is my personal work and does not necessarily represent the official policies of the United States Information Service. Nevertheless, I wish gratefully to acknowledge the generous cooperation I received in preparing the work from my colleagues in Washington and overseas.

Particular mention must go to four very special colleagues—my wife, Lynn, and to Jack, Steve and Bill Dizard, three young men who graciously observed "quiet hours" in our home while the book was in preparation.

WILSON P. DIZARD

American Consulate-General
Dacca, East Pakistan

CONTENTS

1

THE BATTLE FOR WORLD OPINION

Hardly a day goes by without an event reflecting misunderstanding of or unfriendliness toward the United States and its policies. The unpleasant signs of anti-Americanism that seem to recur with such regularity are particularly dismaying for us, a people who have raised back-slapping brotherhood to a national virtue. Our tendency to look upon our reputation in terms of a global popularity contest is peculiarly American; it is also more than a little naive.

Whether we are first, second or seventeenth in such a contest is considerably less important than whether we can count on the friendship and support of the free world in the coming years. Such friendship and support has been important in the past; it is imperative today.

The 1960's are the years of the cold war showdown. The Russians and the Chinese Communists are no longer middleweight upstarts trying to punch their way to recognition; they are heavyweights looking for a final decision. Linked with their new strength is a growing conviction that they are winning the psychological offensive in their battle to defeat us. It is not without significance that the wrecking of the 1960 summit meeting by Premier Khrushchev's dramatic walkout was followed by a step-up in the Communists' cold war offensive, from missile threats to propaganda broadcasts.

Their ideological differences patched up at least temporarily, the Soviet and Chinese Reds are today meshing their operations for a climactic phase of their struggle against the free world. They are determined to win in the 1960's. Accordingly they are mounting a massive campaign of psychological pressure on world opinion aimed at convincing it that the era of American ascendancy has been displaced by the new age of Communism.

The Communist campaign is being waged on a broad front, from lunik space satellites to the glad-handing tours of Red potentates throughout the globe. It has scored some notable successes. While it has also suffered some failures and near-misses, they offer us only wry comfort. The successes have been such that the Soviet Union—and, increasingly, Red China—can now project itself as a world power that has already overtaken the United States in some fields and is rapidly closing the gap in others. The Communist claims are sung raucously to the song of "peaceful co-existence", a powerful theme in a world anxious to move beyond political tensions to the more immediate problems of economic and social development. So powerful is this theme that one day it may be written that the free world destroyed itself because of the myth of a peaceful expanding Communism and a second-rate, unconcerned America.

In the battle for world opinion we face an audience whose image of America is confused and uncertain. On one side it seems that our influence is dwindling while our policies are being undermined and misunderstood. On the other hand, we have the impressive fact of a world that has a genuine desire to know America—what it is like, how it works, and how it affects other people.

The French intellectuals may complain about the *Coca-Colization* of their culture and Oxford University dons may agree, as they did recently, to the proposition that Columbus should never have discovered America, but they are in the beleaguered minority.

No other culture has ever succeeded quite so well or so quickly in making a global impact as has the United States in the middle decades of the twentieth century. The political revolution that has resulted in independence for thirty-five nations since 1945 is based more directly on our ideas and techniques than on those of any other country. In the economic field we have set the pattern for the postwar upsurge in production and trade throughout the free world. Beginning with the Marshall Plan in Europe, our economic aid programs have laid the groundwork for far-reaching development. The many and varied benefits of our expanding private business activity overseas have nurtured the grass roots of the free world economy. From Kobe to Cologne, American techniques and methods constitute standards to emulate in almost every field of endeavor.

Despite the propaganda success of sputniks and other Soviet scientific achievements, we are still regarded as the primary source of technological advances. There are no machines better known or respected than jeeps, Singer sewing machines and California-built jets. Outside the Communist bloc, the dollar bill is the world's universal currency for all practical purposes. Everywhere English is studied, read and spoken largely because it is the language of Americans. In the broad field of culture we are upsetting old rules and hoary traditions more than ever. In the more traditional arts the experimentation that characterizes our cultural life is having a powerful influence.

Even in Russia our influence remains a dominant factor. No other country on earth pays closer attention to American technological progress. Says Nikita Khrushchev for quotation: "We want to be as rich and as powerful as you." Daily his countrymen uninhibitedly make carbon-copy versions of our ideas, methods and devices, from machine tools to the Red-styled version of Disneyland being built in Moscow. It may be Americanization with a vengeance but it is there and it works.

There is so much that is comforting to our national ego in the pattern of follow-the-Americans that it comes as a rude shock when we encounter some of its concrete limitations as reflected by resistance to our policies abroad and in the disquieting results of public opinion surveys. Although overseas surveys present a varied pattern of foreign attitudes towards us, their findings are consistent on the main points. They show a friendly image of America and Americans in general but they reveal sharply varying attitudes toward certain of our policies and practices. America and Americans are generous, friendly, dynamic, youthful—but . . .

Is the United States doing all it can to prevent a new world war? Forty-eight percent of Britons polled on this question answered yes, but only one-third of the Norwegians and 16% of the French agreed. In another recent poll our ability to outstrip the Communists in peaceful competition has been seriously questioned. Only 37% of the West Germans, 28% of the Italians and 9% of the Frenchmen polled thought we could surpass Russia. These are the opinions of allies, part of the NATO alliance which constitutes the strongest strategic commitment we have overseas. In neutralist African and Asian nations, skepticism about American motives and abilities is often more acute. In a study of Indian attitudes several years ago most of the Indians polled labelled Americans as "powerful" or "masters and rulers". None checked off "peace loving".

Such political misunderstandings are matched by doubts about our economic and social system. For most Americans capitalism is attractive because it provides a larger share of material goods for everyone; to European or Asian city dwellers, it may appear a system for exploiting the poor to make the rich richer. A steady drumbeat of criticism pounds out against a wide range of American life—the treatment of Negroes, our moral standards, the apparent commercialization of cultural values, the whole confused and contradictory image of a country that is powerful, immature, uncertain and even hypocritical. It provides bitter logic to the story told by a Frenchman to a *Newsweek* correspondent about a visiting Parisian who tried to locate the American concentration camps in which, he had been told, "intellectuals and militant workers" were incarcerated.

These misunderstandings come from general ignorance of even the simplest facts about the United States. It is probably true that half the world's population has never heard of the United States or knows it only as the name of a large foreign country. To use Dr. Gallup's familiar polling cliché, the "Don't Knows" still outnumber those who have any clear concept of us. For most people overseas, particularly outside of Europe, America is beyond comprehension. Their concerns are bounded geographically by their village and perhaps a nearby market town, socially by their family and clan, and imaginatively by folk patterns, by gods and goddesses, and by heavens and hells that make our own traditions seem pale by contrast.

For most people time and thought are circumscribed by the necessity to grow or earn their own food or die. Life is that direct and simple. The idea that a foreign country called the United States—or the Soviet Union — has anything to do with their interests doesn't occur to them. Little by little, fortunately, the barriers to such ignorance are being broken down every day. The first radio in a village often means a jolting leap from the fifth to the twentieth centuries. Pretty much the same is true of newspapers, magazines and films. The United States and other "foreign" ideas become known and even familiar. The familiarity is often superficial, emasculated by existing patterns of thought. Under Red rule millions of Chinese are learning about the United States but they learn to know us simply as the enemy. In other countries the image of America is more friendly but it is often vague and erroneous.

Only a few years ago we could—and did—conduct our affairs as if popular impressions about us did not really matter. Today we are aware that overseas public opinion is a key factor in our survival. The Communist challenge of the 1960's has given us a sobering new respect for its importance. "The most enduring influence affecting American foreign policy," says the London *Economist* in a look at the next decade, "is a profound lack of confidence in the staying power of Western public opinion when exposed to a sophisticated challenge from its potential foe." This view is somewhat exaggerated but it correctly identifies the essential need we feel for world acceptance of our policies.

We are the first world power to have a primary regard for the opinions of others in terms of our survival and theirs. Julius Caesar could set up bases in Britain with little consideration of what vociferous anti-base Britons thought at the time. Today the anti-missile base descendants of Caesar's opposition are an important consideration of ours in maintaining the bases we operate jointly with the British in their country. William Pitt literally bought the support of European monarchs during the Napoleonic wars with only a passing thought as to whether they or their subjects were pro-British. In Pitt's hard-headed view he was buying the use of territory and troops, not coffee-house opinion.

We deny ourselves the luxury of ignoring the opinions of others. Our world-wide system of alliances and bases depends directly on what other people think about us. Increasingly our foreign policy takes overseas attitudes into account; more and more it undergoes litmus tests for the sake of detecting psychological effects abroad. Even where a policy is adopted with the knowledge that opinion may be against us—the uproar over the famous U-2 "spy plane" incident in 1960 is a good example—our primary effort is to persuade world opinion to approve or, at least, accept what we are doing.

Our strategic military power rests, as it has since 1945, on the superiority of our capacity for retaliatory nuclear destruction as compared to the power of the Soviet Union. The practical significance of nuclear power is being profoundly modified, however, by the course of world events. The reconstruction of Europe and the resurgence of Asia, Africa and Latin America have created an unorganized, non-nuclear third force whose most potent weapon is its popular opinion. While this third force does not have a veto on the nuclear intentions of the two super-powers, it has a significant voting strength in the United Nations and other key forums. Faced with a stalemate of an undeclared nuclear armistice, American and Soviet policies are increasingly concerned with winning the loyalties of the decisive third force. If we lose out it will be because of our fatal miscalculation of what is happening in the world today and our relationship to it.

The focal event of our age is the three-layered revolution—political, economic and social—that is sweeping the earth. In the past, revolution occurred in specific places separated by long periods of time.

Today's revolution is a universal one. As Janet Flanner says, it is "a new strong wind blowing for all men of different colors on different parts of the globe . . . with a steady unending velocity unlike the limited cyclonic gust which brought about the libertarian French Revolution." A billion and a half people in underdeveloped countries want their political revolution, industrial revolution and social revolution all at once. They are exerting their energies to catch up in a few years with everything the west has achieved in five centuries. The political revolution is virtually accomplished: more than thirty-five nations have gained independence since World War II. The industrial revolution is well under way and the social revolution is just beginning.

The effect on all the peoples involved is as explosive as if a pressurized cabin had split open. They are judging us almost exclusively by the part we take in their advance. They are measuring the Russians in the same way—and here our traditions are serving us in good stead.

The free world's revolution is grounded solidly in the American experience. More than any other people, we have laid its foundations, defined its standards, given it political support and material assistance. Moreover, we are in a sense the ideological propagandists of all time, telling everybody that freedom, prosperity and social equality are attainable realities for one and all. We have not been shy about pointing to our own national experience in this connection. Having conducted the world's oldest experiment in political and social freedom, we have an instinctive feel for the new surge toward freedom in the rest of the free world. By contrast, Communism is the counter-revolution, scavenging on the still-powerful remnants of old ideas and tyrannies in an effort to gain the strength to impose its imperialist will.

Theoretically we should be winning the struggle for world opinion hands down. The unpleasant fact is that we are not. Our frustration over this situation leaves us confused and irritated. It also adds fuel to the low fires of the isolationists who still roam the land, preaching retreat to an air-conditioned Fortress America. For the present their arguments have few takers. But nagging questions posed by our allies remain. Why is it that what is so obvious to us is so little apparent to them? Why is misinformation so resistant to information?

In the *Brothers Karamazov,* Dostoevski offered what might be a reason for our troubles: "If the people around you are spiteful and callous, and will not hear you, fall down before them and beg their forgiveness; for in truth you are to blame for their not wanting to hear you". Americans are not inclined to accept such self-despair and abnegation. Over and above our own human inadequacies, we insist that there must be some other explanations for our difficulties in the battle for world opinion.

The simplest and most limiting difficulty is that in our attempts to persuade the rest of the world we are dealing with minds distinctly different from ours—minds based on different social, political, and cultural experiences.

In writing of the tensions between the Irish and the British during the nineteenth century, historian G. M. Young points out that the greatest failing of his fellow-Englishmen was in not recognizing that time and circumstance had created an Irish mind: "What we would never remember, Ireland could never forget". The result was eventual political failure for the British—not so much because of their policies as because of their sheer cultural obtuseness. The British record in raising living standards in Ireland during the latter days of their occupation was generally commendable. In their Empire way they were doing what they thought was right; but in doing it they were setting themselves against what the Irish themselves, rightly or wrongly, thought was important. The neat agricultural schemes of the British were taken for mere tricks to deflect Irishmen from their true destiny.

The British relationship with the Irish generally had the rough virtue of being direct. It was that of colonizer and the colonized. Our dealings with foreign countries are not so simple. They are as bewildering and complex as any ever faced by any nation. We have diplomatic relations with 95 countries, mutual-defense alliances with 40 and economic assistance agreements with 60. Some of these continually enlarging relations are as old as the republic; others are as new and as politically fragile as our ties with the 13 African states created in 1960. We deal with countries run by Communists, emperors, generals, self-styled descendants of God, by men who consult with astrologers before they speak to our ambassadors and by others who consult with the House of Commons. We deal not with a single foreign mind but with hundreds of separate national minds. Their minds—*what they think*—matters to us profoundly. No concern of theirs seems too small or remote to be completely beyond our interest; no disaster or success occurs that does not have some relevance to our policies.

Inevitably, we fall somewhat short of the serenity that we tend to expect of ourselves. Like the Victorian English with their Irish problem, we sometimes fail to remember that which other people never forget. We, too, are hurt when we find ourselves treated with hostility by those we befriend.

How does the foreign image of the United States differ from our own image of our nation? Are we the new Athens? The new Rome or the new Carthage? Or are we a new breed of world leader, not to be measured by old gauges? The response to these questions varies around the globe.

In the west, where economic and cultural standards approximate our own, we are accepted as part of the consensus. Our differences are primarily those of interpreting our common interests. Since 1945 U.S. foreign policy has been most successful in Europe and Latin America in developing a mutually-agreeable standard of political, economic and military interests. Even in the cultural field, where Europeans and Latin Americans have judged us most severely in the past, the breach is narrowing. Seventy years ago Oscar Wilde expressed the feelings of generations of European intellectuals when he said: "America is one long expectoration". But recently the august London *Times Literary Supplement* could summarize the European appreciation for American civilization in another way:

"We in Europe take the vitality of the arts in America so much for granted that we seldom pause to assess it for the remarkable phenomenon it is. . . . It is possible to defend the argument that it is more important to design a society than to plan and execute a work of art; for the past century the Americans have been so busy building their own society to meet their own needs that they might excusably have neglected the arts for the practical sciences. What is impressive is that they have found time for both. If neither a Bach nor a Michelangelo has as yet appeared in Detroit, a splendid mass of evidence has been assembled to point the way".

European and Latin American public opinion can be sharply critical of American policy at times but it is a debate conducted in the framework of a shared heritage. The west, however, comprises less than 40% of the free world's population. We need the west's support but it is in the new nations of Asia and Africa that we meet the greatest challenge to our strategic interests. Here the image of America is newest, strangest and ever-increasingly important. Suddenly and totally we have found ourselves involved in the outcome of a series of revolutions whose success or failure will determine our own survival. We are learning the hard new facts about areas that most of us dismissed until a few years ago as the primary concern of the British, the 'natives' and the roving editors of the *National Geographic.* We have become involved hurriedly and reluctantly, often with little comprehension of our long-range commitment in these areas.

One of our errors has been to underestimate the psychological impact of our new presence in Asia and Africa. For years we accepted the idea of "stomach Communism" as the key to Asian and African difficulties. Put three square meals a day into Asian and African bodies, so the argument went, and all would be well. The Communists and the other trouble-makers would be routed and progress would abound. The economic revolution in Asia and Africa is still limited in scope but it has moved far enough to disprove this theory. In the new ground rules of economic development in poorer areas, complexities begin when starvation has ceased to be a day-to-day obsession and is replaced by expanded thoughts of a materially and socially richer life. The effect of raising per capita annual income from $110 to $150 in an Asian country is primarily psychological. It leads only to a question of "when does the next $40 increase happen". The "revolution of expectations" suddenly becomes the focus of attention as the tempo increases. A generation ago the family breadwinner in Asia and Africa saw little hope of raising his living standards or those of his children. Ten years ago he began to see some hope of his children raising their standards. Today he has hopes of raising his own standard of living before he dies.

This acceleration of expectations paces the lives of the people of Asia, Africa and Latin America today. They are beginning to make a forced march from their own dark ages to the twentieth century. In the sociologist's phrase they are the transitionals, a group in motion from a feudal pattern to an ill-defined modernism, whose main problem is the psychological need to adjust comforting old traditions to driving new pressures. There are countless personal tragedies as people lose their old moorings and are unable to find new ones in the confused strange world of imported western values and techniques.

How much change of habit and thought will be necessary before they can adjust themselves to the personal requirements of their new expectations is a matter of debate but change there will be. The Nigerians can learn to make watches without yodeling like the Swiss, but they cannot do it without showing a more Swiss-like respect for the fractions of a second. Precision and the other ingrained habits of modern industrial society are not European or American monopolies but they have been consistently undervalued by Asians and Africans in their race to catch up with us.

Too often the outward appearance of westernization is accepted by us as the reality. The most common characteristic of the east is the facade of the west, whether its form is Japanese beatniks, Burmese jazz bands, Egyptian airline hostesses or the thousands of new factories which are carbon copies of those in Philadelphia and Milan. As Arthur Koestler has noted: "The motorbus which carries the traveller at 5 a.m. from Bangkok airport to the center of the capital of Thailand has a loudspeaker through which American crooners purr at him, and makes him wonder whether his journey was really necessary. The Arabian desert is ploughed by Cadillacs, and the exhibition of Eskimo handicrafts at the airport of Anchorage, Alaska, bears the same hallmark of the Late Woolworth Period as the idols of Krishna, made of plastic, which are worshipped in Indian homes." There is nothing inherently western about an oil refinery in Cairo or a Willys jeep in Madras except its physical construction. They are imported items which do not bring with them attributes of technological efficiency, political liberty or social responsibility as we understand them. They can be operated by people who believe in transmigration, Communism, clan law or ritual murder as readily as by those who believe in parliamentary democracy and dental hygiene.

What does this superficial acceptance of western products and techniques mean to us ? It means that instead of symbolizing the adaptation of western concepts to eastern needs, the facade of westernization often masks a deep-rooted resistance to our ways. This masquerade is perhaps the most frustrating phenomenon preventing us from reaching the Asian mind. It is unwittingly led by an emancipated elite who accept the convenience of modern technology and science but feel no affinity for other forms of western influence. Their attitude is only imperfectly described by such phrases as anti-western, neutralist or nationalistic. Rather they reflect a psychological maladjustment that operates somewhere in their collective unconscious. Many Asian and African intellectuals have had the personal stamina and intelligence to work out a satisfactory relationship between their own rich cultures and the new impact of the west, but a great many have not. They have instead tried to solve their problems by retreating to never-never lands of ancient glories, building up in their imagination Asian versions of reconstructed Williamsburgs and local imitations of the Daughters of the American Revolution. Their precepts very often take the form of extreme racialism with its opportunities to attack the west on this sensitive score. For others there is a return to strict forms of religion or puritanical standards of conduct.

Inevitably such solutions by escape or retreat prove unsatisfactory. They lead to a neurotic personal outlook that is translated into the patterns of alternating passivity and violent political actions which form so much a part of the day-to-day reality of Asia and Africa. More than any other single element, this instability threatens to undermine our attempts to bridge the political and economic gap between ourselves and the new leadership of Asia and Africa or even to communicate effectively with them.

Here we find ourselves face-to-face with a direct Communist challenge. The Reds face the same problem in trying to reach the Asian mind as we do, and they are giving it the same serious attention we are, perhaps even more. The headlines blazon their attempts to make political and economic beachheads in the area; but these efforts are only incidental to the overall psychological pressure the Communists are building up throughout Africa and Asia. Their targets are not the workers and peasants of Marxist mythology but rather the new managerial and intellectual elite. In addressing this target group they subdue the abstractions of Marxism and present instead a picture of Soviet society that is soothingly attractive.

In his deeply-informed book, *Communism and Nationalism in the Middle East,* Walter Lacquer describes the effect of this approach on the new Asian elite: "The turn of events has shown them that in the Soviet world the technical intelligentsia is one of the privileged classes and that its privileges are likely to continue, if not actually increase, in the future". For the Asian technician and intellectual the Russians offer a potent appeal, holding out to them the tantalizing prospect of economic prosperity with specific guarantees of personal power for themselves."

Our own offers of advice and aid sometimes appear impersonal and vapid by comparison. We do not make big promises nor do we guarantee immediate personal gain. We say that economic and social development are tough, complex jobs. The Communists say they are easy. We tend to talk about the long road ahead; the Communists talk about short-cuts. Their appeal is immediate, with an eye to current propaganda value rather than delayed benefits or long-range advantage. The Communist approach may be shot full of hypocrisy but it is an implacable challenge for us in the current struggle to determine whether the new nations of the east accept longterm partnership with the west or whether they lapse into a pattern of dictatorship and local imperialisms followed by annexation to the Soviet or Chinese Communist blocs.

In this conflict for loyalties, we are inclined to look for a day of decision. We visualize some abstraction labelled "Free World Opinion" marching to the polls to cast a vote for the Americans or the Russians after carefully weighing the two candidates. The truth is that the decision is being made every day. Unfortunately for our love of a fair-and-square contest the battle for world opinion is going to be long and frustrating with no half-time, no decisive scores and no trophies. Outside of Europe and Latin America there is no rush to choose sides between the Communist bloc and ourselves, even among nations who are fully aware that their continued sovereignty depends upon our protection.

The decision will unfold slowly and unevenly. It will be determined by the opinions of hundreds of millions of individuals as to whether our leadership in the 1960's coincides with their own interests. We are certain that it does, but what is obvious to us is not always apparent to others. In the past we sometimes seemed to state our case in terms of an anti-Communist campaign intended to save ourselves first and everyone else later. At the other extreme we have sometimes appeared in the role of international moralizer, dispensing advice in the language of theology and offering economic aid as conscience money. Although these impressions are false, they have been imprinted upon the minds of many overseas who are otherwise well-informed. Distortions of our intent are, in fact, satisfying to many foreigners whose mythology of America, like all mythologies, stems from what they want to believe rather than what is true. It is their predilection to believe what they want that accounts for the success of the Communists in developing an image of America as a money-grabbing, race-baiting, immature society. Contradictions between this image and the known facts do not bother the Communists or their willing audience.

It is relatively easy to select evidence of almost any trait, good or bad, from American life. Our virtues and faults are dutifully recorded by all the devices of democratic discussion. Never has sin, both public and private, been more carefully documented by the sinners themselves. The most telling criticisms of the United States do not come from the pens of French intellectuals or Moscow propagandists—but from ourselves. There is a ready audience abroad that does not wish or is not prepared to understand the reasons for our self-criticism. Foreigners can titillate over the reports of the late Dr. Alfred Kinsey on American sexual inadequacies with only a passing sense of their own failings in this field. Human nature being what it is, they are not inclined to give the same attention to the latest report on American economic-aid programs or our scientific achievements.

We will always be judged overseas on inadequate and often erroneous information. This is a disadvantage but it is not a fatal one. We cannot expect foreigners to be walking encyclopedias of information about the United States any more than we individually need to know all the details of Japanese foreign policy or German coal production. The ideas we need to get across are essentially simple ones.

Americans are old hands at this sort of thing. We are by nature propagandists with an endowed sense of what to say to get people to act. We laugh at the soap ads and then proceed to buy more soap than any other people on earth. Santa Claus is an obese and hairy old fraud in our book but we support him as an indispensable bit of seasonal propaganda. We were the first nation on earth to declare our independence with a document that appealed for the supporting opinions of a candid world rather than for alliances or economic aid. We have been talking that way ever since. "An American cannot converse," said de Toqueville. "He speaks to you as if he were addressing a meeting". We spend half our lives telling one another, personally or through a vast system of media outlets, to buy this, support that, believe her, forget him and accept them. These appeals are not confined to ourselves. Ideologically we have never paid attention to the twelve-mile limit. We are always shipping our ideas overseas.

Benjamin Franklin goes to Europe to evoke British understanding and French support for the ideas and ideals of his countrymen. Lincoln writes to English factory workers to gain their understanding of our civil war. South American revolutions are planned in Harlem; the Czech republic sees the first light of day in Pittsburgh; missionaries leave New England and teachers leave the Middle West to go abroad to start schools and hospitals that become outpost symbols of America. To the western and Christian tradition of spreading the word we have added new techniques and new dimensions. Above all we have set off a worldwide revolution around the concepts of universal political liberty, economic prosperity and social equality. The Communist counter-revolution will fail eventually because it cannot cope with this force. But we can fail by default first if we do not recognize that our own role is more than acting as a political mediator or providing economic and military aid.

Our destiny is to give a mind and a heart to our age. To fulfill this destiny we must win the loyalties of free men everywhere and, eventually, of all those who would be free. The great moments of our tradition are those when we have acted with dramatic rightness to arouse the conscience of all listening men, free and slave.

What is the image of America abroad today? What are we doing to clarify it? Is what we are doing enough to match our high responsibilities? That is what this book is about.

2

DECIDING WHAT TO SAY

The warning comes up like thunder across the banquet tables and lecterns of America:

We are the most peace-loving nation on earth—but the word is not getting across to the man-in-the-street and the man-in-the-rice-field overseas. They are swallowing the Communist line that we are imperialists and war mongers. It is the greatest fraud in history—and we are its victims. Somehow this must be stopped. If we are to win the cold war and protect our loved ones, we must sell America overseas.

The language is the language of the most sales-minded nation on earth and the anger is real, as real as the frustration that fuels it. Why do we find ourselves constantly checked when the answer lies in putting across a few simple ideas?

Why indeed? The answer is not in any lack of concern for the problem. Commissions, committees, working groups, seminars, conferences and investigations—all the means that Americans use to dredge facts from one another have been turned to the task of examining the problem. Nor does the answer lie in any lack of effort. The entire foreign policy machinery of our government has been overhauled in the past decade to meet the new strategic importance of what others think of us. Increasingly our foreign policy is formulated and presented in terms intended to persuade overseas opinion. An official information service costing $100 million a year explains our policies in over eighty countries around the world. Never before has a democratic people devoted so much effort, nor its legislators appropriated so much money, to tell other peoples about itself.

Yet, all this effort and all this money have not eliminated our doubts about our impact abroad. Our queasiness was reflected to an extreme in the attention given the late Senator Joseph McCarthy of Wisconsin when he attacked the overseas information program in 1953. Less glaringly, it is reflected in the thoughtful criticisms of Walter Lippman and other responsible observers who have questioned the propriety and value of programs designed to persuade overseas opinion. Another reaction is found in the partisans of greater efforts to "sell" America abroad. Although their enthusiasm may be exaggerated, they are testifying to the American faith in the force of an informed public in the decision-making process. If we can rally support in Topeka, why can't we do it in Tokyo? The question poses a number of non-sequiturs and it also ignores many of the factors involved in reaching the foreign mind but it does offer a proposition that merits examination.

It is the proposition that the United States has an overflowing abundance of the know-how and of the skills for merchandising ideas that could sell America to world opinion if applied overseas. The prospect is glittering: the solution of our international problems by getting everyone on our side. The argument is usually presented with a sigh: "If we could only harness one-tenth the effort and imagination to this problem that we give to selling soap, we would have it solved." Why don't we do it? Senator McCarthy's charge was that the government is riddled with Reds and incompetents. The advocates of the hard-sell in our overseas policies blame our diffidence on the lack of imaginative, bold programs for harnessing the new techniques of persuasion to our public-relations problems abroad.

The techniques which they extol are indeed formidable, both in themselves and in their promise. Their practitioners have moved far beyond old ideas of direct persuasion. In the occult new science of "social engineering" persuasion is an antique concept. The new discipline sees the mass mind as capable of being manipulated to believe almost anything the manipulators want by pouring the right stimuli into its collective eyes and ears. If you can condition the mass mind in Topeka, why can't you do it in Tokyo?

The social engineers have scarcely been slowed down by the refusal of the mass mind to behave as predicted; they have scored enough limited successes to convince themselves and an increasing circle of their clientele that their practices have universal and inescapable application. Their vocabulary reveals their methods and aspirations: it is replete with such phrases as psycho-persuasion, motivational research, the engineering of consent, social physics, communications engineering and group psychodynamics. Never mind if the appearance of a motivationally-researched TV commercial is the signal for millions of viewers to get up and go to the kitchen or the bathroom. *We'll sell 'em the next time, Chief.* The new opinion manipulators are, above all, persistent in the face of the imperfect human material with which they have to work. We are assured that the kinks will work themselves out in time. One of the "kinks" that needs to be worked out is the strong anti-democratic and anti-humanist thread that runs through much of the writing and practice of the new social engineers. The danger of our society falling under the spell of the new manipulators is remote but their influence is already strong enough to raise questions about their place in a democratic social order. Their presumption to control the mass mind—whatever that is—is profoundly undemocratic.

Fortunately the social engineers have been too busy at home to consider turning their talents to the problem of influencing the mass mind overseas. They are being preceded in this area by the advocates of what is known as "psychological operations" and "psychological warfare". Drawing upon the theories of the social engineers, the "psywar" advocates call for a master plan of operations designed specifically to impress the rest of the world with American power and determination. What we must do, they argue with athletic vigor, is to take the propaganda ball away from the Communists. They contend that we can gain the initiative for a relatively small cost by using psychological techniques which are more effective than the slower-moving diplomatic, economic and information techniques we now use. In recent years there have been a number of proposals for giving major status to such psychological operations in the American government. One of these, known as the "militant liberty program," was sponsored by the Defense Department. The American Legion has proposed a department devoted to "unconventional propaganda warfare" as a Cabinet-level "psychological command post". There have been a number of suggestions for a "Department of Psychological Warfare" capable of matching Soviet propaganda at all levels.

These proposals are predicated largely on the success of U.S. military commanders in utilizing battlefield psywar techniques in World War II and in the Korean conflict. Tens of thousands of Axis and Communist soldiers were induced to surrender through leaflet and loudspeaker appeals made by psywar units in combat areas. In the latter phases of World War II psywar successfully encouraged defeatist tendencies in hundreds of thousands of enemy soldiers. In other instances psywar had little or no success and in some cases its effect boomeranged. Perhaps the most unfortunate episode in the short history of psywar was the offer made by an American commander in Korea to pay $100,000 to the first Communist pilot who delivered a MIG jet plane intact to United Nations forces. To his offer was added the gratuitous promise of a Hollywood starlet to go nightclubbing with the "lucky" pilot. The only result of these offers was to provide the Communist propaganda mill with some ready-made documentation of American dollar-worship and cynicism.

Whatever the value of psychological operations in the military sphere, there is considerable doubt about its application to the general problem of world opinion. Experience has shown that psywar's results are uneven at best and that they usually have an effect only on people who are under heavy emotional pressure in restricted situations. Another condition of success is that the advice given be the dominant advice, preferably to the exclusion of all other "messages". The conditions we face in reaching world opinion are quite different. No matter how important we may think our message is, it is only one of scores of appeals being made—and very often ours is accorded an embarrassingly low priority by our audiences.

The greatest weakness of both the social engineers and the psychological warriors is their persistent tendency to see psychological operations as something separate and apart from our everyday acts which can be isolated and made to influence the rest. There is a psychological implication in every act but it has no life apart from the act. We can have specific psychological objectives and plans but they have no validity unless they are an ingrained part of our overall objectives. Both the social engineer and the psychological-operations enthusiasts have, in their different ways, added to our knowledge of dealing with mass persuasion by their imperfect and often exciting application of psychological and psychiatric techniques; but they have overreached themselves in promising an elixir cure to our public-opinion problems overseas. Their success lies in limited applications of their methods in specific situations, not in general application to the complex problems involved in winning world support for our policies.

In the larger effort of world persuasion we have been hindered rather than helped by the preoccupation of many people with the search for sureshot techniques to deliver our message. *If we could only apply motivational techniques in France . . . if we could only drop ten thousand copies of the Sears Roebuck catalogue by balloon into Communist countries . . . if the Egyptians could only meet some of our fine young high school youngsters . . .* the list goes on and on. Each supplicant envisions the quick conversion of the unconverted and they all disregard the problem of content, of what we say. It may be unfair to accuse the proponents of the hard sell of giving no consideration to the content of their message. Content is implied when they call for a loud, clear message. Nevertheless, their emphasis is always on the container, not its content, as if the very ingenuity of their containers will make up for any possible defects in what it is being asked to convey.

Preoccupation with techniques has been a hallmark of our search for answers to the problems posed by hostile or indifferent public opinion overseas; it is indicative of a serious weakness in our approach. If we are to give a mind and a heart to our age—and nothing less will meet our needs—then we must focus our attention not on techniques but on the more fundamental problem of what we can say to convince people abroad. Our means of persuasion must be determined with our policies and be suited to them. What we do and what we say cannot be separated. The United States cannot conduct propaganda operations by creating illusions in the outmoded style of obscuring some facts and emphasizing others. Our society today is a glass house in which all our actions are seen and judged by world opinion. We cannot hide developments as the Soviet Union does through its absolute control of internal affairs which permits the reeling out of a "line" on the state-controlled radio. In a phrase, we can't fool anyone; the Lincoln wisdom about the percentage factor in deceiving people still stands. We will win our point in the battle of world opinion only because our goals and their implementation are compatible with the actual interests of the rest of mankind.

Our attraction for world opinion is defined by the purpose of our society. We are not going to be defeated by what the world thinks of our tariff laws or our China policy. The decision will hang on the validity of our total claim as a democratic world leader and on the concurrence of our interests with those of other people. In turn, this will depend on whether we are capable of describing ourselves and stating our case in terms that are meaningful to people overseas.

"France was a land, England was a people but America, having still about it that quality of an idea, was harder to utter." Thus did F. Scott Fitzgerald see the problem of expressing his native land. Although he was an astringent critic of American society, he wrote in the great tradition of all those who have tried to give it meaning, from the authors of the Mayflower Compact to Jefferson and his bold egalitarianism, Whitman and his soaring verse, Lincoln writing speeches on envelopes and Huck Finn on a raft, thinking about freedom from the widder woman. Put them all together, with all the enthusiasts and critics who have ever written or spoken about American life and the formula is incomplete, "having still about it that quality of an idea". What can you say about America to describe it in its plenitude? Despite four centuries of development and a national talent for organization, the outstanding characteristic of American society is still its incompleteness. Is incompleteness our essential quality? Is our society a continuing consensus that does not aspire to a final synthesis of its individual and communal affairs? These are important questions for us in our national life and they have a direct bearing on our position as a world power.

The problem of defining America in terms understandable abroad is no longer an academic exercise. We live in a shorthand age where we have already had twenty years to make our leadership appeal on the world stage and where we may have precious few years left to speak out forcefully enough to maintain the support we need for our national survival. We are beyond the point where we can beg the question by offering a simplified version of American conduct or by explaining that American life is complex, requiring a deep understanding of our history and culture. A clear and credible explanation is needed now. If we appear disorganized and incoherent to our overseas audiences, we will lose their attention before we can make our purpose clear. We will then be scoring points in an empty stadium if at all.

Are we capable of defining realistic national goals and driving through to their completion? There are powerful forces who question our ability to do so. The Soviet and Chinese Communist leaderships not only doubt our capability but are basing their long-term strategy on these doubts. Their most damaging propaganda theme to the free world is American inconstancy and unreliability. They document the theme in an authoritative manner with case histories of all the divisive forces and centrifugal tendencies in American life. We comfort ourselves in the mythology that Communist propaganda is lies; in reality, it is often truth rattling around in a cage of deceit. The Communist tactic of driving a psychological wedge between us and our free world allies will be an increasing threat in the coming years, and it will have its effect whenever they can show clearcut examples of American weakness.

Even more serious than the threats of Communist propaganda are the natural doubts that many foreign observers have about our sense of purpose and our staying power. Too often we seem intent upon documenting ourselves as a people who are frivolous or uncaring. The much-maligned free spending, long-winded American tourist is more a stereotype than a reality but he is a commonly accepted image overseas. In business our appearance sometimes seems to betray a lack of seriousness. While other nations have sought influence abroad through such devices as mining concessions, our first move often appears to be the construction of a luxury hotel or a soft-drink bottling plant. The fact that these are practical enterprises and that we can also do our share of concession-seeking at times does not cancel out the public impressions associating us with entertainment and frivolity. Much of what foreigners see or read about us raises the question in their minds of whether we have a serious national or individual purpose.

Such doubts were anticipated over a century ago by Alexis de Toqueville in his perceptive commentaries on American democracy: "Foreign politics demand scarcely any of those qualities which are peculiar to a democracy; they require on the contrary the perfect use of almost all those in which it is deficient. . . . A democracy can only with great difficulty regulate the details of an important undertaking, persevere in a fixed design and work out its execution in spite of serious obstacles." De Toqueville's observations on the weaknesses of democracy have been echoed, with contemporary variations, whenever we have faced a national crisis but they take on special meaning in these years when we face the monolithic disposition of total force by the Soviet Union.

Timorous doubts as to whether we can afford the "luxury" of waste and delay inherent in our political system have given new impetus to those scattered forces in our society that are pressing for a near-totalitarian mobilization of our forces to match the Soviet threat. Pressure for such mobilization increased in 1957 when the

Russians demonstrated their clear superiority in rocket technique by launching the first earth satellite. Since then—and particularly in the debate revolving around the 1960 Presidential election—the proponents of a more austere democracy, with fewer liberties and more state control, have been turned down in favor of a general national resolve to improve the quality of our society at home and abroad within the framework of our present liberties.

Still the misgivings raised by de Toqueville's criticism remain. Do we have the ability to "regulate the details of an important undertaking, persevere in a fixed design and work out its execution in spite of serious obstacles"? Translated into 1961 terms, can we agree firmly on our goals; can we marshal our resources in a way that will satisfy our domestic needs as well as those of our free world allies and, eventually, the captive peoples behind the Iron and Bamboo Curtains?

The strength of our response will determine the form and direction of American society in the next decades. We will need to explore areas of national planning that are strange and even startling to most of us. Such strategic planning is a relatively new concept for us. Only in the last fifteen years have we developed the organizational implements for such planning. The first instrument for our early efforts was the National Security Act of 1947. The Act gave evidence that we clearly recognized the need for strategic planning and also accepted the task of organizing our resources to meet the demands of world leadership. It benefitted from the lessons learned during World War II when the mobilization of our resources was carried out by superimposing jerrybuilt war agencies upon a peacetime structure with resultant confusion and delay.

The new legislation provided for a National Security Council to advise the President on overall national strategy, particularly in international affairs. Although the President retains his constitutional power of final decision, the National Security Council has become the basic instrument for the development of national strategic goals and the policies to support them. Members of the Council, after the President and Vice President, include the Secretaries of State and Defense, assisted by the Chairman of the Joint Chiefs of Staff, the Director of the Central Intelligence Agency and several other Cabinet-rank officials. The Council has a planning board, composed of second-line officials of the agencies represented on the Council itself, which prepares "policy papers" on national problems for consideration by the Council. Each paper includes an estimate of an existing problem prepared by government intelligence agencies and policy planners, together with an evaluation of possible courses of action. The papers form the basis for weekly NSC discussions on the current state of American strategic policy.

In facing the problem of world opinion, the Council performs the vital function of defining national goals and establishing responsibility for their achievement. Increasingly since 1947 the Council has concerned itself with the psychological impact of our policies abroad. The Truman Administration made specific provision for this function in 1950 when it set up the Psychological Strategy Board to advise the Council on ways and means of getting stronger acceptance of American policies by world opinion. Although its purpose was sound, the Board was sometimes over-dependent on the philosophy of the psychological warriors who tended to see its operations as something apart from the regular flow of plans and policies. The Board was abolished in 1953 after less than two years of operation in an extensive reorganization of the NSC structure by the new Eisenhower administration.

During his 1952 election campaign Mr. Eisenhower stressed the need for better integration of psychological operations into overall national strategy. "This would mean," he declared in a campaign speech in October, "the selection of broad national purposes and the designation within these purposes of principal targets. Then it would mean this: Every significant act of government should be so timed and so directed at a principal target that it will produce the maximum effect. It means that our government in this critical matter will no longer be divided into airtight compartments. It means that in carrying out a national policy, every department and every agency of government that can make a useful contribution will bring its full strength to bear under a coordinated program."

The new Administration put these concepts into effect by strengthening the National Security Council structure. A planning board was set up with a broad charter for coordinating all of the Council's affairs. At the same time, the Administration showed its concern for the importance of psychological strategy by removing the government's overseas information program from its second echelon position in the State Department to independent status as a separate agency. The administrative center or headquarters of the organization, located in Washington, is known as the United States Information Agency.

USIA is the planning and logistic bureau for the government's overall psychological strategy operations. The United States Information Service is the designation given the two hundred foreign posts of the agency which are maintained in principal cities throughout the world to carry out the nation's information and cultural programs abroad.

Establishment of the United States Information Agency in 1953 gave new status to information and psychological factors in the formulation of our strategic policies. Moreover the agency was given important responsibilities in the National Security Council framework.

This and other changes in our foreign-policy machinery in recent years have brought the United States a long way down the road toward the integration of its resources for the effective conduct of a modern foreign policy. Coordination among diplomatic, economic, military and propaganda elements within the National Security Council framework is now a day-to-day reality. We have had this advantage for less than a decade. The new arrangement is still in its formative years and, like any adolescent, it is both weak and strong. Its strength is that it provides a forum for the integrated planning and disposition of our strategic resources. Its weakness is inexperience in the magnitudinous problems of coordinating hundreds of intricate policies under a committee system. In a typical National Security Council meeting, its members may be asked to advise the President on such varied problems as the American schedule for lunar exploration, the size of next year's military budget, our defense of the off-shore islands of Formosa and plans for a global television network. Each of these policies must be decided on the basis of opinions from a dozen government agencies whose views are inevitably colored by their own particular interests.

Aside from overcoming these inherent difficulties in forming a clear-cut policy directive, the National Security Council must also establish a healthy balance between tactical and strategic considerations. The primary concern of the Council is advising the President on long-range strategy. However, day-to-day problems demand immediate action and they divert attention from the consideration of basic strategy. The annual Congressional budget process shortens the focus within which long-range programs can be planned. Unforeseen events such as a revolt in a Soviet satellite or temporary difficulties with one of our important allies require urgent decisions and a flexibility that is sometimes difficult to achieve in the Federal government's administrative structure. Such factors tend to restrict the perspective in which basic policies are judged.

Many informed observers inside and outside the government have concluded that our strategic needs during the 1960's require a revision of the National Security Council and other elements of our strategic policy machinery.[1] Some of the most fruitful thinking on the subject of policy organization is being generated in Congress. In 1959 the Senate authorized a subcommittee on "national policy machinery" to study the problem of strengthening our strategic planning mechanism. Several months later the Senate Foreign Relations Committee began a parallel study. The varied proposals that have emerged from these and other studies share a number of ideas.

There are many who have felt that the present committee system of the National Security Council should be modified by a more direct line-of-command control in the formulation and execution of strategic policy. Both of the Senate committees have envisioned an expansion of State Department influence over strategic planning. The Foreign Relations Committee study, prepared by the Brookings Institute, calls for a new "Secretary of Foreign Affairs," with three other Cabinet-rank secretaries under him who would be responsible for political, economic and ideological operations in a new Department of Foreign Affairs—an expanded version of the present State Department. In 1960 a special Presidential committee headed by industrialist Mansfield Sprague made a study of the particular role of the information program in our overall strategy.

Whatever the final outcome of these proposals for strengthening United States strategic operations, it is obvious we are moving toward an era of more intensive planning particularly in international affairs. In our multivocal, democratic way we are beginning to match the Communist apparatus for conducting a protracted political, economic and psychological struggle in which military operations are a muted last-resort threat. There will be no magical change in our world position as a result of any revisions in the mechanics of

---

1. Some observers do not agree. One of these, *New York Times* military expert Hanson Baldwin, has taken to task those who lay our strategy troubles on alleged faulty organization in Washington: "This is always an easy out. It is easier by far to draw blueprints for the ideal state than to find the administrators, the policy-makers, the wise and learned men of character and integrity and ability to run it. We have, in too many areas, a bureaucrats' paradise in Washington, but blueprints are no solution; they are, at best, an aid; the men are what counts."

our strategy planning. The same stickling problems will still be with us. No amount of streamlined policy-and-action planning is going to wipe out the dilemmas we face in dealing with disarmament, the Chinese Communists, the missile race or the future of eastern Europe. The delusion that policy machinery comes equipped with its own built-in ability to produce "the right answers" is peculiarly persistent in American bureaucracy. The cause of this delusion often lies in an exaggerated attachment to the committee system. Our reliance on committees to arrive at decisions-by-concurrence is a typically pragmatic American approach to the complexities of decision. When we go beyond this and depend upon concurrence to protect us from all possibility of error we may be evading responsibility. The result may be policies and actions whose chief virtue is that they are agreed to, not that they are effective.

What the new disposition of our resources *can* do—assuming it is guided by wise leadership—is to minimize the danger of inadequate definition of our policies and actions. In standing up to a monolithic Communist threat on the one hand and the equally pressing problems of providing positive leadership for the free world on the other, we must not be handicapped by the lack of coordination that comes from acting from the components of policy rather than from its totality. We seem uncertain of ourselves, we confuse our friends and we leave the way open for the Communists to misinterpret our apparent indecision for lack of will. The problem may be illustrated by a Mutt-and-Jeff story. Mutt asks Jeff what water is made of; Jeff tells him that it is two parts hydrogen and one part oxygen. "What?" says Mutt. "Ain't there no water in it?" In defining the component parts of our national policy, we face the same type of question from our friends and enemies: ain't there no national purpose in it? The need to define our total purpose will become increasingly urgent during the 1960's as the Communist leadership concentrates its efforts on undermining our support among our free world allies. Any positive speculation must assume that the Communists will not start another overt "limited war" as they did in Korea and that they will not start a general war. Although we have to keep up our guard against these possibilities, they do not correlate with basic Communist strategy. The Communist method was expounded by Lenin when he wrote: "The soundest strategy in war . . . is to postpone operations until the moral disintegration of the enemy renders the delivery of the mortal blow both possible and easy." This is the essence of Communist strategy. It reveals

Communism as a counter-revolution to the free world's current political, economic and social revolutions. The Communist approach is to break down hostile or neutral opinion until it is too fragmented to resist the final violent effort to establish Red hegemony.

Despite the battle cries of our home-bred psychological warriors, we cannot turn back the threat by trying to match the Communists in the field of propaganda skirmishes. We might gain some short-range tactical advantages if we did but any such undertaking on our part would end in self-defeat in the long run. In the first place, the American government lacks control over communications media and public opinion, which is a most essential element in conspiratorial propaganda activities. Secondly, the Communist approach is essentially destructive, designed to destroy the democratic order. Its application to our policy would not only be ineffective but also counterproductive. Finally, it does not fit in with the nature of our message, which is an open appeal for support not merely of specific policies but of our overall purpose.

As exponents of a free world we have to present our case in an open society where our deficiencies as well as our assets are exposed. As with Oliver Cromwell's famous instructions to the artist painting his portrait, the picture of America overseas has to include the warts along with the rest. Our long-range gamble is that our purposes and our actions can be made clear enough to convince the rest of the free world and, eventually, people in Communist-ruled territories that our essential interests are the same as theirs. Despite a considerable amount of wishful thinking and Fourth-of-July rhetoric, these similarities are not self-evident to most of mankind. This is due partly to the basic difficulties we face in reaching the foreign mind but it is due also to the complexities of our own society and its apparent lack of forceful purpose, as force and purpose are understood by more ancient societies with different standards and mores. Americans know that our civilization is built upon an elaborate, largely unwritten theme of consensus. What keeps us together is not any concord of race, creed or assorted privileges. Even when we disagree we do so within the consensus, letting it move and adapt itself to new variations as the needs of our society change. We understand this instinctively but it is difficult for us to convey an understanding of our social harmony to the rest of the world. From the geographical and psychological distances at which they listen to us, they hear only the many discordant voices of America that seem to ring above the steady quiet beat of national agreement that integrates our society.

Our strategic interests will not be met by psychological warfare tricks or propaganda gambits as such. Nor will it be served by sweetness-and-light attempts to win a global popularity contest through policies designed to win limited public-opinion support in certain areas abroad. Our purpose will be served by explaining as precisely as we can who we are, what we intend to do and how we intend to do it. As Mr. Cromwell said, warts and all. This is our propaganda for the 1960's and for the 1970's and the 1980's. It is based on the only sound structure a democratic society can give it—the identity between its own interests and the interests of the people we are trying to persuade. It requires precision in definition and imagination in execution.

Clear purpose. Precise actions within this purpose. Imaginative explanation of both our purpose and our actions. These are the basic elements of our message to the world. Much of what the world hears about us is the reverberations of our own free society in its continuing domestic dialogue through newspapers, films and other media. Supplementing this, echoing it and amplifying it, is our national effort to provide the rest of the world with a credible description of our purpose and our actions. This is the job assigned to the United States Information Agency. As we have seen, it is a newly important factor in our conduct of foreign relations but its antecedants go back deep into our national history.

3

WORDS AT WAR

The United States has been in the international propaganda business, off and on, for a long time. In all our wars as well as in many of our peacetime policies, we have sought popular support abroad for our ideas. Since our current activities have developed from this history, a look at our past propaganda operations is in order. They go back to the American Revolution, when propaganda played a crucial role in the war for independence.

Political pamphleteering, posters and slogans helped start the revolution and then kept it going until victory. Without knowing one cliché of psychological warfare verbiage, the revolutionists applied all its techniques from surrender leaflets to whispering campaigns. The small directorate that planned the strategy in Philadelphia was composed of men fully aware of the need for overseas sympathy and support.

When Benjamin Franklin went to France in 1776 to gain backing for the Revolution he left his comfortable silk clothes at home and moved about the Parisian salons in a rough woolen suit. Delighting all with his "plain American ways," he played the homespun philosopher with such astuteness and presented the American case so effectively, that he won what he was seeking—a pledge of French support against the British. His mission to Paris was both a diplomatic success and a stunning venture in international propaganda.

During the early years of new nationalism, our geographical isolation and general preoccupation with continental expansion deflected concern for what other peoples thought of us. Our political popularity abroad was a dormant subject until the Civil War when both the Union and the Confederacy engaged in various types of propaganda in an attempt to gain support for their respective causes from European countries. Outlawing of the African slave trade by the Confederacy in 1861 was clearly an attempt to modify European criticism, but the South was thwarted in this purpose by an earlier piece of propaganda—*Uncle Tom's Cabin.* In both novel and play form, Mrs. Stowe's antislavery arguments were read and seen by hundreds of thousands of foreigners throughout the world before the outbreak of the war. Subsequently the Confederacy maintained agents in the principal European capitals for the purpose of promoting the Southern cause. On the Union side, Abraham Lincoln served as his own propaganda chief. He understood the impact of the slavery issue and he played upon it in his own subtle way. One of his most successful projects was to send such persuasive emissaries as Henry Ward Beecher and Archbishop John Hughes of New York to Europe to propagandize for the Union. At the same time over a million booklets explaining the Union position were circulated throughout the continent.

Lincoln also took the unprecedented step of making direct appeals to foreign audiences outside the normal channels of diplomatic procedure. In two famous public letters to British workingmen he argued the anti-slavery cause with compassion and effectiveness. The letters shocked the British government; the Foreign Minister, Lord Russell, wrote to his ambassador in Washington, fretting that there were no precedents to guide either of them in handling the matter. In an age when the affairs of state were handled among aristocrats in their salons, the idea of a direct appeal to the working classes of one country by the head of another government was considered bad form.

It was not until World War I that the United States established an official propaganda service. Known variously as the Committee on Public Information and the Creel Committee after its chairman, George Creel, the organization was authorized in 1917 by President Woodrow Wilson for the purpose of whipping up domestic support for the war and also for conducting international propaganda operations to match the German effort in this field. Creel and his aides brought to their job a lively if somewhat primitive idea of the value of propaganda. Writing of the Committee's work after the war, Creel noted: "Back of the firing line, back of the armies and navies, back of the great supply depots, another struggle waged with the same intensity and with almost equal significance attaching to its victories and defeats. It was the fight for the minds of men. . . . Our effort was educational and informative throughout, for we had such confidence in our case as to feel that no other argument was needed than the simple, straightforward presentation of facts". To a modern observer Creel's analysis seems unsophisticated. Much of his organization's output was in fact heavy-handed and lacking in credibility.

The activities of the Creel Committee, together with anguished post-mortems on the reasons why we went to war, gave the American people a disturbing, though somewhat inaccurate, introduction to the force of propaganda in the modern world. During the 1920s and 1930s, considerable evidence of the influence of Allied and German propaganda was accumulated. Many Americans were convinced that our gullibility in the face of this propaganda had led us unwisely into the war. Their feelings were largely a rationalization for the letdown of inflated hopes that had motivated Americans to believe they were fighting the "war to end all wars". Nevertheless this rationale contained enough truth to make propaganda an emotional catch-word.

The study of propaganda became an important concern for the academicians. They brought to it the exciting, imperfect techniques of the new social sciences. Unfortunately they also brought their own private technical vocabulary ("diffusion and restriction tendencies," "catharsis of insecurities," etc.) which left the average citizen groping in a semantic fog. One of the leading practitioners of propaganda analysis in its formative years was Professor Harold D. Lasswell of the University of Chicago, who issued his first book on the subject, an analysis of propaganda techniques in World War I, in 1927. During the next dozen years Lasswell and his disciples prepared a series of ground-breaking studies in propaganda, including the classic *World Revolutionary Techniques* which probed the strengths and weaknesses of Communist Party propaganda.

Indicative of growing interest in the subject was the founding of an Institute for Propaganda Analysis at Columbia University in 1937. The Institute was to be no academic ivory tower. The purpose of the organization was to provide the average man with a continuing exposé of the hidden forces that were trying to shape his life and thought. There was little objective analysis of propaganda as such. The Institute based its investigations largely on the assumption that all propaganda is false and that it would therefore collapse from sheer exposure once its true sources were made known; from here it was but a short ideological jump to the premise that a good share of the world's troubles could be short-circuited if we knew enough to resist the propaganda that sustained them. For four years, before it closed down shortly after Pearl Harbor, the Institute applied these postulates in analyzing such subjects as the Spanish civil war and the Rudolph Hess flight to England. Although its reports had little effect on the events it sought to expose and destroy, the work of the Institute for Propaganda Analysis did lead toward more thoroughgoing and objective appraisal of propaganda problems.

When the United States entered the war in 1941 immediate consideration was given to a war propaganda program. Long before we initiated any plan for such operations the American government was alerted to both Allied and enemy capabilities in this field. Reports of Nazi propaganda effectiveness were widely circulated in this country before the war as were accounts of British efforts in counteracting this phase of the Axis offensive. During the two years of uneasy neutrality before Pearl Harbor, the Roosevelt administration took several steps towards recognizing the new importance of propaganda in foreign affairs. Nazi attempts to undermine our influence in Latin America through economic and propaganda penetration became an increasing threat after 1939. In August 1940 the administration formed the Office of the Coordinator of Commercial and Cultural Affairs between the American Republics with a newcomer to government service, Nelson A. Rockefeller, as its chief.[1]

Under Rockefeller's aggressive leadership the new agency initiated the first full-fledged American overseas propaganda operation. All in all, its activities were quite successful. "Cultural affairs officers" were assigned to embassies throughout Latin America and our first government-sponsored foreign libraries and binational cultural centers were opened. Student exchange activities were encouraged. Latin American newspapermen and other opinion leaders were invited to the United States to see for themselves what this country and its people are like. The Roosevelt "good neighbor" theme was repeated in radio broadcasts and newspaper articles prepared by the Rockefeller office.

Spurred by the increasing Nazi threat to our security the Roosevelt administration established in 1941 two additional information offices by Presidential decree. One was the Office of Facts and Figures, directed by poet Archibald MacLeish and concerned primarily with enlisting domestic support for the defense program. The

---

1. Two earlier and somewhat ineffective attempts to meet the pre-war threat of Nazi influence in Latin America were an Interdepartmental Committee for Scientific and Cultural Cooperation and a Division of Cultural Cooperation in the State Department, both set up in 1938. The Rockefeller organization's title was changed in July 1941 to the Office of the Coordinator of Inter-American Affairs and in March 1945 to the Office of Inter-American Affairs. After the war its activities were eventually absorbed by other bureaus of the State Department.

other was the Coordinator of Information under the direction of Colonel William J. (Wild Bill) Donovan who later became head of the wartime cloak-and-dagger Office of Strategic Services. Among other duties, Colonel Donovan's office was authorized to carry out propaganda activities overseas. This phase of its operations, directed by playwright Robert E. Sherwood, was just getting under way at the time of the Pearl Harbor attack in December 1941 when it suddenly became the focus of a hastily expanded propaganda program. On February 24, 1942, Sherwood put the shortwave "Voice of America" radio on the air for the first time. "The Voice of America speaks," he announced. "Today America has been at war for seventy-nine days. Daily at this time we shall speak to you about America and the war. The news may be good or bad. We shall tell you the truth."

The initial attempts to build up a government propaganda service after Pearl Harbor were soon snagged in bureaucracy and in the personal ambitions of a variety of experts, real and alleged. The organizational tangle was resolved in June 1942 when President Roosevelt called in Elmer Davis, a newspaperman and radio commentator, to direct a new Office of War Information. The OWI was charged with the task of coordinating all government information activities domestically and internationally except in Latin America. (Information and cultural activities in Latin America continued to be carried out by the Nelson Rockefeller office until the end of the war.) OWI absorbed the Office of Facts and Figures; Robert Sherwood continued as director of the overseas operations.

The history of OWI is wrapped in the personality of Elmer Davis. A twang-voiced Hoosier, Davis was an enigmatic man who combined a flair for writing slick magazine fiction of the blandest sort with a shrewd astuteness in political affairs. He took over his OWI job with the deceptively simple conviction that he was in the information business but he soon found out that a considerable portion of the war planners in Washington took a different view. They were perfectly willing to let OWI grind out don't-aid-the-enemy posters and pamphlets but they drew the line on substantive information about America's policies or objectives. The result was a series of battles royal between the tough-minded Davis and other Washington officials. When a military commission refused to release details of the trial of eight Nazi saboteurs, Davis carried the fight to the White House and won. In other battles he lost.

A great part of Davis' troubles lay in the nature of the Office of

War Information itself. An amalgam of four other agencies, it was set up with no direction other than a vague charter to produce win-the-war enthusiasm. Coordination between the OWI and the State Department, its logical source of guidance, was conducted largely by telephone between Washington and New York, where most OWI officers were located. This indifferent approach to guidance seriously handicapped the OWI. It was weakest at the point where it should have been strongest—in providing an authoritative, credible account of American war and post-war aims. The greatest fault lay at the highest levels of government where the win-the-war objective often pushed aside any serious projection of post-war planning. As a result we unnecessarily confused our friends and encouraged our enemies. The OWI did publicize such ringing declarations as the Atlantic Charter with its famous acclaim for the four freedoms; but noble sentiments alone are not enough to maintain the hopes of people in occupied areas. When these people began asking more specific questions, the noble messages lacked definition and seemed to lose validity. Too often the clumsy application of high-sounding phrases led to disillusionment. The immense grinding of these badly-meshed political gears in the war years was a lesson against letting vague expressions get too far ahead of workable policy.

Having been denied any high-level participation in setting government policy, the OWI and its myriad operations abroad concentrated on providing general information about the United States. Their material was eagerly sought after by vast numbers of foreigners, many of whom were getting their first view of America and its power in the form of soldiers and military equipment. The OWI took advantage of this intensified curiosity to provide a pioneer program of comprehensive information about the United States. Unfortunately the material was occasionally too innocuous and smacked too much of the advertising writer's touch. Its blandness once prompted an OWI hand to suggest, in a moment of exasperation, that the war be re-christened "The War That Refreshes".

Overseas where OWI posts operated under the newly-minted name of "United States Information Service," its activities were more virile and direct. Unrestrained by the direct cautionary hand of Washington and New York, OWI posts in combat and occupation areas were under the control of military theater commanders who were becoming increasingly aware of the value of propaganda and psychological warfare. Some commanders particularly appreciated the influence that radio could have in softening up enemy morale and bolstering the hopes of occupied peoples. The British had taken an early lead in this field and we followed close behind with a series of high-power transmitters scattered throughout North Africa and Europe. Radio proved to be a highly satisfactory tactical weapon in a number of instances. When the provisional Italian government surrendered in September 1943, there was a question of whether the Italian navy would follow suit. An OWI transmitter in Algiers was pressed into service to broadcast news of the government's surrender and to give instructions for the fleet's own surrender procedure. The broadcasts were made on a frequency normally used for international distress calls. Within three days the fleet sailed into Malta intact in accordance with the radio instructions.

Perhaps the most dramatic story of radio persuasion was a joint Navy-OWI project for broadcasting special programs to the German submarine fleet. A German-speaking Navy officer, using the pseudonym of "Commander Robert Lee Norden, USN", opened his series of broadcasts by building up a careful reputation for accuracy in reporting "inside" developments in the German submarine fleet. His information was based on carefully-selected intelligence reports and he soon had an attentive listening audience among the German submariners. He then began to turn the propaganda screw with remarkable results. He reported on frictions within the Nazi fleet command and on its exaggerated claims of Allied shipping tonnage sunk. Soon the German government shortwave services began to pay Commander Norden the tribute of answering his "lies". Further confirmation of the effectiveness of his broadcasts was found after the war in official German naval correspondence where his broadcasts were described as having "a crushing effect on the morale of German naval personnel." [2]

The OWI and the armed forces were not always so lucky in aiming messages at the enemy. Sometimes their activities were so poorly executed that they were even counterproductive. Occasionally they lost credibility completely by relying on shaded facts which could easily be refuted. Sometimes there was a touch of the ridiculous. The OWI once circulated matchbooks with a message in French about the Four Freedoms of the Atlantic Charter. "Freedom from Want" was translated as *liberté corporale* which to most Frenchmen repre-

2. Examples of OWI effectiveness during the war are given in detail in Edward Barrett's excellent book on the early days of the information program, *Truth Is Our Weapon,* Funk and Wagnalls, 1953.

sented a personal liberty that did not need to be included in any Charter.

By the end of the war the OWI had 13,000 employees in its domestic and overseas offices. It was a conglomerate staff of newspapermen, advertising executives, foreign refugees, professional enthusiasts and a handful of assorted oddballs. Unavoidably the organization suffered from its quota of misfits in spite of screening efforts. The antics of a few incompetents gave the organization a tarnished name it did not deserve. (One radio operator, hired to send Morse-code news to North Africa, garbled the translations so badly that the OWI office in Algiers responded: "If must send with foot, please use right foot.") Much of the attack on the OWI was politically inspired. For columnist Westbrook Pegler, the OWI was "a hide-out for privileged intellectual New Deal cowards and Communists." The ratio of New Deal Democrats on the staff was undoubtedly higher than the national average, thanks in part to political patronage and in part to what Arthur Krock has ruefully called "the superior articulation of the left". Most of the OWI staff was made up of professionals from journalism and other media fields who applied their talents without political motives to a job they did not always fully understand (just what *do* you say to a Bulgarian?) and who were just as happy to get back to their old job on the paper or on Madison Avenue when the war was over.

Their personal eagerness for peacetime work was matched by the zeal of a large part of official Washington to get rid of the Office of War Information after the defeat of Japan. The war was over; there was nothing more to explain. The OWI was dissolved with more than indecent haste; the war ended in August 1945 and the organization was ordered liquidated by the end of the year. Threatened with total extinction, the information program was transferred to the State Department. All its activities were sharply reduced; the Voice of America radio operation, which had been broadcasting 3200 live programs weekly in over forty languages at its wartime peak, was cut almost in half.

Under the persistent prodding of Assistant Secretary of State William H. Benton, who was then in charge of the program after the OWI was disbanded, the Truman administration agreed to retain at least the framework of an information service. A number of U.S. Information Service posts overseas were shut down completely while those remaining reduced their scale of operations. In supporting the information program, even at a reduced level, the administration battled the ill-concealed prejudice of many Congressmen as well as the whole tenor of American opinion which in 1946 was anxious to forget as much as it could about foreign problems. At one point the House of Representatives actually eliminated all funds for the program; it was saved from extinction only because President Truman and Secretary of State George C. Marshall persuaded the Senate to restore the appropriation.

Congressional and other opposition to the information program's continued existence changed in 1947 as a result of international developments. It was apparent by that time that the Soviet Union had no intention of following through on its wartime agreements with its allies concerning post-war problems. The attempted Communist take-over in Northern Iran, the Greek civil war, together with Soviet pressures in Eastern Europe and Germany, furnished proof for all but the most obtuse that the United States and its free world allies faced a new threat to their security. This realization had profound effects on our foreign policy with its new stress on mobilizing free world resources to meet the threat. Fortunately for the future of the overseas information program, 1947 was an off-year in Congressional elections. Following what has come to be traditional practice, dozens of Congressmen visited foreign countries during that summer and fall. Their reactions to the military and economic situation abroad varied but they all recognized the deplorable state of misunderstanding and misrepresentation of the United States and its policies. The net result of their reaction (" Something must be done to put America's story across.") saw the legislative light of day in the form of the Smith-Mundt Act.[3]

The Smith-Mundt Act is the basic charter for the present overseas information program. It states that an information program is an integral part of the conduct of American foreign affairs and outlines the areas in which the program is to operate. Included in this was much of the old OWI concept of information-media activities as well as an important innovation—government-sponsored visits of foreign leaders and professional specialists to the United States. The plan for travel grants to these foreign leaders supplemented a parallel proposal, introduced by Senator J. William Fulbright in 1946, for the exchange of students financed by foreign currencies received from the sale of American war surplus material. The Smith-Mundt Act was no dreamer's document. It was a clear-cut directive that has

3. It became law in January 1948.

stood the test of a dozen years' buffeting. Major credit goes to its primary sponsor—a shrewd, practical-minded Republican Congressman from South Dakota, Karl Mundt, who has had a proprietary interest in the information program ever since. (The Smith of Smith-Mundt, Senator H. Alexander Smith, a New Jersey Republican, is now retired.)

The Smith-Mundt Act was an important development in the history of our overseas information program since it gave the program permanent status. However, it was, to use the Washington bureaucratic phrase, only a hunting license—a Congressional authorization to do something without the money to do it. From a post-war low of its fifteen million dollar annual appropriation in 1947, the information program was boosted to only $25 million in the Spring of 1948, an amount which permitted little more than the maintenance of overseas libraries and the operation of a small Voice of America radio facility. One of the most immediate results of the Smith-Mundt Act was a Congressional investigation.

Lord Bryce, the Victorian commentator on American political institutions, once wrote that the single most important contribution made by the American government to political science has been the Congressional investigations. Officials of the information program can take some consolation in the fact that they have advanced, in no small measure, their nation's contribution to the art of government. Per dollar appropriated, the program has been one of the most pawed-over aspects of our government. This is due in part to its newness and strangeness, in part to the incompetence of some of its personnel and in part to the fact that it constitutes a sitting duck for politicians determined to score a point against their opponents. Any program that spends money broadcasting to the Egyptians and demonstrating square dancing to the Siamese is wide open to a political uppercut from time to time, no matter how loud and long it protests the rightness of its ways. In the main, Congressional investigations of the program represent a conscientious effort for improvement. The headline-making attacks on the program have, in the past, usually been launched by individuals who were out to make a political point or who simply were uninformed. Typical was the charge of one Congressman, long since pastured back to his Idaho home by the electorate, who announced in 1951 that "Red influences in the State Department" caused five Voice of America radio transmitters to be assigned call letters spelling "I lie" in Russian. A weary State Department spokesman patiently explained that the call letters of the station were assigned long before the VOA existed, that they were not heard overseas and that, incidentally, they did not spell "I lie" in Russian. This explanation could be made for the record but not quickly enough or forcefully enough to catch up with the original charge. The pattern was repeated with major-league trimmings in the McCarthy investigations of the Voice of America a few years later.

Congressional investigations were not yet uppermost in the minds of information program planners in 1948 and 1949. They were concentrating on an expansion of the program under the leadership of its new head, Assistant Secretary of State George V. Allen, a career diplomat. Congress increased program appropriations in 1949 to over $30 million, permitting the program to build up to effective strength after three lean-budget years. Most notable aspect of the build-up was an expansion of program activities in the Middle East and Asia. In four short years since the end of the war over six hundred million Asians had gained independence from colonial rule. Freed from the inhibitions that had previously marked its operations in areas controlled by our European allies, information posts were established in many Asian cities and expanded in others in order to meet the demands imposed on our policies by the lusty new public opinions of the independent nations.

Meanwhile the form and function of the entire program was being changed by the quick pace of other political events abroad. The *coup d'état* in Czechoslovakia, the defeat of nationalist forces in China and the Berlin blockade gave new urgency to American countermeasures to meet this new strategy of Communist imperialism. Our countermeasures included the information program; in April 1950 President Harry Truman called for a "Campaign of Truth" especially designed to expose Soviet "big lie" techniques. Several months later when the outbreak of the Korean War underscored the need for a stronger U.S. information effort overseas, Congress appropriated $86 million for USIS activities, almost three times more than it provided the year before. Particular attention was given in these appropriations to strengthening Voice of America radio transmitting facilities.

The tripling of the appropriation in 1951 called for an intense shifting of organizational gears once more from neutral to high. The program, now being directed by Alabama newspaperman Edward Barrett, expanded quickly in some areas but was stymied in others. It was hard to recruit people fast enough to handle the needs created by the expansion; by 1951 hundreds of foreign jobs were still unfilled and a score of posts were understaffed or unopened. The organization was being forced too hard for its own good. Nevertheless the overall record showed success, particularly in the field of anti-Communist operations. The Russians tacitly acknowledged its effectiveness by installing a complex electronic system to jam Voice of America broadcasts in Communist-bloc countries and by closing down USIS posts in Prague, Sofia, Bucharest and other satellite cities.

A noteworthy postwar innovation in the information program was a commission of distinguished private citizens appointed by the President to oversee program operations. Known as the U.S. Advisory Commission on Information, the group has served as a helpful critic of our overseas propaganda activities for almost fifteen years.[4]

In examining the information program's efforts to reorganize its activities to meet the new Soviet challenge, the Commission declared in 1950: "Events in the past year have made a United States government information program more important than ever. . . . It is in the information field that we meet the rival forces head on. The Soviet Union, for example, places by all odds its heaviest reliance on 'propaganda', spending enormous sums and using its best and most imaginative brains. Other governments are acutely conscious of the importance of information programs and are spending more in proportion to their capacities than is the United States in telling its story abroad. The passage of the Smith-Mundt Act and its accompanying appropriation were a recognition by the Congress of the importance of this task. Under the legislation a good beginning has been made. But in the view of this Commission the task is far more important than has hitherto been recognized. . . . "

The enthusiasm of the Commission was not shared by other critics both in and out of Congress during 1950 and 1951. The Truman administration attempted to win stronger bi-partisan political support for the program by appointing a leading Republican, Dr. Wilson Compton, president of the State College of Washington, as administrator of the program. But it was soon obvious during the 1952 Presi-

4. The committee's competence can be measured by the high level of its membership which in 1960 included Sigurd Larmon, chairman of the board of Young and Rubicam; Philip Reed, chairman of the finance committee of General Electric; Erwin D. Canham, editor of the Christian Science Monitor; former ambassador Lewis E. Douglas, and Mark A. May, chairman of the commission and director of Yale's Institute of Human Relations. The commission reports to the President on the information program's progress regularly.

dential campaign that the Republicans considered the information program as a likely candidate for reform. In a campaign swing through California, Dwight Eisenhower said: "We must realize that as a nation everything we say, everything we do, and everything we fail to say and do, will have its impact in other lands. It will affect the minds and wills of men there. . . . We are not going to win the struggle for men's minds merely by tripling Congressional appropriations for a super-loud Voice of America. Rather it will be the message we give the Voice to speak. Rather it will be the spiritual strength, the understanding, and the compassion which we Americans can summon to put into that message. Rather it will be the planned and effective use of every means to appeal to men and women everywhere."

No one doubted, on the day after Adlai Stevenson sent his congratulations to President-elect Dwight Eisenhower, that there would be many changes in Washington or that these would encompass the information program. None but the most perceptive, however, could have guessed that the dominant figure in overhauling the information program during the months ahead would be Joseph R. McCarthy, the junior Senator from Wisconsin.

Within days after the Eisenhower administration took office in January 1953 the information program became the object of four simultaneous investigations. One was conducted by the Administration itself, two by the Senate and one by the House of Representatives. The Administration investigation was a quiet, concerted effort to clarify the function of the program as part of an overall plan for improving coordination in foreign affairs. The House of Representatives' investigation was concerned primarily with finances while the Senate Foreign Relations Committee under the leadership of Senator Bourke Hickenlooper of Iowa paralleled the Administration's own efforts. The investigation carried out by the Senate Government Operations Committee under Senator McCarthy's direction, however, came as close to laying low the information program as any event in its short history.

I was given the somewhat dubious advantage of being assigned back to Washington from an overseas post in time to watch the entire funereal proceedings. During the black days of the spring of 1953, the organization sagged and groaned to a halt. There was little direction to the operations and no inclination on the part of the underlings to start anything. The Campaign of Truth crusade was stopped short. Many of the shiny knights who initiated it had fled or been voted out of office while the troops left behind were wondering what they were doing in this army. Day in and day out the investigators poked around the camp, trying to prove that the Saracen enemy was not somewhere over the horizon but right here in the ranks. Worst of all, more and more of the folks back home who were paying for the crusade seemed prepared to believe Senator McCarthy's charges.

One of the wry amusements of our staff at the time, aside from speculating what was going to happen next, was to make up fanciful USIS documentary films for foreign showing. One such masterpiece was called *Napalm—the Story of an Idea*; another was *A Day in the Life of a Smalltown Call Girl.* Even these forays of misdirected talent were no compensation for the dreary course of the McCarthy investigations. Most appalling and ironic of the developments was the attempt to prove that the organization was riddled with Reds and sexual deviates. In their search for proof, the McCarthy investigators were aided by a self-appointed group within the service which referred to itself as the "loyal American underground". (The implication, of course, was that the rest of us were bomb-throwing Bolsheviks.) One by one, members of the underground made their appearances as "friendly witnesses", each with a tale of sinister influences. One young secretary burst into the headlines with the revelation that she had been importuned to join a free-love colony in Westchester by her Voice of America boss. It turned out that he had suggested she might be interested in buying land in a cooperative housing venture. But the facts never caught up with the original juicy charge; nor did any of the actual faults in the information program ever get a serious hearing before the McCarthy committee.

Over and above its effect on the information program, the McCarthy investigations dealt a serious blow to our international respect. Informed public opinion abroad expressed its astonishment at a minor legislative leader who apparently had the power to call the tune for the American government. Foreign newspapers, particularly those with political axes to grind against the United States, did not spare the more spectacular details of the investigation either in their news stories or in editorials. Raymond Aron, one of the few leading French intellectuals who has taken a consistently realistic view of the necessity for French-American cooperation in world affairs, attended a McCarthy hearing and announced that he was unable to see how he could honestly continue to defend the United States against those who maintained that our political life was characterized by fear and hysteria. Around the world high-pitched criticism accompanied the investigations, particularly when it was learned that some of the books removed from USIS library shelves as a result of the investigation were burned. In Berlin, a professor walked into our library there and announced he was boycotting it until the books that had been removed were restored. In Oslo the newspaper *Verdens Gang* declared editorially that "McCarthy and his associates have damaged the cause of the United States much more than any Communists they could conceivably uncover." The American Embassy in Tokyo received a query from a Japanese scholar on the subject of American "thought police".

The most actively vociferous overseas commentators on the McCarthy investigations were those of the Communist propaganda apparatus. Their theme was simple and effective: American hysteria, American weakness, American immaturity. McCarthy, they declared, was merely exposing what enlightened people already knew, that—in the words of Radio Warsaw—"despite all the VOA yappers, the constructions of Socialism are growing, that the power of the democratic world is increasing and that all attempts at diversion are paralyzed".

"For whom does the bell toll?" asked a Radio Prague commentator with a rhetorical flourish. "The bell tolls today for the Voice of America".

This gratuitous death-knell was premature, however. Within the space of several weeks in the late Spring of 1953, the pressures on the information program were gradually relieved and the long uphill fight back to normal operations was begun once more. The McCarthy investigation adjourned without smoking out a single Communist, although it forced the suicide of at least one employee and the resignation of a number of conscientious officials who had stood up to the Senator. The center of interest now shifted to the Congressional appropriations committees. After considerable debate Congress appropriated $85 millions for the program, a sum that required a cutback in operations all along the line including a 25 percent reduction in the work force. Morale in the organization was low and there was little stimulus for high-flying ideological campaigning. High fliers, the investigations proved, were fair game.

Slowly, then quickly, this hesitancy changed. In August the information program was transferred from the State Department and made an independent agency known as the United States Information Agency. The new agency continued to receive policy guidance from the Department but it was free to operate its own program. Overseas the United States Information Service posts continued to operate under the control of the American embassy in each country but they received their operating instructions and funds from the Agency in Washington. In the following months the quiet efforts of the Eisenhower administration's own appraisal of the information program bore fruit in a series of directives giving USIA a more prominent place in the foreign-policy mechanism of the government. For the first time the overseas information program was to participate officially in both the formulation and the development of foreign policies. Here, at last, was recognition of the growing importance of popular persuasion in foreign policy. It was a big step forward from the time when OWI took its policy cue by telephone from a minor State Department official.

With this new look in the design of policy planning went a new viewpoint. In a speech before the American Society of Newspaper Editors in Washington, President Eisenhower boldly outlined his concern for the need for disarmament both as a step towards reducing international tensions and as a means for freeing more funds for world economic development. He challenged the Soviet Union to back up its peaceful words with deeds in this field. The death of Stalin in March 1953 and the East German workers' revolt in June added urgency to the President's appeal. It was a message worthy of major exploitation and the new Information Agency was ready to go to work on it.

The organization benefited from some vigorous new leadership, including its new director, former New York radio executive Theodore Streibert. A bluff, gruff man who had a habit of saying precisely what he thought, Streibert took on his job with no interest in postmortems about the former glories or failings of the information program. He started fresh and he showed a sure sense for giving the program what it sorely needed—firm leadership and a solid administrative framework. His accomplishment may be summarized by saying that he gave all of us working for him the feeling that we were in the information *business*. By the time Streibert resigned to return to private business late in 1956 he had built up an organization that had confidence in itself and in its long-range mission. Appropriations were relatively stable; USIA was participating more in the formation of policy; plans could be made for the day after tomorrow with assurance.

Streibert's replacement as director of the Information Agency was Arthur V. Larson, a distinguished labor-law expert who had also served the Republican Party as ideological adviser and speech writer. His close identification with the more political aspects of the Eisenhower administration did not sit well with the Democratic majority in Congress and he resigned after less than a year in the job. In November 1957, George V. Allen, who had headed the program ten years earlier as Assistant Secretary of State for Public Affairs, was recalled from his duties as Ambassador in Athens to take over direction of the Agency.

Allen brought to the job not only his twenty-seven years' experience as a diplomat but also new ideas on the role of information activities in our overall strategy. He placed greater emphasis on the value of the information program as a long-range policy instrument rather than on its tactical value in meeting day-to-day public-opinion problems overseas. Speaking before a Congressional committee in 1959, he summarized his views:

"It is my conviction that this Agency can make its most important contributions to the foreign policy objectives of the United States through its long-range programs. These should help achieve a clearer understanding of the American people, their character and the institutions that underlie American policies... Under all conditions we would need to give an account of ourselves overseas. The need is particularly pressing in these times. Where political stresses and strains make normal healthy interchange between peoples and between governments difficult, the Agency needs to bend every effort to keep open the channels of information and of ideas. It needs to keep books, magazines, films and discussions before the people of other countries. We need to show others an advanced democratic nation in action. We need to demonstrate sympathy and understanding of social, economic and political problems. We need to give people everywhere a sense that here is one great, active nation dedicated to man's best aspirations. I have been responsible for this program for something over a year now and during that time my chief concern has been to give proper emphasis to the things that will build confidence in us through better understanding. One thing I have done is to insist on representing the United States adequately with books and other materials that make people think more carefully about us—for that which men think about is that which men understand and remember. I am convinced that it is basic understanding that will do our work best."

Under Director Allen's administration, the Information Agency underwent a subtle change in the approach to its job. The new emphasis was on the longer look, on cultural and ideological programming that may seem unspectacular from day to day but which promises greater returns in deeper understanding of American policies and motives abroad. Beyond its implications for our national strategy this approach reflects a more mature attitude on the part of the Agency and of the American government generally in propaganda matters.

In December 1960, George Allen resigned from government service to become head of a private research institute. He left a USIA organization that was more conscious of its responsibilities and more confident of its ability to carry them out than at any time in its history. Because of his long experience and prestige earned in over thirty years in the Foreign Service, he was able to strengthen the information agency's relationships with the State Department in Washington and with the Department's diplomatic establishments abroad. I believe—and I think that most of my colleagues would agree—that our organization became of age during George Allen's three-year term as its director.

Never before was the sensitivity of the American people regarding their overseas image so exposed as it was during the last weeks of the 1960 election campaign. Both parties dug in on the issue, with both Democrats and Republicans stressing the need for a "new image" of America to win the confidence of people abroad.

Whatever judgment future historians may make on American prestige in the seventh decade of the twentieth century, there seems little doubt that the disquiet which Americans have shown over the issue in recent years was an important factor in President Kennedy's election victory. His call for a more vigorous approach to meet the threat of "the lean, hungry enemy", as he described Communism, struck a responsive chord in the inner consciences of millions of Americans.

It is highly significant that the Kennedy Administration has expressed concern for the role of the USIA program in its review of foreign policy operations. This concern was reflected in the selection of Edward R. Murrow as director of the information agency. Mr. Murrow brought to his new assignment strong experience in the information field together with the assurances of the new Administration that it intended to give high priority to USIA's activities.

By what means do we reach people overseas with a valid statement of our intentions? What do we say and how do we say it? Is what we say and do good enough to match our responsibility as a democratic world leader whose leadership is based on the freely-given support of the rest of the free world? A closer look at the mode of our information operations abroad will provide some of the answers to these questions.

4

FROM PENNSYLVANIA AVENUE TO LUANG PRABANG

Two blocks west of the White House on Pennsylvania Avenue is an unassuming grey-brick building that might be classified architecturally as Warren Harding Gothic. It is headquarters for the U.S. Information Agency, parent organization of more than 200 U.S. Information Service posts scattered from the staid precincts of London's Grosvenor Square to the up-country Laotian city of Luang Prabang.

In Indonesia the U.S. Information Service is called Kantor Penerangan Amerika Serikat. In Greece it is Amerikaniki Iperisia Pleroforion and in Argentina, the Instituto Cultural Argentino-Norteamericano. From Reykjavik north of the Arctic Circle to the steamy Indonesian port city of Surabaya the USIS sign is a familiar landmark for millions of people. Its offices and libraries receive tens of thousands of visitors every day; millions more listen to its Voice of America radio programs and read its news releases, magazines and other publications. It teaches English to the Japanese, explains developments in atomic energy to the Swedes and describes the Constitution to the Nigerians. In the Far East it broadcasts its message through the most powerful radio transmitters in the world and in Tehran it relies on bicycle messengers. In Turkey it shows films about Tennessee in railroad-car cinemas and in the Carribean it shows them on passenger liners. It once asked for, and got, the King of Thailand's permission to use music he composed for one of its films. It publishes books in such languages as Urdu, Gujarati, Telegu, Farsi, and Tagalog about Tom Sawyer, space satellites and Walt Whitman. In Moscow it distributes a Russian language picture magazine every month that changes hands briskly at three times the official newsstand price. It does all this so that the world may get to know Americans and their ideas better.

By any standard measurement ours is the biggest information service of its kind in the world. For all their alleged superiority in the arts of propaganda, the Russians have nothing like it in size, extent or in openhandedness although they are trying to imitate it where they can. When an American critic of our foreign policy wants to make his most telling point he usually declares that we are not reaching down to the grassroots to convince world opinion about ourselves. No one has ever quite defined where the world's grassroots are but every day USIS posts open their doors for business in such cities as Khorramshahr, Dar-es-Salaam, Mogadiscio, Tegucigalpa, Hue, Bamako, Chiengmai, Belo Horizonte, Enugu and Moulmein.[1] These towns are as varied as their exotic names and the public opinion problems that the officers of our information service find in each of them are equally diverse.

Conakry on the West African coast was a dozing seaport town under French administration until 1959 when it became the capital of the new nation of Guinea. The USIS post there is housed in a large white reconverted bank building just off the city's main square. Directing its operations is a former newspaperman, Hal Tufty, who has been in information work since 1955. After a tour of duty in South Asia, Tufty was selected for his Conakry assignment partly because of his fluency in French, the *lingua franca* of the new nation. Conakry is one of a score of posts that has been opened in Africa since 1954 as a result of the creation of new nations there. From his high-ceilinged office adjoining the library, Hal Tufty directs a program whose purpose now is to demonstrate to the native leaders of Guinea that the United States respects and supports the development of their country. Working with Tufty are eight Guinean employees and an American assistant, Will Petty, a young Negro who entered USIS in 1959 after spending two years in West Africa as an exchange student in the Experiment in International Living program. The yearly budget for the Conakry post is $75,000; this is a substantial figure for an information operation in a small country but it is considerably less than the funds and personnel available to the Russian, East German, Red Chinese, Czech and Hungarian delegations who have established themselves in Guinea since independence.

On the first floor of our office in Conakry is the library which is patronized by a continual flow of visitors all day. The only lending library in the country, it has won a place of highest respect among literate Guineans. There are no newspapers in the country except for a bulletin issued by the government. Tufty and his assistants place material in the government bulletin and supplement it by issuing their

---

1. These cities are located in the following countries respectively: Iran, British East Africa, Somalia, Honduras, Vietnam, Mali, Thailand, Brazil, Nigeria and Burma.

own pamphlets and also photographs which are posted in public places throughout the country. One of the most popular USIS publications has been a colorful cartoon pamphlet describing the 1959 visit to America of Guinea's first president, Sekou Toure. Films are also used in Conakry to acquaint Guineans with America. When Hal Tufty can get away from the office he travels into the interior by jeep to meet with provincial leaders and other Guinean opinion makers. He usually takes a projector with him and a copy of the film that the Agency in Washington made about President Toure's American tour. Although the film has been seen many times throughout Guinea it is still a big hit. Seated in the night-darkness of their village squares, the Guineans follow every detail of the film's description of the reception their new leader received in the little-known country of America across the sea.

Three thousand miles west and south of Conakry in Rio de Janeiro, our information programs have been in operation for almost twenty years. Aldo D'Alessandro, the athletically built post director, came to the information service in 1942 after a long career in commercial radio. D'Alessandro's official title, like that of other USIS post directors, is public affairs officer. He oversees the operations of nine posts throughout Brazil, including the latest one at the country's new capital, Brasilia. He also supervises a program for providing assistance to the Brazilians and resident Americans who operate binational cultural institutes in twenty-seven cities. These Brazilian-American Institutes are lively centers of activity; in addition to a full range of cultural and social events, from violin recitals to puppet shows, they teach English to over 50,000 persons a year. In the industrial and commercial center of Säo Paulo the local institute has five thousand members and is an important element in the city's cultural life.

The main job of D'Alessandro and his twenty-two American assistants is to contact and converse with Brazilian opinion leaders from editors to parish priests. The conversation almost invariably gets around to American policies as they relate to Brazil and usually includes some commentary on our coffee-drinking habits. How much coffee we drink and what we pay for it is an important subject in a country whose economy still rests, despite a large program of crop diversification, on the coffee crop. Assignment in Brazil has made USIS press officer Lafe Allen a self-educated expert on the world coffee trade. He has to know the facts and figures in order to handle press queries competently. Although coffee is a perennial topic for Americans and Brazilians, it is only one facet of our relationship with them.

They want to know, too, what our attitude is toward their plans for strengthening Brazil's economic and social foundations. Convincing them of American interest and concern is an important part of the USIS job in Brazil.

There is a similar job to be done some ten thousand miles east of Rio de Janeiro in Dacca, the moist, hot capital of East Pakistan. Our information post here is familiar to me since it is currently my assignment to direct its operations. There may be more interesting work somewhere but I would be hard put to name it. Packed into an area no bigger than Arkansas, East Pakistan contains almost 50 million hard-working people, 80% of whom are illiterate, most of whom suffer from endemic diseases such as malaria and dysentery, many of whom live at a near-starvation level and all of whom are citizens of one of the largest new nations of Asia. Combatting ancient scourges and giving hope for modern development is a massive Pakistani-American program to raise economic, social and health standards. To tell its story and get across its purpose is our business. I have a staff of nine first-rate American officers and 120 Pakistanis, together with a respectable $400,000 annual operation budget. In addition to our main offices on bustling Topkhana Road in Dacca we operate six smaller posts in provincial cities. Since the Bengal jungle separates the Dacca office from all but two of the cities, we usually rely on river boats or planes to reach them. During the long monsoon period every summer even these modes of transportation are occasionally inoperative.

Climatic and geographical difficulties do not prevent our materials from reaching all parts of East Pakistan. In addition to hundreds of columns of press material placed in local newspapers every month, we issue a twice-monthly newspaper describing Pakistani-American events in detail. The paper is no propaganda throwaway; it is sold to over twenty thousand subscribers in two language editions, English and Bengali. Through the press, films, libraries and other media we tell the story of America's role in Pakistani progress.

Conakry . . . Rio de Janeiro . . . Dacca . . . three different cities with three different information problems but each sharing a common theme—the identification of American aspirations with those of the local population. It is the most difficult and delicate of themes to express without sounding the false note of condescension or insincerity. Yet it is the most important single thing we have to say, the most effective way in which we can give a heart and mind to our age.

No two information programs overseas are alike because no two political situations are alike. However, there is a common pattern to

USIS operations since they are always circumscribed by our overall policy objectives. Each of our foreign posts is part of the American diplomatic mission in the country of its location. Our ambassadors are directly responsible for all official activities of the U.S. Government in their respective countries of assignment and this includes what USIS says and does. The country director for USIS activities, the public affairs officer, is a senior member of the ambassador's staff. He sits on the embassy "country team", a committee under the ambassador's direction that coordinates all our official activities in the country. Participation of the public affairs officer on the country team assures full consideration of public opinion factors both in local embassy actions and in the policy recommendations that the ambassador makes to Washington. The scope and nature of our information services are carefully tailored to the embassy's estimate of what type of program can best advance our political objectives in each country. This determination is made every year when USIS and the embassy draw up a "country plan", which is a detailed outline of objectives and activities of the country information program for the coming year. The "country plan" is then sent to Washington for approval. Once approved by USIA and the State Department it becomes the charter for information activities in the country. Our major informational objectives in most free world countries can be summarized in four phrases:

1. To provide an image of the United States as a leader in the free world whose fundamental interests are similar to those of other free world countries.

2. To document American life as a reflection of a vigorous democratic society whose goals are similar to those of other free world nations.

3. In countries where the United States has economic and military aid programs, to publicize the extent and purpose of these programs.

4. To point up, where necessary, the danger of Communism as a new form of imperialism that threatens the freedom of independent nations through internal subversion and external aggression.

These major objectives are adapted in each country plan to meet specific local conditions. In the early days of the information program many posts felt a compulsion to say something about everything. In the new professionalism that now characterizes the program this compulsion has gradually been modified. Our most effective information efforts are those that concentrate on a relatively few ideas and express them succinctly and with conviction.

USIS has to work within the political climate it is trying to influence. This involves a considerable amount of discretion, especially in countries where information activities by any foreign government are suspect. (There is a reasonable basis for this suspicion in some instances. The information offices of a number of foreign governments have often served as "covers" for intelligence operations.) As part of the American diplomatic mission our activities are not usually hampered in most free world countries. There are, however, some instances where restrictions are in force. The Indian government has been reluctant to permit further expansion of information services by any foreign nation in recent years. We have nine posts in India and would probably have more if we were not bound by this general restriction.

Occasionally programs are curbed for our own political reasons. An awkward instance occurred some dozen years ago in an Asian country where we quietly stopped distributing copies of the Declaration of Independence at the suggestion of local officials. The list of our grievances against an eighteenth century British monarch described too accurately the grievances of present-day opposition groups in this particular country against their own king. All too often we are placed in the dilemma of having to moderate our message of freedom in order not to embarrass less-than-freedom-loving governments with whom we are necessarily allied. The dilemma becomes all the more acute when we are pressed by progressive, non-Communist elements in friendly countries to reconcile alleged American support for totalitarian regimes with our democratic claims. Since we do not presume to choose internal governments for other nations, there can be no easy answer to such apparent contradictions.

Next to what we say, our most important decision is whom do we speak to. We cannot address ourselves directly to everyone overseas. In India there is one American USIS officer for every ten million Indian citizens. Even in the unlikely event that the information service should be given funds to send several thousand officers to India they would be able to reach only a small portion of the local population. There are other cogent reasons why overexpansion would not work, the most important being the fact that the Indians would not want thousands of us "foreigners" pleading our own national causes in their country. We can put our ideas across in India and other countries by working together with the local opinion makers who are sympathetic to our cause. They can explain our case to their fellow citizens in their own languages and with a fuller understanding of their national mentality than any American could ever have. The battle for public opinion abroad is essentially a struggle for the loyalties of the leading opinion makers in each local situation. The bulk of the Communist propaganda machinery is aimed at opinion-making groups and so are most USIS efforts. Exceptions occur when the confirmed hostility of opinion-making elements make it necessary to appeal directly to mass opinion. This explains the Communist use of mass-movement appeals in free world countries where they are adamantly rebuffed by the ruling opinion leadership. By the same token we use direct appeal to mass opinion through our shortwave radio operations beamed toward Iron Curtain countries. Occasionally there are political situations even in free world countries that require us to circumvent hostile opinion leadership through appeals to a mass audience.

Identifying the opinion leadership in a given country or city is a difficult business. In one country the group may be narrowed down to a few dozen people; this was certainly true for many years in Saudi Arabia. In more than one African country the opinion makers constitute a group of tribal chieftains who could fit in a small room. In other countries the opinion-making group must be numbered in the tens of thousands. As societies advance economically and politically opinion makers become more numerous and more difficult to identify. The patriarchal type of opinion makers of tradition-oriented societies gives way to more sophisticated and subtle variations of opinion makers as caste and family disintegrate. There are, of course, some obvious candidates for the opinion maker group in any country. These are the top government officials, newspaper publishers and editors, broadcasters, religious leaders, professional men and the like. Other opinion makers come in a great variety of occupational shapes and cultural sizes. Throughout Southeast Asia there are thousands of astrologers who play a vital role in both private and public decision making. Whatever the limitations of astrology, the astrologers cannot be ignored by anyone concerned with opinion in Asia. Doctors are another highly influential group, particularly in countries where health conditions are serious and medical men are few.

Whoever the opinion makers are, it is the job of USIS to see that they are identified and that they are made aware of our position on key issues. Particularly in the press and communications fields USIS officers must personally know the top people and keep in regular contact with them. Others are contacted less frequently. Most posts maintain an address list of their contacts, broken down by occupational categories. When the embassy wants a policy statement or other important information given wide distribution, it may be mailed to all those on the address list. When I was serving in Greece, a country of 8,000,000 people, our post had an address file containing the names and addresses of over 35,000 persons, grouped in such categories as civic leaders, writers, industrialists, doctors and—my favorite category —"Miscellaneous Intellectuals."

The strategy of concentrating our information operations on a relatively small group of opinion makers has been questioned by some critics on the ground that it is inadequate to the need for matching Communist propaganda efforts in free world countries. The problem they raise is real. The Soviet Union invests heavily in grass-roots propaganda through the foreign counterparts of its own Communist Party and through other front organizations. This tactic reflects historic Communist use of mass "popular front" movements as a means of neutralizing and eventually overmatching what is known in Marxist-Leninist jargon as "the ruling circles" of non-Communist countries.

Reliable estimates indicate that the Soviet Union and its satellites are currently spending about $500 million a year on propaganda directed at the free world, not including the considerable sum needed to jam non-Communist radio broadcasts. The Chinese Reds are relatively late starters in the international propaganda field but they have gone into it with the same intensity that has marked the rest of their aggressive strategy. In 1959, the Chinese Communist international radio services surpassed those of the Voice of America for the first time in the amount of program-hours broadcast.

A major portion of the Communist effort involves training a native Communist leadership for subversive political propaganda work in countries throughout the free world. Hundreds of such potential leaders are groomed every year in Moscow and other Communist capitals for jobs directing Red enterprises from newspapers to local party cells. This strategy gives the Soviet and Chinese leadership a native-led propaganda and agitation channel that can be exploited to identify local grievances with Communist goals. Whatever the surface advantages of such a policy, any attempt on our part to try to copy this Communist strategy of grass-roots agitation would be disastrous. It would involve, first of all, a massive shift in our traditional policy of non-interference in local politics which would be resented by other free world countries. It would also mean giving up any hope of maintaining positive democratic leadership. We would tragically confirm the already-held suspicion that we regard smaller nations as pawns in an overall struggle with the Communists.

Furthermore, in point of pragmatic fact we could not match agitation efforts of the Communists. Their strategy is based on a conspiratorial mechanism; ours flows from a free society which cannot hide anything.

The use of conspiratorial tactics on our part would result in immediate loss of prestige and ultimate failure. Our best strategy is to present our ideas openly. By concentrating our efforts on broad opinion leadership, we stand a better chance of building up general confidence in American motives and action than if we concentrated on a "professional" pro-American faction which could be counted on, through one form of pressure or another, to parrot our line. There may be some tactical advantages to having an obedient "party line" following but such a tactic does not meet our overall need for broad international support for our policies.

We seek everybody's support, and we run our information services to accommodate this fact. USIS offices are usually situated on the main street in the busiest part of the cities and towns where they are located. They operate on an "open door policy" and every day uncounted thousands of people walk through their doors. Some come to look at picture books in the libraries; others drop in to discuss specific business affecting the United States; the great majority of visitors, however, come simply because they want to learn more about us.

Our posts are divided into two sections, one for information activities and another for cultural. The information section serves as the embassy press office and supervises our film, radio, exhibit and publication programs. In larger posts an American officer may be assigned to each of these specialized media activities. The extent of the individual media operations in any particular country depends primarily on their relative effectiveness in getting across the American message to the people there. At my post in Dacca the film program is the largest of our media operations because films have proven to be the best way to reach both small opinion leader groups and mass audiences in East Pakistan. Some posts concentrate their efforts on other media. In African and Asian countries the exhibits program is often the best means of putting across an idea. Our officers have developed several do-it-yourself systems for mounting simple photo exhibits that are compact and demountable to facilitate their use in back-country areas. One of these, developed by exhibits officer Herb Rosenthal in Turkey, involved nothing more complicated than a few brightly-painted sticks and some cord from which the pictures were suspended.

In most posts the main business of the information section has to do with the local press. The information officer is the anonymous "American embassy spokesman" who provides the press associations and newspapers with our viewpoint on current issues. Our press offices have a high priority on the "beats" of most political reporters overseas. In turn our officers have their own "beats", covering all the important newspapers and magazines at regular intervals to talk with the editors. USIS press offices are an integral part of the most extensive non-commercial press service in the world—a daily news file prepared at USIA headquarters in Washington and transmitted by radio teletype circuits to local posts overseas. The press file's material consists largely of official American statements such as Presidential speeches, State Department announcements and the transcripts of conferences such as the President's press conference. These are made available to editors and other opinion leaders abroad as background material to give them an accurate account of our official position on leading issues.

In addition to dealing with newspaper people our information officers assist thousands of people who visit or write USIS every day. A good part of any officer's day is spent answering questions. Many of them can be answered by giving the questioner a copy of a handy compendium of facts and figures entitled *Facts about the USA* which has been prepared by USIA and has been translated into many languages around the world. There are many other queries, however, that cannot be answered "by the book".

Complementing our information and media efforts is our overseas cultural operation. Cultural relations are one of the oldest aspects of diplomacy. The number of ballet dancers and poets traded between two countries was once a rough indicator of their mutual relations. Exchanges of artists were a generally harmless exercise in good will that appealed to the tribal customs of the diplomatic elite. In modern times cultural relations have become a more business-like part of international diplomacy. The bigger nations have developed elaborate programs to display their cultural achievements on the international stage. The purpose is to impress; none have used artistic devices more lavishly for this purpose than the Soviet Union and the Chinese Communists. The Soviets ship ballerinas and circuses all over the world; the Chinese are not far behind with theatrical troupes, pianists, scholars and tumblers. In the free world the British have developed a large, sophisticated program operated from a chain of British Council cultural centers in principal cities abroad. The French have been operating similar organizations for many years.

The United States was the last of the great powers to enter this field officially. Private attempts to strengthen American cultural relations were made by several binational organizations before World War II; such groups have existed in Latin America since the 1920's. However, early efforts were scattered and were given almost no official support. The pace changed at the beginning of World War II when programs were set up for meeting enemy cultural penetration in Latin America and other areas of the world. Cultural attaches were assigned to embassies where they became a part of the new U.S. Information Service operations. Simulated by the postwar Fulbright scholarship program, the State Department set up a full-fledged cultural division in 1947. The program has grown steadily since then.

If any one aspect of our cultural activities could be selected as spreading our influence widest and deepest it would be the world-wide system of libraries we maintain. If a USIS post has nothing else, it has a library. In dozens of places it is the only free lending library available. In addition to 162 overseas libraries we have extension services and book-exchange agreements to supply material to thousands of other foreign outlets. Our library operations stand as quiet proof not only of American scholarship but also of the breadth and variety of American ideas. Supplementing them is the program for encouraging the production and distribution of American books, both in English and in translation, for commercial book outlets overseas. The other major cultural activity is the so-called exchange program which assists in sending American students abroad for study and in bringing foreign students to American colleges and universities. Most of the fifty thousand foreign students now studying here have received advice or other assistance from our posts abroad in planning their studies here.

Over and above these organizational tasks, our cultural attache must be responsive to the local cultural scene wherever he is stationed. His assignment may be in sophisticated Paris or in exotic Kabul; the problem is essentially the same, that of keeping open the lines of American communications to the local intellectual elite. Usually cultural officers have doctorate degrees or the other academic merit badges which permit them initial access to this elite.

As might be expected, our activities have been tightly restricted in the Communist bloc for many years. Immediately after the liberation of Eastern Europe in 1945 we opened information posts in Czechoslovakia, Poland, Rumania, Hungary and Bulgaria. Under the agreements the western allies made with Stalin during the war these countries were to be permitted to reestablish themselves as independent nations. USIS operations in these countries were part of a western effort to meet the problem of growing Soviet pressure on the newly-formed governments. Our libraries and other information facilities were well patronized not only because of their services but also because of their symbolic appeal as windows on the west. Although they were operated with discretion, these posts were soon recognized by Soviet authorities as a distinct hindrance to their plans to communize Eastern Europe. One by one they were arbitrarily closed down by Soviet-dominated governments; the unsubstantiated charge against the posts was that they were "spy centers" and "imperialist propaganda machines." In August 1951, all operations were ended in the Soviet satellite countries when the center in Budapest was eliminated by the Hungarian government. In recent years there has been a small but significant resumption of American cultural and informational activities behind the Iron Curtain.

In Warsaw the American embassy operates a modest information and cultural program that includes the distribution of a Polish-language magazine, *Ameryka,* and the operation of a small exchange program. We have no operations in Rumania, Hungary, Bulgaria or Albania; nor are there yet any prospects for any. Even if we should be invited to establish full-fledged information centers behind the Iron Curtain as part of a Communist gambit on "relaxing tensions", we would be reluctant to do so without firm guarantees of reasonable protection for our personnel, local as well as American. One of the tragic aspects of the closing of our offices and libraries in the satellite countries a decade ago was the harassment of our local employees by their Communist governments. They were forced to report to the police regularly on their own activities and those of their American employers. Since most of them were anti-Communist and pro-democratic, this requirement was distasteful to them. A number of them were summarily jailed as "lackeys of the Americans" and on other vague charges. Many of those jailed have never been heard from again; it can be assumed that at least some of them were executed because of their USIS activities.

Since 1955 when the Soviet government decided to step up official contact with the west, the American embassy in Moscow has carried on a small cultural and informational operation to implement the various agreements we have signed with the Russians in these fields. The original agreement on exchanges of delegations in various arts and sciences was signed in 1958. Two years later the agreement was extended until 1961 and was broadened to include new fields such as summer language study programs and an exchange of information on the peacetime use of atomic energy. Under these agreements, 59 cultural and scientific delegations from the United States visited the Soviet Union in 1959; they ranged from the New York Philharmonic Orchestra to a group of 22 housebuilders. In the same year 68 Soviet delegations visited the United States. During the same year, two showcase fairs were sponsored by the American and Soviet governments in Moscow and New York respectively. Our Moscow embassy also supervises the monthly distribution of 50,000 copies of a Russian language *Life*-type picture magazine produced by the Agency. The Russians produce a similar magazine for distribution in the United States under the quid-pro-quo terms of our overall cultural agreements with them. Although still slim and tenuous, the lines of cultural communication between ourselves and the Soviet peoples have at least been opened through these arrangements. How long they remain open and how effective they are in terms of our interests is a matter of conjecture. The real test of their value to our strategic interests is whether the ideological grip which the Soviet leadership has over its people will be loosened by these new contacts with the west.

The twelve hundred officers and technicians who serve overseas at USIS posts are a variegated group whose only common attribute is that they entered the business as amateurs. Despite the increasing importance of overseas information work in modern diplomacy there is no school or university in the United States that gives specific training in the complexities of modern-day propaganda. The officers manning our posts abroad have learned the business on the job.

Most of the information officers have journalistic backgrounds, although many of them came from the film and radio fields. The cultural officers came mainly from college campuses or other teaching jobs. There are more than two hundred women in our foreign information service, most of whom are secretaries. Many of the others are librarians although a number of other professional assignments are also held by women. Ruth Tryon was an information officer in Hungary in 1951 when, together with another embassy officer, she was declared *persona non grata* by the Hungarian government on trumped-up espionage charges after she had been named in the treason trial of Archbishop Josef Groesz. Dynamic brunette Patricia Van Delden became the first woman director of a country operation in 1958 when she was appointed public affairs officer at our embassy in The Hague.

A USIS officer is normally assigned to a number of different foreign countries during the course of his career. His assignments alternate between those labeled "hardship" and "non-hardship," the designations indicating relative conditions of health, climate and isolation. Within the "hardship" category, distinctions are made as to degree of inconvenience, and appropriate compensation is paid to all our Foreign Service personnel serving there. Known as the "hardship post allowance", this compensation runs as high as 25 percent of an employee's salary. My present home, Dacca, is a "25 percent post". It is also the subject of a somewhat apocryphal story about the rigors of the Foreign Service.

The climatic and health disadvantages of Dacca are all carefully outlined in the State Department's report that is made available to any American being sent to the city. One day a newly-recruited officer was informed that he was to be assigned to Dacca. He read the post report and blanched at the prospect. Mosquitoes, snakes, dysentery, monsoons—it did not look good and he told the personnel office he would prefer another post. "All right," said the personnel chief. "We have another post out there that you may like. It's called Chittagong. Take a look at the post report and let me know." The officer took the report home only to read of more mosquitoes, snakes, dysentery and monsoons, plus the following paragraph under the section entitled Entertainment Facilities: "There are no adequate entertainment facilities in Chittagong but you can get up to Dacca for holiday weekends."

Regarding the many difficulties of living in such isolated places, you have to be philosophical, as the old Scotch lady said, and not think about them. A few of the difficulties cannot be forgotten or wished away. Education of their children is a real concern for most Foreign Service families. In about half of our posts overseas school facilities range from good to excellent; in others, they are fair or non-existent. George Butler, an experienced Latin American hand, tells of one information officer and his wife who sent their little boy to a local American school south of the border a few years ago. He came home the first day and proudly displayed the books that had been given him. It was a dog-eared collection. One of them, a civics book, had a portrait of a distinguished-looking gentleman opposite the title page captioned: "Our President—Warren Gamaliel Harding". Despite forty-year-old books and other handicaps, our sons and daughters usually thrive surprisingly well on their nomadic life. They can expect to receive about a third of their education in the United States since officers are rotated between Washington and foreign assignments.

Health is another problem in some foreign assignments although both the State Department and USIA have recently won Congressional approval for legislation to provide better health facilities for Foreign Service personnel. Nevertheless, health casualties of personnel still complicate somewhat the problem of keeping our offices in Asia and Africa fully manned.

A more sporadic occupational hazard is riots. Because of their central locations USIS offices and libraries are the best known and the most conspicuous official symbol of America in many foreign cities. Their accessibility is a functional advantage in day-to-day operations but it becomes a practical disadvantage in moments of political crisis when demonstrations and riots flare. If the demonstration is directed against an American policy or one we are associated with, our information office often becomes a target for the demonstrators. In most cases only a window may be stoned or some tempers frayed but occasionally the damage is more serious. In Taipeh in 1957, a Chinese mob was incited to riot by a rumor of alleged injustice in a legal case involving the shooting of a Chinese "peeping Tom" by an American sergeant. Our information office was gutted and parts of the building were pulled apart by the screaming mob. Public affairs officer Ralph Powell and three of his assistants—James Moceri, Alex Boas and Philip Carroll—remained in the building to protect classified records until other help could be summoned. They were all injured in the ensuing melée with Boas suffering heavy wounds.

These attacks are not usually intended against USIS specifically; the rioters in most cases are students, the most regular clients of our libraries. During the Lebanese riots of 1958 students attacked our office there and the Coca-Cola bottling plant, each in its own way a popular symbol of America in local student circles. The logic that impels a student to throw a brick at our library one day and borrow a book from it the next is obscure but commonplace in many foreign cities. Local opinion circles do not necessarily support either the logic or the destructive action of these riots. When the library in Athens was bombed in December 1958 during the Cyprus crisis, responsible Greeks showed their chagrin over the action by sending packets of books to our embassy to replace those destroyed in the blast. Whenever U.S. government property is destroyed, the local government is billed for the damages in accordance with standard diplomatic practice.

Living abroad in strange surroundings requires psychological stamina and flexibility. In 1958 the Agency took special recognition of this factor when it instituted psychiatric examinations of all prospective candidates for foreign assignment as well as of their wives. Notwithstanding such precautions the quality of the Agency's personnel is still uneven in spots, primarily because of the difficulty of determining standards for measuring a successful officer. Professional ability is only a partial guide. An excellent record in commercial media as a reporter, magazine editor or radio producer does not assure fitness for information work overseas with its special requirements in regard to personal characteristics and attitudes. Some essential qualities can hardly be judged until an officer is on the job. In recent years the Agency has been more candid in recognizing errors in personnel selection and in bringing about the resignation of employees whose work is marginal. Annual "performance rating" reports on employees, a standard government procedure, are the main basis for judging work performance. In 1958 some 116 of the USIA's employees were, to use its bureaucratic phrase, "encouraged to seek employment elsewhere".

Prospects for developing a professional career corps were enhanced in 1960 when the Agency set up a "career Foreign Service Reserve" corps. This new system partially replaces the procedure of designating USIS officers overseas according to ratings normally used to designate State Department administrative personnel. The new Foreign Service Reserve corps is regarded by the Agency as a stepping stone toward Congressional approval of some form of a permanent USIS career corps similar to that of the State Department corps. To facilitate the transition, USIS Reserve Corps officers were selected after a series of oral and written examinations in a manner similar to the State Department's selection system. The end result may be some form of integration of the Agency's and the Department's officer corps. The decision will depend on the outcome of a series of current discussions about returning Agency activities to the State Department where they were located before 1953.

Allied with the Agency's "career Foreign Service Reserve" program is its Junior Officer Trainees program instituted in 1954 to select and train young men and women for Agency careers. Only a few candidates enter the trainee program each year but it has consistently been bringing in valuable new talent and fresh ideas. Trainees are given ten weeks of initial training in Washington and nine months of on-the-job training at a foreign post before they are accepted into the Agency's officer corps. In-service training at both government and private schools are provided for more seasoned officers to strengthen their professional qualifications.

One type of in-service training is the program for language-and-area studies designed to fit officers for service in a particular country or area. The past decade has seen a significant increase in the amount and the quality of such studies being offered in American universities.

Harvard's Russian Research Center and the University of Pennsylvania's South Asian studies center are two that are well-known both for academic research and for preparing government and private employees for work in critical areas. The State Department's Foreign Service Institute in Washington is known especially for the teaching of the "exotic languages" of Asia and Africa. The Agency has been stepping up its program for assigning officers to such studies.

Almost all USIS officers have studied one foreign language, usually one of the "world languages" such as French, Spanish or German. There are many officers who speak two or three languages together with a few like Eastern European specialist Joseph Kolarek who speaks four. Nevertheless American Foreign Service personnel still reflect our national weakness in language training as compared with the educational traditions of other world powers. Language facility is especially important in the information services where officers work so directly with local officials and opinion leaders. To speak his language is often the greatest compliment that can be paid a foreign editor or government leader. In 1960 over 400 USIS officers received on-the-job language training at their posts and 122 were assigned fulltime to language schools in the States for study sessions ranging from three to eighteen months. Those who pursue the more extensive courses are expected to spend at least six years in an area where they will use their newly-acquired ability.

The main burden of maintaining close touch with the day-to-day situation at each foreign post is shouldered by our seven thousand local employees who are usually native citizens of the countries where they work. In the main, they are dedicated and intelligent experts who provide their American supervisors with a continuing estimate of what the United States can or should say in their countries. It would be difficult to function two days without this advice. No American, not even one trained in area studies, can hope to match the natural instinct of a good local political observer. The real test of the effectiveness of a local employee is how well he relates this instinct to an informed understanding of American purpose. Over the years USIS posts have developed a valuable group of employees who are expert in this field.

In order to strengthen their understanding of the United States and its policies, some of the most promising local employees are brought to the States for a three-month orientation tour. In all more than 200 employees have toured the United States and examined Agency operations in Washington during the past decade. They return not only better informed but also more enthused about their work.

While our information activities are flung out all over the world even more widely than the ubiquitous embassies and consulates of the State Department, Washington is still the center for administrative and coordinating activities of our information service. Whatever is done in the field depends upon daily communication, by dispatches and telegrams, with USIA in Washington.

As we have seen, our strategic policies are based on Presidential decisions made within the National Security Council framework. The day-to-day translation of these policies into world-wide information operations is handled by the Agency in close cooperation with the State Department. Because American foreign policy is complex and far-ranging, such coordination is required to assure that what we say through our diverse media outlets is both accurate and timely. Soviet propaganda would be quick to pick up any discrepancies in our output. Except for fast-breaking news events, most decisions on our information output are made at the "guidance meetings" held every morning between representatives of the two agencies. Through these daily meetings, too, USIA can examine proposed policies and suggest means for strengthening them in terms of acceptance by public opinion overseas. Increasingly the emphasis in these considerations is on the overall tone of our output, in other words, on the general impression we are creating. The way we say something is almost as important as what we say.

In recent years "hard sell" propaganda techniques have been

gradually abandoned in most areas in favor of a straightforward presentation of the facts—good, bad and otherwise—without psychological embroidery. Ten years ago, under the emotional impact of the "Campaign of Truth", our information output was often consciously propagandistic with a concentration on such themes as the villainy of Communism and our military strength. Contrary to good intentions or pious claims of "objectivity", USIS media were often obtuse both in approach and execution. Paradoxically, it was the 1953 McCarthy investigations and their attempt to "prove" that the information services were "soft" that brought about the reappraisal leading to more cool-headed and objective programming.[2]

The McCarthy hearings failed to prove "softness" but they did point up the ineffectiveness of a great deal of our "hard sell" propaganda. Sobersided experts assigned by the new Eisenhower administration to study the role of the information program recommended in the late spring of 1953 that the program concentrate on the presentation of straightforward information without benefit of propaganda flourishes. The same recommendation was made by several Congressional and private study groups who were examining the program at that time. The resultant change in tactics was a major victory for those who saw the overseas information program as a long-range effort to provide a responsible explanation of our policies and to build confidence in our leadership.

Once policy and guidance lines are decided upon between USIA and the State Department, the Agency takes over the job of giving them form and function through our world-wide communications facilities. USIA media departments, which are located in Washington, include radio (the Voice of America), press, film, television, libraries and exhibits. In order to assure a coordination among the various media, representatives of each sit together at the regular policy-planning meetings.

The Voice of America is the only medium that sends material directly to an overseas audience. Almost all of its broadcasts originate in the Washington studios. They are beamed overseas by eight sets

2. It must be said in defense of the administrators of the information program in the late 1940's and early 1950's that they were following government policy in their stress on anti-Communist and similar themes. It is well to recall that the American government faced a serious problem at the time in convincing many of its free world allies and others of the threat to their own continued security of Soviet intentions in Greece, Iran, Germany and Korea.

of transmitters located on the east and west coasts. All other media departments prepare material which is sent to USIS posts for foreign distribution. Our overseas posts receive a variety of material on a regular basis from the Agency's press and publications service, motion picture service, television service and the information-centers service which provides Stateside support for the library system and certain other cultural operations. Embassy cultural operations in the field are handled through USIS but in Washington there is a division of responsibility between the Agency and the State Department. A separate cultural division within the Department is responsible for cultural-exchange programs.

A sizeable administrative structure is required to supervise the USIA program and its diverse overseas activities. The budget for the Agency has hovered around the one hundred million dollar mark in recent years. The books have to balance every year to the satisfaction of the Agency's own auditors, to the satisfaction of the U.S. General Accounting Office and of the Bureau of the Budget. Congress also keeps a watchful eye on the program. Congressional attitudes toward the Agency and its work have been generally favorable lately. Experience and maturity in the information business have brought about a new sense of reality on the part of both Congress and the Agency. Most Congressmen support the program in principle and in appropriations. Nevertheless there are still some outstanding hold-outs: Senator Allen J. Ellender, the Louisiana Democrat, has been a lively critic of the program.

A number of Congressmen specialize in Agency affairs because of their membership on the appropriations committees that pass on its budget every Spring. Chief among these is Rep. John Rooney, chairman of the House sub-committee that determines the budgets of USIA, the State Department and certain other government departments. Rooney, a Democrat from Brooklyn, is in his own words a supporter of the information program. He is also one of its most consistent and perceptive critics. He knows how the program works and he has an instinct for spotting any inflated claims made about the program. The new stability that exists in the Agency's relations with Congress permits it to operate at the steady pace essential to its success. The early pattern of alternating big and small budgets was a serious handicap. Both the Agency and Congress have learned their respective lessons in this regard. USIA has become moderate in its budget requests and Congress has shown a corresponding willingness to honor its requests.

There is a new professionalism and steadier sense of purpose in our information operations today whether it involves talking over the Voice of America, showing a film to a group of Mexicans or providing a reading room for a Nigerian city. Each of these operations has its own special set of possibilities and limitations in projecting an effective image of America. How this is done, medium by medium, is the subject of the next seven chapters.

5

RADIO ROUND THE WORLD

"The rebels have seized the radio station. . . . " is a familiar phrase in reports of foreign revolts. It points to radio as a citadel of the power to influence public opinion. In the United States, television has relegated it to a secondary position but in many countries radio is still a developing and revolutionary force. Not everyone can read, but anyone can listen. The arrival of the first radio in a village marks the end of political and cultural isolation. The soothing impersonal voice, with its tongue of a thousand dialects, brings news and disturbing ideas from the outside.

Radio is the world's most widespread communications medium. There are over 300,000,000 radio sets in operation around the globe. About two-thirds of them are in the United States and in Europe; the rest are widely dispersed in other areas. There is a radio for almost every adult in the United States but in India there is only one set for every two hundred Indians. There are more radios in Great Britain than there are in Africa, the Middle East and South Asia combined.

Comparative ratios of set distribution are however, misleading guides to the growing influence of radio outside of Europe and America. A better indication of the power of the medium is its startling rate of growth. The number of radio stations in newly developing areas of the world has doubled in recent years. At the present rate of sales, the number of sets in Asia and Africa will more than double in the next five years. Moreover, radio has an influence far out of proportion to the spotty distribution of receivers in these areas. Public opinion surveys show that most Asians and Africans tend to give more credence to what they hear over the radio than to what they read in newspapers. The disembodied voice issuing from a three-tube receiver is accepted as the authoritative word.

These facts have not escaped the attention of the modern practitioners of propaganda throughout the world. Radio offers them special advantages. For one thing it is the most direct and inexpensive way of reaching a large audience. Anyone with a reasonably powerful radio transmitter can beam a shortwave broadcast almost anywhere in the world. Although shortwave listening has never been popular in the United States, it is important overseas. Most people abroad who can afford them buy radios with both standard and shortwave bands. Day or night, they can listen to the polyglot siren songs of over fifty nations, each trying to convince the other through news programs, music, Pen Pal Clubs, political commentaries and chatty interviews that they are on the side of goodness and truth.

Radio has featured in international propaganda developments since the 1920's. At that time the Soviet Union, France and other European countries began broadcasting in the languages of neighboring countries. These early broadcasts were mediumwave transmissions, limited in range to a few hundred miles. In 1927 the first significant use of shortwave transmissions that could span oceans and continents was made by the Netherlands government when it inaugurated a shortwave service to its colonies. Other European powers and the Soviet Union soon followed suit with their own international shortwave services. In 1932 the British Broadcasting Corporation began its famed Empire Service in English. By the outbreak of the war in 1939 BBC was broadcasting in nine languages to all areas of the world.

The United States has been a latecomer to the shortwave radio field. Unlike most other systems, American radio developed primarily as a commercial service with minimum government regulation. Since commercial radio relies on local advertising revenues for its existence, there is little incentive for private broadcasters to enter the shortwave field. The first venture of our government in the field was the initiation of broadcasts to Latin America in 1940, but it was not until February 1942 that an official overseas shortwave service was organized to reach beyond our own hemisphere—an action dictated by the needs of war. The "Voice of America" radio, operated by the pre-OWI Coordinator of Information, began transmissions in German. Within a few months, VOA was broadcasting in most of the major world languages under the aegis of the newly formed Office of War Information. As with most wartime projects, the Voice started off with a crash-program confusion that sometimes hindered its effectiveness.

Hundreds of commercial radio people flocked to the OWI colors to operate the new shortwave services. They brought to the job all the flair and imagination of American radio techniques. It was a novel listening experience for foreign ears and they generally liked what they heard. VOA's early problems were not in attracting listeners but in deciding what the United States should be saying with its new radio voice. Coordination with the State Department on political guidance was often weak. Department officials were inclined to show disinterest in what they sometimes regarded as the radio antics of the OWI office in New York. The geographical distance between New York and Washington did not help matters; there was an even greater distance between the traditional attitudes of our diplomats and the free swinging enthusiasm of some OWI officials.

Inevitably, there were slip-ups when the Voice was saying one thing and the State Department was saying another. An instance of poor coordination occurred in 1943 when an OWI Italian language radio program broadcast a commentary in which Italy's King Umberto was referred to as a "moronic little king". No one in Washington apparently had bothered to inform OWI that the allied powers were conducting delicate negotiations aimed at Italy's surrender and directly involved with the position of the royal family. The episode served to force both the State Department and the OWI to adopt more adequate controls over what was being said by the official American radio system.

The OWI began its shortwave operations with an almost total lack of transmitters capable of beaming a radio message overseas. When the war began there was only fifty thousand watts of shortwave commercial transmitting equipment in all of the United States. This is no more power than a single large commercial station has these days. The National Broadcasting Company, Columbia Broadcasting System and a few smaller radio systems controlled our prewar shortwave transmitters. Most of them were immediately pressed into service by the new government propaganda planners under the leadership of playwright Robert Sherwood, director of the OWI's foreign operations. Additional transmitting equipment was rushed into production. Before the war ended the OWI had 39 transmitters operating in the United States.

The Voice of America rapidly won a large and faithful listening audience overseas. By 1945 it was broadcasting in forty languages around the clock to all areas of the world. The VOA was by all odds the largest radio operation ever undertaken up to that time. Shortwave broadcasting was important in the wartime effort of the Voice, but its greatest successes were achieved by its mediumwave stations overseas. The directors of these stations showed a realistic understanding of what they could and should say; they were also in close touch with American military commanders and other authorities.

Millions of radio listeners got their first impression of American radio—and of American ideas—from our mediumwave stations. American programming techniques, which had seemed so strange to foreign listeners a few years earlier, became the new standard.

With the end of the war the vast apparatus of the Voice was rapidly dismantled. Remnants of the OWI were transferred to the State Department with orders to reduce VOA radio output. From a broadcasting schedule of 3200 hours a week in 40 languages, radio operations were cut in half. It was the end of the first cycle of on-again, off-again orders that have bedeviled the Voice. From 1947 to 1949 it continued to operate in New York with a greatly reduced staff.

The next cycle of expansion began with the announcement of the "Campaign of Truth" by the Truman administration early in 1950. The new crusade was heralded by a major expansion of shortwave transmitter facilities. Vital to the plan was establishment of additional facilities abroad to boost the signals sent from our transmitters located on the east and west coasts. Thanks to some astute planning during the dark days of 1946 when the OWI was being disbanded, the Voice retained control of some of its transmitters abroad as well as others in the United States.

The budget increases voted by Congress for the "Campaign of Truth" gave the Voice the funds it needed to begin building another effective worldwide system of transmitting stations. Included in the system were the most powerful stations ever built. Located in the Philippines, Okinawa and Munich, they transmitted with powers of one million watts each. By way of comparison, the largest transmitter power authorized by the Federal Communications Commission for commercial stations in the United States is fifty thousand watts. The Okinawa transmitter signal was so strong that when VOA engineers were testing its range they were informed by the Swedish Broadcasting System that the Far Eastern transmitter was interfering with its domestic broadcasts! The overseas transmitters helped in solving one of the most difficult problems VOA engineers face. This is the geographical fact that any broadcast from the United States must 'hop' over at least three thousands miles of ocean before it is heard by an audience on the European, Asian or African mainlands. The Soviet Union on the other hand is broadcasting from the center of the Eurasian land mass and has little difficulty in projecting a good radio signal anywhere in Europe or Asia. Our overseas transmitters are designed to receive a shortwave signal from Stateside transmitters and rebroadcast it at increased powers. In some areas the shortwave signal from the United States is converted to a mediumwave signal by our transmitters abroad since more foreign listeners, like most American listeners, prefer to listen to a program on mediumwave when they have a choice.

In addition to its new land-based transmitting stations overseas, VOA engineers installed a transmitter on a mothballed Maritime Commission ship. The ship was intended to provide the Voice with a transmitter that could be moved to various parts of the world as the political situation warranted. Manned by a Coast Guard crew, it was refitted and commissioned as the U.S.S. Courier in March 1952. A few months later it proceeded to its assignment in the eastern Mediterranean and it has remained there ever since. For over eight years the Courier has been anchored off the island of Rhodes, where it provides the only reliable mediumwave signal of the Voice in the Middle East. For several years discussions have been held with Near Eastern governments with a view to securing a land-based site for a transmitting station to replace the Courier.

Facilities installed in 1950-52 vastly strengthened our signals to many areas. They were still not adequate, however, to overcome the Soviet jamming that was initiated against our Russian language programs in 1948 and reached peak intensity a year later. Plans were made for an even more powerful ring of transmitters to boost the VOA signal into Communist areas. But these plans like many others were halted by the McCarthy investigation and the cutback in information appropriations in 1953. The McCarthy investigators charged that VOA engineers were sabotaging the radio operation by building new transmitters whose signals could not be heard overseas. The charge involved highly technical data and the McCarthy investigating team called on engineers who in one way or another seemed to support the Senator's claims.

After the Voice was transferred to the new United States Information Agency in the summer of 1953 its center of operation was moved from New York to Washington. The original selection of New York was based on the fact that it was the largest radio center of the country. However, this advantage was overbalanced by coordination difficulties between the radio people in New York and policy advisors in Washington. The VOA studios were moved to Washington in 1954 and installed in the Health, Education and Welfare Department building in the Southwest section of the city.[1] A small bureau is still

1. Guided tours of the VOA studios are conducted daily for vistors to Washington.

maintained in New York for special events programming. It was several years before the Voice recovered from the morale-shattering, budget-cutting events of 1953. Although the number of languages broadcast by the Voice was reduced to 34 as a result of the budget cuts, many programs were later reinstated. By 1960 Voice languages increased to 36—only slightly less than its Campaign of Truth heyday.

Of all the USIS media, the Voice was the last stronghold of the hit-'em-hard school of psychological warriors. The radio operation was looked upon by them as an anti-Communist device whose primary usefulness was to strike back at Soviet lies. The result was too often a strident, high-pitched program that delighted in making sophisticated political points without concern for the reaction on the average listener who lacked both the background and the interest to understand them. This preoccupation with hitting back harmed the Voice's credibility at times as well as its chances for an extensive listening audience.

In the sobersided reappraisal that took place in 1953 when the USIA was set up, this pugilistic tone was changed. From now on the Voice was to be concerned primarily with factual news coverage and features on American developments. The anti-Communist campaign was relegated to its proper place as one aspect of the American viewpoint. The result has been a more professional air in VOA operations, which is favorably reflected in its increasing overseas audience. Today the average Voice broadcast consists of 50% news and commentary and 50% general feature programming. The news programs are not much different from those broadcast by any American station except that events of particular interest to the local audience are stressed in foreign language broadcasts. The commentaries are usually expositions of certain aspects of American policy, although special series deal with United Nations affairs, economics, and other major topics of world interest. Features are specially prepared by the various language services of the Voice and are custom tailored for their particular audiences. Many language services have a weekly question-and-answer feature to discuss queries submitted by listeners. Recent developments in science, medicine and cultural life are also featured.

Together with their more quiet tone has come a shift in the geographic pattern of VOA broadcasts. During World War II and for several years thereafter most broadcasts were directed to audiences in western Europe and Latin America. Since then the pattern has changed radically in favor of broadcasts aimed at the newly independent peoples of Asia and Africa and those behind the Iron and Bamboo Curtains. Broadcasts to Europe have been cut back severely. At one point during the budget-cutting years following 1953, broadcasting to Latin America was virtually eliminated but this curtailment has been reversed since the recent reappraisals of our Latin American affairs. There are more broadcasts in such exotic languages as Bengali, Urdu, Farsi, Amoy and Tamil—all major languages in Asia.

Another recent trend has been toward an increase in transmissions in English. For many years English was the stepchild language of the Voice; in the cycle of budget cuts, it was always among the first of the language services to be reduced. This was done on the assumption that foreigners preferred to listen to broadcasts in their native languages. Studies of shortwave listening habits have since shown that foreign listeners place more credence in the language of the originating country. In other words, for those who understand it, English is the most credible and authoritative language the Voice of America can use. Psychologically, a foreigner listening to a VOA English broadcast has the feeling that he is getting a direct American viewpoint at least, whether or not he agrees with what is being said. He may not get quite the same feeling when he hears the same viewpoint broadcast in his own language; there may be a lingering suspicion that what is being said is designed to impress him. Another reason for extending our English programming is that English is rapidly becoming the second language of most educated people in non-English-speaking countries.

In 1958 the Voice of America began a world wide experiment to provide more news programs in English on a round-the-clock basis. The initial success of the venture has led to a steady increase in VOA English broadcasting. Late in 1959 VOA further expanded the English-listening audience potential when it began to transmit a special series of newscasts in simplified "Special English" for listeners who are less than fluent in the language. The "Special English" newscasts are announced at a slightly slower pace than regular English transmissions and their vocabulary is limited to approximately 1200 words. As an incentive to its less-than-fluent listeners, the VOA English Service has prepared a special dictionary of these words.

The new emphasis on English broadcasting permits VOA to make better use of the excellent educational and documentary shows prepared by commercial stations in the United States. They are supplemented by VOA's own English language productions, including a first-rate series of American plays presented by VOA in cooperation with the American National Theater and Academy (ANTA). Among the distinguished stars who have appeared on the ANTA series are Helen Hayes, Ed Begley, Mildred Dunnock, Walter Abel and Martha Scott. Another special series entitled "Forum" features distinguished American scientists and artists in talks on the contemporary American cultural and scientific scenes.

The most popular of the English language programs is "Music USA" featuring light music recordings. Begun in 1954 as an experiment to attract a young audience abroad, Music USA is now a permanent two-hour nightly show beamed to a world-wide audience. Its musical presentations are divided equally between popular music and jazz with program notes for both supplied by Washington disc jockey Willis Conover. Rock 'n roll and other noisy fads are pointedly bypassed as are any temptations to capitalize on the program's popularity by insinuating a propaganda line into it. The propaganda is the music itself, particularly the jazz sessions which attract the greatest listener attention overseas. Although Music USA's listenership is worldwide, its most attentive audience is behind the Iron Curtain. Bootlegged jazz records—many of them recorded on old X-ray plates—sell for exorbitant prices on the Moscow black market. Listening to Willis Conover is a status symbol of revolt against Communist conformity among young people in the Soviet bloc. When George Wein, producer of the Newport Jazz Festival, visited the Soviet satellites in 1959 in search of musicians for an international jazz band he reported that "Eastern Europe's entire concept of jazz comes from Willis Conover."

The 39-year-old Conover, whose deep, bottled-cream voice is establishing an overseas vocal trend known as "the Conover accent," has his own ideas on the reason for the popularity of jazz. "It is a cross between total discipline and anarchy," he points out. "The musicians agree on tempo, key and chord structure but beyond this everyone is free to express himself. This is jazz. And this is America. That is what gives this music validity. It is a musical reflection of the way things happen in America. We are not apt to recognize this over here but people in other countries can feel this element of freedom. They love jazz because they love freedom."

Music USA is only a small part of the Voice of America's service to its major audience target—the eight hundred million people under Communist rule. Radio is the most strategic medium we have for reaching behind the Iron Curtain; most of the news that flows through the "underground" news-and-rumor channels in the Communist empire is based in large part on free world broadcasts. American transmitters are the main originators of these broadcasts. The Voice of America beams about 56 program-hours of news and other features into Communist countries every day; another 120 program-hours of broadcasts are sent by two private American organizations, Radio Free Europe and Radio Liberty. There are similar though somewhat smaller efforts by many other free world countries. The Britsh Broadcasting Corporation with hours of daily programs has a considerable Iron Curtain audience. The Greek state broadcasting system, sending from an antiquated five thousand watt transmitter in Athens, has a small but steady listenership for its daily fifteen-minute shortwave news programs to neighboring Communist countries.

The Russian language transmission of the Voice was initiated in 1947 after the short period of our postwar political honeymoon with the Soviets. The program was a low-keyed news-and-commentary report on American developments but this was too much for the Soviet leadership. In 1948 the Soviet government began a systematic campaign of jamming VOA broadcasts beamed to its territory and by 1950 jamming was extended to VOA broadcasts beamed to eastern Europe. Jamming is one of two effective devices that the Communists use to discourage listening to free world broadcasts in their territory. The other device is to restrict radio listening to sets which cannot receive foreign programs. Most of these sets are wired speakers that can only receive the local Communist station on a closed-circuit system. Fifty-five percent of the radios in Communist countries in 1959 were wired speakers. At that time there were three wired speakers for every wireless set in the Soviet Union; the ratio in Communist China was closer to one for one with new radio production in that country reportedly confined largely to wired speakers. Wired speakers are also common in the eastern Europe satellites.

The number of wireless sets in the Communist bloc remains high, however, and it is primarily through jamming that the Red leadership can discourage their owners from listening to free world broadcasts. Jamming is an electronic device that interferes with normal radio listening by broadcasting unpleasant, high-pitched noises on the same wavelength as the program selected for jamming. Listening to a jammed radio program has been described as trying to hear a normal conversation in a roomful of screaming children. Occasionally jamming is accidental as when two radio stations inadvertently broadcast on or near the same frequency. International telecommunications agreements have kept the airways generally free from such broadcasting clashes. Most jamming these days is well-planned and purposeful. In the early days of jamming, the interfering noises were created mechanically by broadcasting recorded unintelligible noises or even music and voice programs on a radio frequency used by the station being jammed. In recent years the Communists have developed special transmitters which create the jamming noises electronically. Jamming is effective on all types of broadcasts whether they are shortwave, longwave or mediumwave.

There are two types of jamming operations—by ground wave or sky wave. Ground wave jamming is carried out by a radio wave that travels along or over the surface of the earth. Its usable range is only about one hundred miles, making it effective in a relatively small area. Although low-powered transmitters can be used in this type of jamming many of them are necessary to cover any sizeable area. Skywave jamming is used to interfere with powerful shortwave transmitters that are capable of blanketing tremendous areas by radiating their signal into the ionosphere to be bent downward in a reflected ray returning to earth at some distance from the transmitter. Skywave jammers attempt to interfere with these reflected signals.

Jamming is prohibited under existing international telecommunications agreements signed by the Soviet Union and almost every other country on earth. When the Russians began their jamming operations against the Voice of America early in 1948, the State Department took immediate steps to point out that their action was contrary to international law. The Soviet Foreign Ministry answered two American notes in the Spring of 1948 by blandly denying that Soviet transmitters were using Voice of America frequencies. The Soviet Union continued to brush off the issue the following year when it refused to reply to an American protest to the International Telecommunications Union on stepped-up Communist jamming. In 1950 the United States pressed the issue before the United Nations General Assembly which passed a resolution in December of that year condemning jamming as a denial of the free flow of news and ideas and called on U.N. member states "to refrain from such interferences with the right of their peoples to freedom of information." The resolution also requested member states to "refrain from radio broadcasts that would mean unfair attacks or slanders against other peoples anywhere and in so doing to conform strictly to an ethical conduct in the interest of world peace by reporting facts truly and objectively."

It was evident in the debate on the resolution that the Soviet Union had no intention either of relaxing its jamming operation or of eliminating the abuse and slander that marked its radio propaganda operations. Its U.N. delegation, supported by the parrot voices of other Iron Curtain representatives, charged that the United States, Great Britain and other western countries were engaged in psychological warfare against their countries. The Soviet Union, said one Russian delegate, "has the right and the duty . . . to paralyze the aggressor in this radio war."

USIA and other government agencies have spent considerable time and money to develop counter-measures to Communist jamming. There is no magical solution to the problem. A technique that is successful today may be blotted out by increased jamming tomorrow. Voice of America engineers realized early in their counter-jamming operations that the most effective approach was one that was versatile, incorporating a wide range of engineering, operating and program techniques. They have made extensive use of such technical devices as heterodyne filters, speech clippers, exalted carrier-type receivers and other engineering methods. The most effective pattern of surmounting jamming interference is through the use of high-power transmitters which are difficult to jam and through the simultaneous transmission of the same Voice of America program from different transmitters employing many different frequencies. This "saturation broadcasting" has proved to be effective in penetrating areas outside large Soviet and satellite cities. The concentration of jammers in and around large cities still presents a difficult electronic problem for our engineers.

Beginning in 1957 Soviet bloc countries gradually relaxed their jamming of some free world broadcasts. The first break in the Communist jamming cloud occurred when the Polish government diminished and then stopped its jamming activities in the weeks following the 1957 Poznan riots as the Poles gambled and won in their struggle to loosen Soviet control. During those heady days a number of deputies in the Polish parliament rose to argue against jamming on the grounds of its high cost and also because it was a violation of the people's right to a free flow of ideals. Such challenges to authority were new and strange to a parliamentary body that was still Communist controlled but on the jamming issue a majority of deputies carried the day.

At about the same time but without benefit of parliamentary debate, the Soviet government also began to modify its jamming practices on a selective basis. In May 1956 it ended jamming of BBC broadcasts only to resume it a few weeks later. It was not until 1959 that the Russians adopted what seems to be a new policy of limited jamming. They stopped jamming Voice of America Russian language transmissions on the day that Premier Krushchev arrived in the United States for his famous tour. Following the signing of a cultural agreement between the Soviet and British governments in February 1960, jamming of BBC Russian language transmissions was ended. Although BBC authorities hailed this Soviet gesture as one "normalizing relations in the field of broadcasting" as called for in the agreement, they and their American counterparts were aware that the new Soviet policy on jamming could be reversed at any time.

This was demonstrated in the weeks following the "U-2 spy plane" incident and the failure of the Paris summit conference in the summer of 1960. The Russians stepped up their jamming operations on a selective basis, although not to the level they had reached during the 1950's. USIA estimates that the Soviet Union still has more than 1500 jamming transmitters at 300 sites within its own borders. There are an additional 750 such transmitters at about 90 locations in Czechoslovakia, Hungary, Rumania and Bulgaria. The installation of this number of jammers represents an initial investment of about a quarter billion dollars, together with an annual operating expenditure of about $185 million which is more than six times the amount that USIA spends to originate Voice of America programs every year. Soviet experiments in relaxing jamming in recent years have had no effect on the Chinese Communists who continue to jam every free world broadcast beamed to their territory.

There has been a good deal of speculation on why the Soviet Union has relaxed its jamming policies. The Russians themselves ascribe their motives to a desire to "relax world tensions" but their decision may involve domestic considerations as well. The Soviet leadership has demonstrated that it recognizes the need for some loosening of restrictions aimed to isolate its people from western influences. This development is undoubtedly being forced, in a subtle manner, by the growth of an educated, inquiring middle class which is beginning to chafe under Marxist ideological restrictions. The easement in jamming activities by the Soviet government could well be interpreted as a small but significant step towards meeting the demands of this group.

The Soviet policy of relaxation in jamming has never extended to Radio Free Europe (RFE) and Radio Liberty, the two private American organizations that beam transmissions across the Iron Curtain. Radio Free Europe began its broadcasts in 1950 in an effort to provide an unofficial free world contact with the eastern European satellites. Three years later, Radio Liberation (now Radio Liberty) began similar operations aimed at the Soviet Union. Because of their unofficial status RFE and Radio Liberty are unhindered by the diplomatic restraints that govern the Voice of America and other official western radio sources. In their broadcasts to the Communist bloc from stations located in western Europe, both organizations have developed a hardhitting form of reporting that has occasionally opened them to criticism for irresponsibility. These criticisms reached their height on both sides of the Iron Curtain during the post-mortems on the 1956 Hungarian freedom revolt. There was extended debate over Radio Free Europe's alleged incitement of the revolters, promising them help from the West that could not be materialized. Although these charges were later disproved they provided grist for the Communist propaganda mill.

In recent years there have been a number of proposals—some of them from high-placed sources in the American government—that RFE and Radio Liberty should be closed down because they are stumbling blocks in the path of our major goal of establishing a more normal relationship with the Communists. The advocates of this course point to a number of tactical errors which both RFE and Radio Liberty have made in the past in their propaganda approaches to eastern Europe. The main argument of those who oppose the continuation of the two organizations, however, is that they are cold-war anachronisms preaching, at least by implication, a doctrine of liberation-from-Communism that is both dangerous and misleading. Critics point out that whatever justification talk about liberation and "rolling back the tide of Communism" once had, it is highly unrealistic in the 1960's when there is little chance that the Soviet Union will countenance any significant relaxation of its control over the satellites.

These are persuasive arguments that raise fundamental issues about our long-range strategy with regard to the Communist bloc. First of all, do we accept Soviet hegemony over its satellites or do we intend to hold to the principle of self-determination? This is the context in which the future of RFE and Radio Liberty has to be argued. Their purpose is not to lead a crusade toward "liberation". The idea that eastern Europe will rise at a signal given from a microphone in Munich or New York is too far-fetched to be considered. RFE's true role, and one which it performs with distinction, is to replace the opposition that Communism has destroyed. It does this not only with news and opinions that cannot otherwise be heard in Communist countries but also with music, religious services, variety shows and even a "radio doctor" who prescribes treatments for individual listeners and mails them American and European drugs that are unavailable or in short supply in the Soviet bloc.

As long as radio remains our principal means of communication with people in the Soviet bloc, the activities of RFE and Radio Liberty are both legitimate and necessary. It is difficult to assess their effectiveness since it takes place primarily in the minds of people. There is no doubt that the programs are listened to and that they are a living electronic witness to the interest of the western world in the fate of people living under Communist rule. The two organizations, together with the Voice of America and other free world radio transmissions, also have an important indirect effect on Communist policy. So long as the Communist leadership knows that its people have access to uncensored news from the outside, its own power to suppress unpalatable news is limited. Broadcasts from the free world also keep the people of Communist countries informed about one another in ways which are helpful to their political and economic interests. It is more difficult to dragoon the peasants of one Communist country into collective farms if they know that their agricultural colleagues in Poland are given an opportunity to farm privately. RFE, in particular, does extensive cross-reporting of activities within the Communist bloc.

RFE and Radio Liberty are a source of tension in our relations with the Communist leadership but it is a form of tension that can be extremely useful in furthering our objectives. By building up pressures within Iron Curtain public opinion they exert an influence on the Communist leadership to modify its repressive policies. Looked at in this light, RFE, Radio Liberty, the Voice of America and other western broadcasts into the Soviet bloc are desirable elements in our overall strategy of steady slow pressure on Red leaders to modify their plans for a totalitarian world state.

A special problem for the Communists in restricting free world information in their territory is RIAS, the famed USIS station in West Berlin. RIAS stands for Radio in the American Sector, a name it adopted in 1945 when the station was set up because Soviet occupation authorities had monopolized the main Berlin station for their own broadcasts. RIAS started out literally as a series of public address systems mounted on trucks and driven around the shell-pocked streets of the conquered city broadcasting the latest news. A transmitter was soon installed in the American occupied sector of the city and RIAS began its unique and sometimes stormy career as an American station transmitting from an island of freedom one hundred miles inside the borders of Soviet-controlled eastern Europe. Since then it has held a special place in the political struggle over Germany through its ability to challenge the Communist monopoly of information in East Germany. Broadcasting around the clock RIAS has a loyal audience of East Germans who listen in spite of more than 500 Communist jamming stations aimed at it and in spite of the steady campaign of abuse and veiled warnings by Communist authorities against listening.

RIAS is responsible in large measure for the continued flow of escapees from East Germany to the West although it has never actively encouraged defection. Under normal circumstances RIAS is a model of low-key effective informational programming. It attracts its East German audience with straight news reporting and a wide variety of music and feature programs including the services of a full-fledged symphony orchestra. RIAS has been providing such special services as an educational series for East German teenagers designed to balance the monotonous diet of Communist ideology they receive in school with more objective facts. These educational broadcasts are geared to the curriculum of Soviet Zone schools so that students have a continuing check on the Red-slanted teaching they receive. For adults RIAS has a "University of the Air" series that provides a forum for advanced studies to counteract the academic enslavement characteristic of Soviet Zone universities.

The station maintains a separate identity from the Voice of America although it is supervised by the U.S. Information Agency. Only a small part of its programming comes from VOA headquarters in Washington; most of its programs are prepared by its German staff in Berlin under the general direction of a small group of Americans. The Germans on the staff are given a full measure of autonomy in preparing their programs. RIAS has long since learned the values inherent in being a local, German-flavored station, not an ersatz American voice. There is a particularly German tang to the RIAS political commentaries that are often presented in the form of "political cabarets," the sharp satiric dialogues in which Germans delight. The station has its own political cabaret troupe called the Insulaner which specializes in barbing the political skins of East German officials.

The RIAS success in political commentary results from its close attention to the day-to-day political situation in the Soviet Zone. Its staff contantly probes weak spots in the East German facade, thus keeping the Communist leadership on the defensive. Several years ago the East German press office called in reporters to deny a rumor that German technicians were being shipped off to the Soviet Union to work in factories there. On a hunch, a RIAS staff member telephoned the post office in East Berlin to find out how he could mail a package to a mythical uncle who he said had recently been sent off to Russia. The post office obliged by giving him full instructions. The instructions were made the subject of a biting political satire that evening that included a recording of the phone conversation. Two days later East German authorities retracted their press conference statement.

RIAS usually operates in the political field by indirection. When an East German youth organization announced one day that its leadership would be chosen by free elections RIAS did not propose a boycott or sabotage of the elections. Instead it suggested that members of the organization should support those candidates who favored more sports and entertainment activities rather than political indoctrination. The result was a landslide for the "RIAS candidates".

The station has also pressed its political point more directly. The first such occasion was during the Berlin blockade of 1948 when, day in and day out, RIAS underscored the determination of the United States and its allies to maintain the independence of West Berlin even to the extent of sustaining the city's population by airlifted food and other necessities. At a time when Communist propaganda was trying mightily to convince the East Germans and other satellite peoples that West Berlin's days were numbered, the station won new respect for itself and for the west by reporting the truth. The mere presence of RIAS and its message of hope in West Berlin at the time was a major factor in maintaining the morale of the West Berliners themselves.

RIAS also featured in the East German workers revolt of June 1953. It did not encourage the revolt in its broadcasts but it spread the news that set off the spark when it reported a call of the West German trade unions for a general strike. The following day, the day set for the general strike, saw the first violence in East Berlin. Despite a censorship clamp-down by the Communists, the riots took place too close to the West Berlin zone to be hidden. RIAS broadcast details of the rioting and the revolt spread through the Soviet Zone. By massive application of Soviet force the rioting was suppressed but the situation in East Germany has never been the same. "The East Germans," says one German observer, "proved to themselves that men can be men even under totalitarian dictatorship."

The Communists maintain an elaborate radio station of their own in East Berlin which outdoes RIAS in cultural presentations but not in the all-important virtue of credibility. At the height of the Berlin crisis in 1959 RIAS received over 75,000 letters a month from East Zone listeners notwithstanding the ever-present danger of Communist postal inspection.

RIAS is the only radio station that USIA operates overseas. However thousands of hours of the Agency's radio materials are broadcast on foreign radio stations every week through the efforts of local USIS posts. Almost every post has a small radio studio where local programs are prepared for placement on local stations, usually without attribution to USIS. In Latin America, more than eighty thousand hours of such programs were placed in 1959. Through special arrangements with the Columbia Broadcasting System USIA provides tape recordings of the New York Philharmonic and Metropolitan Opera performances to hundreds of stations overseas each week.

Many local networks and individual stations overseas take advantage of USIS offers to provide special-events coverage from the United States which they could not otherwise afford. If a Cabinet minister from a Far Eastern country is visiting New York or Washington, the Voice of America studios in those cities will prepare a special interview with him in his own language for use by radio stations in his own country. The Voice of America also provides foreign stations with a script service on such subjects as labor, medicine and agriculture. Adapted to local conditions and the local language, these scripts provide an inexpensive and effective means of getting news of American developments on foreign stations.

Sometimes requests made by foreign stations are highly specialized. Several years ago in Greece the military radio station network director told me that he was having trouble with a science-fiction show his stations were running. The show featured an American scientist named Peter Look who was adept at blasting off to the moon, Mars, Venus and other planets in search of adventure. Unfortunately the network's sound-effects department was lacking in space rocket noises. Could we help him? A query was put to Washington and within a few days we turned over to him some authentic Cape Canaveral rocket noises that permitted the indomitable Peter Look to blast off on his adventures with more authenticity than ever before.

How important will Voice of America shortwave broadcasts be in the future? There is a rapid decline in shortwave listening in more prosperous countries where television viewing has supplanted radio listening. As television networks spread across national boundaries and oceans, international radio broadcasting will diminish. Nevertheless the next decade will bring an overall increase rather than decrease in the shortwave radio audience. The increase will occur mainly in Asia and Africa where the present number of radio sets (about 100 million) can reasonably be expected to increase 20% yearly in the next ten years. Furthermore, radio transmissions will continue to form a free world information link with public opinion in Communist-dominated areas for many years to come.

One good reason for at least maintaining, if not expanding, the present level of our shortwave services is to meet Communist and other competition. Since the end of the war the Soviet Union's international radio effort has been consistently larger than ours. For years the Voice of America was in second place in terms of the number of hours broadcast; currently we are in fourth place, trailing behind the Chinese Communists and the Egyptians, both of whom are saturating Africa and Asia with their broadcasts. While the level of Voice of America radio operations has remained stable in recent years, the Communists have been sharply increasing their already massive schedule of broadcasts. In 1959 they stepped up their schedules by 400 hours a week, a jump of more than 15%. Half of this increase took place in transmissions to the critical Middle Eastern, Asian and African areas. There was also an increase in broadcasts to the United States including a special transmission to teach Russian language lessons.[2]

---

2. Radio Moscow can be heard clearly on the shortwave band in most parts of the of the United States during the evening hours, on practically all meter bands, varying with the seasons. For east coast listeners it broadcasts between 6 p.m. and 1 a.m., EST. In the west it can be heard between 7 and midnight, PST. Some interesting insights on the Soviet image of the United States and its people can be obtained by listening to these programs.

Communist transmissions in the past were usually noted for their dullness but both the Russians and the Chinese have taken some tips from western broadcasters. Their transmissions now include such sprightly features as disc jockeys, quiz programs and give-away premiums.

In order to strengthen its electronic ability to meet its international broadcasting obligations USIA is currently building several sizable new shortwave installations. The largest of these is located near Greenville, North Carolina: It will be our most powerful single broadcasting facility when it is finished in 1963 with a total power of a 4,8000,000 watt output—the equivalent of ninety-six of the largest commercial broadcasting transmitters in the country. The Greenville facility will be able to beam a clear signal to most parts of the world. Supplementing it will be a 250,000 watt shortwave installation being built in Liberia for relaying shortwave programs from Greenville and other Stateside transmitters to Africa and the Middle East. On the debit side the VOA will lose one of its most important overseas transmitting stations when it closes down its installations at Tangiers as a result of a 1959 agreement with the Moroccan government. Replacement or renovation of a considerable number of its 87 transmitters at home and abroad is another priority project for USIA in the coming years; most of the present equipment dates from World War II.

As with any radio operation, the primary problem is always what to say and how to say it. The current emphasis is on straight news programs, supported by low-keyed authoritative comments and features. This is in sharp contrast to VOA's earlier tendency to slug out propaganda points with the Communists and to weight its news in accordance with elaborately-developed "guidance themes." Experience has shown that the effectiveness of these tactics was often negligible. For better or worse people do not listen to the radio to be harangued. Most listeners are sophisticated enough about news reports to recognize whether or not they are being given the straight story. It is this kind of audience we want when radio listeners around the world turn on their sets and hear *Esto es la Voz de America... Etho Phonis Amerikis... Ici La Voix d'Amérique... This is the Voice of America.*

6

GOING TO THE MOVIES, GLOBAL STYLE

"If I could control the medium of American motion pictures, I would need nothing else in order to convert the entire world to Communism."

Thus did Josef Stalin pay tribute to the influence of Hollywood in a conversation with Wendell Willkie in 1942. The Soviet dictator may have overestimated his ability to hold an audience but he had a realistic appreciation of Hollywood's power to persuade.

Whatever the shortcomings of American films, there can be no question of their global influence. "The products of Hollywood," says the staid London *Times Literary Supplement,* "go all over the world, flown in jet aircraft and climbing the goat track. They are dynamic, ubiquitous, brash, shameless, persuasive, compelling the cultures of ancient, alien countries to copy their formula and imitate their style. Here is the Voice of America made visible. . . . "

It is a powerful voice, perhaps our strongest single means of influencing world public opinion. Even literate people overseas usually receive their initial and most lasting impression of the United States from films. The quality of Hollywood films is of direct concern to the USIA in trying to assess and validate the image we create as a nation. To supplement commercial distribution of American films abroad, USIS posts operate the largest non-commercial film network in the world.

Overseas almost everyone who has the price of admission goes to the movies. In 1959 foreign box-offices sold over seven *billion* tickets to film showings. Nearly half of these ticket sales took place in Asian countries; in India alone, more than a billion tickets were sold. While the number of motion picture theaters in the United States has remained more or less constant in recent years, there is a construction boom in theaters abroad. In Taipei the number of theaters has doubled in recent years. There is a new theater built for every day of the year in South Asia. In thousands of small cities and villages around the world, the "cinema" is an open-air enclosure where you bring your own chairs and watch a scratchy five-year-old film run off on a cantankerous twenty-year-old projector. The only difference between the film showings in these theaters and those on American TV at one o'clock in the morning is that foreign audiences are usually seeing the picture for the first time. On an Adriatic island recently, I attended the local premiere of a Greta Garbo film that I had played hookey to see in 1938. It is safe to predict that it will take another decade of intensive field work before the last Laurel and Hardy comedy is combed out of the world's distribution networks.

Old films may go on and on but it is the production of new films that sustains the burgeoning movie industry around the globe. Over 2300 feature films were produced in 1960 in 38 countries. The United States still holds a commanding lead in overall film production although it has slipped behind India, Japan and Hong Kong in the production of feature films. About 150 feature films were produced by American firms in 1959; it is expected that final figures for 1960 will show a total closer to 200. The Soviet Union and its satellites have doubled their production to approximately 200 feature productions annually. Traditional film producers like the Czechs and those Germans now under Soviet rule are turning out quality products that are being distributed increasingly in free world markets.

The rise of the Japanese industry from post-war rubble to its present production of five hundred feature films a year is phenomenal, but the Indian film industry is even more significant in terms of audiences and number of films shown in the vast Asian and African markets. The industry is centered in Bombay where over three hundred films are made in twenty studios every year by improvisation that Hollywood could hardly dream of. India can produce great films such as the prizewinning *Pather Panchali,* made by Satyajit Ray, but the average Indian film is a potboiler with a script cribbed from Hollywood. Lacking a ready-made plot, Indian film makers grind out musical folk dramas including subcontinental versions of the Hollywood Western. Called "mythologicals," they feature Indian gods and goddesses romping through temples in action-packed tales of the victory of the good guys over the bad.

The European film industry has also raced ahead in world markets in recent years. European film distributors originated and developed the art of 'dubbing'—the substitution of the original sound-track voices with lip-synchronized translations in foreign languages. The results have been so successful that most European films distributed overseas are now dubbed in the major world languages as are many Hollywood films. The results are somewhat disconcerting; Fred

Astaire speaking Arabic seems less than real, but dubbed films are almost always financially successful.

When a film is not dubbed, it is usually given sub-titles explaining the story in simplified form in the local language. Foreign film distributors are not above changing the subtitled dialogue of American films to suit the market. If the original dialogue in the film is a little dull or esoteric a good subtitle writer can adapt it to local tastes without much difficulty. There is an unconfirmed report that the Persian language version of *Gone with the Wind* was changed so much that it was difficult to determine who won the Civil War—the North or Scarlett O'Hara.

Despite the strong competition in world markets Hollywood films still maintain their reputation as the steadiest box office draw in most free world countries. Although individual foreign film producers can match and even outmatch Hollywood films at the artistic level, none has been able to maintain the high technical quality of Hollywood productions. All of the important technical innovations from "talking pictures" to Technicolor and Cinemascope have been pioneered commercially and perfected by American producers. The foreign film industry has never equalled Hollywood's mastery of the visual spectacle. Whatever may be the artistic consequences of this emphasis—and it ranges from the outrageous to the excellent—it provides films that people enjoy.

The foreign market has become increasingly important in the economic calculations of the American film industry. Before the war it represented a bonus since the domestic market was big and reliable. Today the overseas market often determines a film's financial success. The ratio of receipts for an average film in 1939 was 65% from domestic distribution and 35% from foreign; today the ratio is about fifty-fifty. In 1959, the American film industry did a $300,000,000 gross business overseas. American producers are now inclined to keep their big foreign audiences in mind in selecting scripts for new films. Twenty years ago they worried about how a film would go over in Dubuque; today, they call for reports from their foreign distributors on box office potentials in Buenos Aires and Singapore. The growing importance of the foreign market is in part responsible for the current trend toward the visually spectacular "blockbuster" films with big stars, big sets and not too much dialogue. The spectacle-for-spectacle's sake may not always win the approval of the New York film critics but it sells tickets in such unlikely places as Belem, Isfahan and Chittagong to movie-goers who do not speak English and who want to be entertained visually.

In an industry where trends are a dime a dozen there has been a consistent post-war drift toward the "international film", produced by Americans overseas, usually with one or more foreign stars. Foreign governments are eager to assist the peripatetic Hollywood producer because of the prestige and the financial stakes to be gained; Egypt, Spain and Yugoslavia have cooperated with American film makers to the extent of lending units of their armies for crowd scenes. Foreign governments can be sensitive, too; a Middle Eastern country, learning that a Cinemascope spectacle about one of its ancient heroes was being made in Spain, lodged a complaint with the State Department. The Department was only mildly shocked when it was told by the producers that they chose Spain because it looks more like the Middle East than the Middle East does.

It is still cheaper to make films overseas although the economic gap between domestic and overseas film production is constantly narrowing. Overseas production allows the use of blocked foreign currencies that American companies have been unable to convert into dollars because of currency restrictions.

Despite the advantages of international film subjects produced abroad, the perennial bread-and-butter product of Hollywood is films made in the United States about Americans. It is from these films that most foreigners deduce their own visual images of what we look like and how we act. To grasp the impact of American films abroad we must detach ourselves from our daily lives and look at Hollywood pictures through foreign eyes. Even an inconsequential Grade "B" comedy provides visual food for thought in terms of the props alone—the kitchens, the clothing and the machines. We may goggle at the picture-postcard scenes in a FitzPatrick travelogue but our wonderment is no greater than that of an Asian audience looking at the interior of an FHA house.

I once went with several Persian friends to see an American detective film at a large theater in Abadan, the oil-refinery center in southern Iran. The audience was composed mainly of technicians from the refinery. As the picture progressed I was disconcerted by their whispering commotion every time an automobile appeared on the screen. I finally realized they were debating the make and the year of each car. They had a greater identification with our technological experience than with the question of whether Dick Powell, who played the film detective, was going to get his man.

What ideas of American life do foreign audiences form from Hollywood? At best their image is only a partial one and therefore is somewhat distorted—as distorted as our image, say, of North Africa drawn from Foreign Legion and take-me-to-the-Casbah movies we have seen. The debate over the pernicious versus the idyllic effects of Hollywood movies has been fraught with more than the usual quota of nonsense. On the one side, we have the defenders of the industry, typified *in extremis* by the following report from *Variety,* the show-business journal:

"The American entertainment world—particularly motion pictures and music—is doing a better job indirectly in selling democracy and America to European nations than the U.S. State Department is accomplishing directly. This is the opinion formed by indie producer Herman Cohen, just returned from eight months abroad. . . . Cohen produced two films in England, 'Horrors of the Black Museum', and 'The Headless Ghost', both for American International release."

One can question Mr. Cohen's general thesis as well as his own film contributions to international diplomacy without, however, going to the opposite extreme and arguing that most American films present a perverted view of American life. The latter argument is usually expounded with solemn head-shaking and accompanied by recommendations that "bad films" should be prevented from entering the overseas market. Its exponents do us the service at least of getting to the nub of the problem. They present us with the choice of a film industry that is reasonably free from an artistic and commercial viewpoint or one that is guided by government directives and eventual control. Pragmatically, the problem is less serious than the dire warnings of the pro-censorship clique would suggest.

American films do reflect American life. Never in history have the mythologies, the shortcomings, the self-delusions and the strengths and the glories of a people been so widely and so forcefully presented as have those of Americans in their films. The reason for the success of these films is their broad range of style, taste and subject matter, both pleasant and unpleasant, sophisticated and soporific. The balance may weigh in favor of the mediocre and the inconsequential because of the industry's preoccupation with entertainment for average audiences. To be fair, the influence of Hollywood must also be measured qualitatively. The upper range of its achievement reaches high toward capturing life in the complex process of film making. Hollywood is successful overseas because it does a better job of touching the instincts of its audience—whether through a musical film or a dramatic love story—than most films of other countries. This is due partly to Hollywood's undoubted mastery of film techniques but also to the fact that its films present an entertainment reality—reality of interests if not of life.

Hollywood films are often misunderstood by foreign audiences when they regard the films as literal interpretations of American life. It may be an interpretation that flatters their own prejudices. Several years ago *Rally Round the Flag, Boys* satirized suburban living and its preoccupation with television, frozen dinners and the female habituation to committee meetings. For a French critic, Jean DuTour of the conservative Paris weekly *Carrefour,* the film was conclusive evidence of "the complete debasement" of the American male. "The film," he wrote, "is one of those documents that the United States produces from time to time that give the alert spectator a frightful picture of their morality and of their way of life. It is an important work because it consecrates this curious fact: the exchange of sexes in America. The women have become the men, and the men have become the women." Mr. DuTour's analysis of a film that was clearly meant to be a caricature is off the mark but it is the kind of reaction that can be expected when it reinforces the critic's opinions.

In recent years both the commercial film industry and the American government have shown an increased awareness of the place of films in molding world opinion. This has resulted in closer liaison between government and the industry on the problem. USIA has taken the lead in assisting to keep producers and scriptwriters informed on foreign events, customs and cultural values that should be considered in the production of films. This is not censorship but rather a healthy cooperation between government and the film industry that results in products more acceptable to overseas audiences.

Industry-government cooperation was demonstrated in 1955 during negotiations between our government and the Soviet government on exchange of films. Agreement to trade films with Russia was in keeping with the Summit conference decision to increase informational and cultural exchange between the two countries. A reciprocal agreement was formalized guaranteeing the distribution of Hollywood films through the Soviet state distributing organization. Our government enlisted the cooperation of the Motion Picture Association of America, the film industry trade association, to assure distribution of Russian films in the privately operated theaters of our country. As a result of the agreement, American films could now be shown in the Soviet Union for the first time since before World War II. For more than fifteen years before the new exchange of films Deanna Durbin had remained the best known American movie star in the Soviet Union.

The film exchange agreement was criticized by some newspapers because the State Department did not get iron-clad guarantees that the films sent to the Soviet Union would not be cut or re-edited, as had been done with a number of pre-war films, to give a distorted picture of American life. Actually, the agreement does contain such a prohibition and the Russians apparently have been abiding by it. The exchange should provide Soviet moviegoers with a closer view of American life than that provided in their own films and other media. Among the films currently being circulated in the Soviet Union are *Oklahoma, Marty, South Pacific* and *All About Eve*. The distribution rights to each of these films were bought for sixty thousand dollars. Reciprocally, the United States bought seven Soviet films at the same price. The exchange started with gala openings on the same evening in Moscow and Washington in November, 1959. Since then arrangements have been working smoothly; indications are that more films may be exchanged when the current series is finished.

An alternative to the anathema of censorship would be self-policing by the film industry itself of films to be exported. The possibility for such regulation in an industry that is becoming increasingly fragmented is dim. A form of policing is carried out, meanwhile, by censorship boards abroad; most countries have some scheme of censorship for films. The British censorship code is particularly harsh: films are divided by category with the most objectionable being classified as "X". (British distributors long ago showed an appreciation of the advertising value of the fact that "X" rhymes with "sex".) British censors usually clip scenes of violence and have occasionally sacrificed the artistic point of an excellent picture through such cutting. The film *I Want to Live,* a stirring psychological study of the problem of capital punishment, was shown in Britain without the climactic scene—an execution in a California prison gas chamber. European countries also classify films according to their suitability for children; theaters admitting underage patrons to films listed as unsuitable are subject to severe penalties. Political censorship, too, occasionally restricts foreign distribution of Hollywood films.

Despite restrictions or inadequacies, Hollywood is undoubtedly the leading exponent of American life among the world's millions. American motion pictures provide the image of America as it exists in most men's minds abroad. I have often thought that, if we could project the average foreign image of the United States on a screen, we would see a mosaic-like composite in which Americans would look suspiciously like Gary Cooper, Marlon Brando, Danny Kaye, Marilyn Monroe, Jerry Lewis and other Hollywood worthies. In any event, the image would be a friendly one, depicting the United States as a strong, variegated and economically advanced country.

Writing of his impressions of American life, Pakistani journalist A. M. A. Azim declares:

"I wonder if Americans themselves fully realize the contribution that Hollywood has made in 'selling' America to other countries, and especially to the Indo-Pakistan subcontinent. There must be countless in my age-group, who are now nearing fifty, who got their earliest and the most lasting impressions of America through the motion pictures, when they were barely in their teens. . . . It is sweet to recall these 'movie' impressions of America—the America of the cowboys and their adventures—the wide open spaces—the America of Mary Pickford, Charlie Chaplin and Douglas Fairbanks. The American typified in my mind was the six-foot, broad-shouldered, slender-waisted specimen of humanity in tight-fitting jerkin and breeched trousers with a broad-rimmed hat. . . . Of course there were villains and crooks in the movie stories. But the villain did not typify the average American in the boyhood image. On the other hand, the hero did. Then came the more serious type of American—still through the movies. He was the village sheriff, wore a top hat, and gathered a half dozen other top-hatted persons around a table to discuss a grave problem. The gathering of the top-hats inspired confidence that the problem, however grave, would be solved; and so it was."

In view of Hollywood's vitality and prolific success in presenting American life and ideas to overseas audiences, it is unfortunate that there are so few private channels for foreign distribution of factual films about the United States. During the 1930's and early 1940's our film makers issued excellent commercial documentaries such as the *March of Time* and *Profile of America* series. The economics of the film industry today cannot support such an effort. The present-day documentary film is usually intended for noncommercial distribution. Nevertheless, it is still big business. In 1958 over 7300 documentary and educational films of all types were made in the United States for a total cost of a quarter of a billion dollars. Such films range from avant-garde documentaries that win respect at international documentary film festivals to straight commercial films glorifying the virtues of the American carpet industry. The proportion of educational films intended as audio-visual aids for classroom use is expanding.

American educational film producers are showing an increased interest in the foreign market. The United Nations Economic and Social Council (UNESCO) has recommended that educational and cultural documentary films should be exempted from customs duties. Thirty free world countries will admit such films duty-free, provided each one is certified to be educational. American documentary producers submit their films to USIA in Washington for official certification. Over 50,000 educational films and filmstrips have been accredited by our information service since 1942.

In spite of existing inducements, foreign circulation of documentary films by commercial American companies remains very limited. There is relatively small profit for the company in overseas sales of documentaries, especially in countries requiring foreign language versions. Compared with the American market where documentary and educational films are booming, foreign sales are marginal.

In order to assure a wider foreign distribution of some of our excellent factual products, USIS has stepped in to assist. The information service runs the largest documentary film distribution network in the world. Operating from 210 film libraries overseas it shows films to audiences of over 500,000,000 persons a year. In any one of the 210 cities around the world where we have a film library, anyone representing a bona-fide organization can walk in and borrow a packet of films and a projector to show them if he does not already have one. For many others residing outside the cities, films are conveniently available by mail.

Most films distributed by USIS are about the United States. The film office in Washington continually screens the output of private documentary producers to select suitable films for overseas use. Of the 531 films screened in the 1959 fiscal year, 21 were selected for regular program use. Another 118 were tabbed for special use.

At each local post, the Information Officer decides which of the selected films should be included in his film library to best serve the program in his area. He receives "test prints" of the films which he, in turn, screens for suitability to local conditions and program needs. If a film is selected for his library, an order is sent to Washington requesting that the film be provided in the language of the country.

The high effectiveness of films in our libraries is due largely to the fact that they are presented in the language of the country where they are shown. In many Asian and African countries USIS has the only significant collection of documentary films in the local languages. This was also true in Greece when I was first assigned there in 1955. We had over 400 films in Greek—the only film library of its kind in the country. Our information service and economic aid mission have since cooperated to help the Greek Government draw up plans for facilities for its own Greek language films.

Foreign language soundtracks are made by processing laboratories located in New York. A particularly appropriate script may be translated and revoiced in as many as 44 languages. The procedure is complicated by the fact that many foreign languages require more words and more time to say the same thing. Greek is one-quarter longer than English. In a film where the dialogue is voiced on a split-second schedule, this discrepancy can cause difficulty.

In the face of various technical, geographical and even political problems, the translation and voicing service in New York can work remarkably fast. During the Hungarian revolution of 1956 our film office in Washington produced a film on the event two days after the first newsreel footage of the revolt arrived in this country. The New York laboratories matched this by producing 24 different language versions of the film in seven days. The film was sent overseas to USIS offices and shown to millions of people while the revolt was still active. The film's timeliness was highly effective abroad. I arranged a showing of the film at a prison in southern Greece where there were a large number of hardcore Communists. Two days later the prison director informed me that twenty of his Communist charges had applied to him for certificates recanting Communist loyalties which they had previously steadfastly refused to sign.

For millions of people in other lands our films are the first motion pictures they have ever seen. The reason for this is that no other film distributor has such a comprehensive system for getting films into remote areas. By mule and jeep and riverboat, we carry films to waiting audiences. In the Central African Federation, for example, USIS delivers films regularly to a large village in Nyasaland where they are shown at a British missionary school. The films are shipped from the office first by train, then across Lake Victoria by ferryboat, and, finally, over the jungle into the village by monoplane. In the delta areas of Pakistan, Burma and Vietnam, river launches are used to transport the films. Our local posts operate over three hundred "mobile unit" trucks to deliver films in rural areas that can be reached on wheels. The arrival of our truck in a provincial village is usually a big event. Special showings are made in schools during the day and, in the evening, the entire village gathers in the square for a community show projected either on the screen we provide or against a higher and larger whitewashed wall.

Increasingly, our films are being distributed under the aegis of local governments and private organizations. In Malaya, the central government operates 104 film trucks that show films to ninety thousand persons in provincial areas daily. A large number of these films are ours. The state-supported film distribution system in Vietnam in 1959 accepted our offer to provide packets of documentary films to be distributed to provincial areas by Vietnamese officials. In Turkey, we assisted the government in setting up the first national audio-visual center to train Turks in film production and distribution methods. Until they could build up their own film library, we supplied most of their films. Our films still form an important part of the center's collection. In a separate arrangement, the Turkish railway system has outfitted a special railway car to show our films. The car is shunted from one station to another throughout the country.

In West Germany many of our films are certified by a government board as educational. This means that when they are shown in commercial theaters, they entitle the theater owner to a slight reduction in his entertainment tax payments. The purpose of the tax reduction is to encourage commercial theaters to balance their programs with educational material. Our film libraries are a major source of supply for the tax-reducing films. As a result over 25 million Germans paid admissions to theaters showing our films in 1959. The films, incidentally, are leased to the German distributors at the going commercial rate—one instance where USIS operations turn in a cash profit to the United States Treasury.

Film distribution is often a valuable means of establishing contact with local organizations. Our film libraries include a sufficient range of titles to provide interesting programs for almost any responsible professional or social organization. There are films on medicine, dentistry, social work, architecture and other professional subjects. The film library is an important implement for the information officer or the cultural attaché in his contact work. Unless an organization is actively hostile to American "influence" the offer of a USIS film on a subject of interest to the group is usually eagerly accepted. If the desired films are not available in the local film collection they may be obtained from Washington by air mail. A special "packet film" service operated from Washington makes professional and other special films readily available to all our overseas posts.

Films are so much a part of our experience that we sometimes forget what an overwhelming experience it can be to see a movie for the first time. This was once vividly brought home to me when I was stationed in Turkey where we had an extensive film program in provincial areas. One evening in a packed village square we showed a film in which a railroad train comes straight down the tracks toward the audience. The villagers panicked and almost destroyed the film equipment in their rush to escape from the train. This incident led to a study of the effect of films on provincial audiences. The findings of the study, which was made in 1951 in Turkey by films officer Monteagle Stearns, were both surprising and sobering. They proved that the average Turkish villager had almost no comprehension of the films. The two examples used in the study were *Blue Ribbon,* a short documentary about a Midwestern state fair, and *Rural Co-op.* Both films contained elements—turkeys, farm machinery and other agricultural items—that were identifiable to Turkish peasants. They identified them, as a matter of fact, but many of them were convinced that the cattle and the machinery were actually brought to their village by the "magic box" film projector.

Their reactions ranged from blankness to confusion. Consider the following impression of the workings of an American rural cooperative obtained from the film by one 25-year-old Turkish farmer who was questioned after seeing *Rural Co-op,* a film about an American poultry cooperative. The interview is recorded as follows:

"Can you tell me what you saw?"

"The factories, the motors for plowing, there was a bottle factory. I saw people who were cleaning the turkeys. It showed the taxi cabs and the city. I saw many things but that's all I remember."

"Were the people you saw in the film Turks?"

"Only one or two."

"Did the people you saw live in the city or in the country?"

"Of course they were city people. They came out of apartment houses and from shops and factories."

"Who owned the factories and shops that you saw?"

"There was a sign, but I could not read it. The factory belonged to the American government. I could not understand who the owner of the shops was. I understood the factory. I understood that they cleaned turkeys and crated them."

"Can you explain how these films were made?"

"The first time I saw the film, I thought there were real people reflected in the mirror. But my friends explained to me how it worked."

"What is a co-op?"

"The boss of a shop is called a co-op, I think."

"The film is called 'Rural Co-op'. Why is it called that?"

"In the film, a man got rich in the village, saved his money and became a co-op."

"Why do they call him a co-op?"

"To show that he is richer, they say 'co-op'."

Of the hundred villagers who were similarly interviewed only one had a clear idea of how motion pictures operated and what films like *Rural Co-op* were about. He was a young boy who had had some contact with the outside world. He had, it turned out, done time in a Turkish reform school.

This study and others that were undertaken later made it apparent that our films were not always getting their points across. What seemed perfectly clear and reasonable to us was murky and incomprehensible to some of our audiences. To assure a common ground of understanding, the Agency launched a program of producing films overseas with local settings and situations. The rudiments for the program already existed as the information services had maintained a small film production operation since the OWI days to supplement the documentary films culled from commercial sources.

The overseas films production program is now a major USIS activity. Since 1951 films have been made in over 40 countries by our film crews. Most of them deal with some aspect of American cooperation with the country where the film is being made. Our economic and military aid activities throughout the world have been documented in this way. The success of such films depends on whether they are given a light or heavy-handed touch. Any film on American aid that stresses the look-what-we-gave-you theme will fail. The most convincing approach is indirect. Typical of this was a series of films on the care of fruit trees in Iran. Produced for USIS by a University of Syracuse crew, the film explained proper tree care with occasional mention of the fact that the methods shown were those used by Point Four experts in their work with the

Iranian Ministry of Agriculture. The Persian farmers got the point—and the United States got the credit.

Cultural understanding is also advanced by means of our film production program. Our post in Tokyo has produced an excellent series expressing American appreciation of Japanese culture. When novelist William Faulkner visited Japan a film record of his trip was made including visits to shrines and bull sessions with university students. The film proved to be one of the most popular documentaries ever produced in Japan. The reason for this is simple: Faulkner showed a genuine and intense interest in the Japanese. He came to Japan to learn as well as to teach and his sincerity was reflected in the film.

Our film crews also cover foreign political events of special interest to our national policy. During the 1956 Hungarian crisis our cameramen shot some of the most effective footage made of the streams of Hungarians who fled their country when the revolt failed. This footage was later incorporated into several films on the revolt and distributed in scores of languages throughout the world. The famous South American tour made by Vice President Nixon in 1957 was covered by one of our camera teams. Their film included the incidents where Communist rioters attempted to storm the Nixon entourage and hit the Vice President with rocks and vegetables. Other sequences depicted the warm welcome he received from the majority of Latin Americans—an aspect of the tour that was sometimes lost in the sensationalized newspaper reports of student demonstrations.

For most viewers abroad as well as at home the primary contact with film coverage of current events is through newsreels shown in commercial theaters. American commercial newsreels enjoy worldwide popularity. Over the years the Agency has developed cooperative arrangements with newsreel companies to provide footage of overseas events. If the footage is timely and newsworthy enough the newsreel companies will take it. In some countries USIS operates its own independent newsreel facilities; in others, it cooperates with foreign newsreel distributors to supply film footage to be incorporated into their commercial product. I had the latter arrangement in Greece where the local newsreel distributor welcomed our newsreel footage and clipped it into his own. In this way he added to his coverage of Greek subjects and we had an opportunity to show Greek-American activities in almost every theater in the country. We chose our subjects with an eye to newsworthiness and visual appeal; in three years of steady production we had only one sequence that was not accepted by the distributor.

In vast Africa we produce and distribute the only newsreel devoted exclusively to African affairs. The film is edited and printed in the United States. Issued monthly under the title "Today", the African newsreel is a twenty-minute report on constructive trends throughout the continent. A secondary theme is American understanding and support for the nations of Africa. A typical newsreel included the following subjects: the visit of President Tubman of Liberia to Sierra Leone, the Premier of Eastern Nigeria receiving an honorary degree from Michigan State University, the Ethiopian police college graduating its first class of cadets, a Negro mother in Milwaukee who is a city official making her official rounds, and American Point Four road building activities in Ghana. Since its inauguration in 1957 the African newsreel has won acceptance throughout the continent. It is shown in 185 commercial theaters every month as well as through hundreds of non commercial outlets. It is not unusual to have two-year-old newsreels still being shown to wide-eyed audiences in back country theaters throughout Africa.

The African newsreel is a tribute to the initiative of the USIS officers in African posts who are called upon to supply material for it. Although few if any of them had previous training as newsreel producers before they entered the information service, they have become adept at coaxing good usable footage from their local cameramen. In its early days each month's production of the newsreel was a crisis usually because the footage from Ibadin or Addis Ababa was lost, strayed or stolen somewhere between its point of origin and New York. Since then production difficulties have been reduced to manageable proportions and the original purpose of the newsreel—to reflect American interest in emerging Africa—is being abundantly fulfilled.

It is not only in Africa that our newsreel production meets difficulties. There could be many a slip between the idea and the product if constant vigilance were not maintained. Once when I was helping to put together a newsreel in a Middle Eastern country we decided to do a sequence on the local monarch receiving an honorary university degree. Our cameramen did a fine job of shooting the event and we turned the footage over to a local commercial film laboratory with a suggestion that the musical soundtrack include "academic music". The next day we went to the lab to preview the newsreel. The King flashed on the screen with all appropriate regalia to the martial strains of Benny Goodman's arrangement of *Buckle Down, Winsocki.* Fortunately it was not too late to substitute an alternative soundtrack.

Another of our film activities that is due for continued expansion is audio-visual aids to teaching. School systems over the world are beginning to recognize that audio-visual techniques are not a luxury but a necessity in mass education. A film or filmstrip properly used can teach certain subjects to more people more effectively than any other teaching aid. We now have operative arrangements for audio-visual film distribution and training with educational systems in over forty countries around the world.

The films program of our government information services is an important supplement to the Hollywood films which provide the rest of the world (and, if the truth be told, ourselves) with a concept of America. The hundreds of millions of people overseas who see our USIS films every year represent a large segment of the vast audience that receives its image of America through the movies. Furthermore, our films provide a factual account of the United States and its aspirations that serves as a balance to the more highly dramatized version of America and Americans presented by Hollywood.

7

TELEVISION — THE NEW INFLUENCE

In 1964 if the nebulous plans of a group of Japanese promoters materialize, the world will see its first global television program. The feature of the program will be the Olympic Games in Tokyo. The Japanese organizing committee hopes to utilize 24 earth satellites to transmit the televised Games simultaneously to all parts of the earth.

This would be pure Buck Rogers fiction if it were not a logical extension of the present international TV boom. It took the newspapers two centuries to become a worldwide medium; the movie industry did it in thirty years. Television has established its global credentials in less than a decade. From a few isolated stations in 1950, it spread to continental-network telecasting by 1954 and to the possibility of trans-Atlantic simultaneous programs by 1961. It is the media success story of the postwar era and it is just beginning. As we shall see, the propaganda implications of this development for the United States are immense.

Television is already big business overseas. There are over 100 transmitters in operation in 70 countries tuned in by over 35 million sets. This is 22 million less than the number of sets in the United States in 1960. But American TV set distribution is reaching the saturation point while the number of foreign sets in use can be expected to double twice by 1966. At that time, there will be only a dozen countries without television. In the other eighty countries, there will be over 1500 transmitters with over 100 million sets and a viewing audience of 400 million persons. International networks such as the pace-setting European network, Eurovision, will be commonplace.

Wherever it goes, television brings its own special impact. Americans, by and large, have come to terms with its pervasive influence but for most of the rest of the world, it is still new and disturbing. Through its sense of immediacy and intimacy, television is the most potent weapon the world's propagandists have during the 1960s. The Communists are giving particular consideration to the propaganda potential of television, both at home and abroad. By 1960

Communist bloc countries had 189 transmitters in operation in their own territories. Although industrial production has priority over consumer-goods production in all Red countries, a significant exception is often made in the case of television receivers. There are over six million sets in operation throughout the Communist world, all tuned in to the televised party line. The Soviet Union has developed its television network with a careful eye to the possibilities of linking it with the European networks. Free World countries who need help in developing their own TV systems will usually find the Communists willing to oblige.

The most striking example of TV's propaganda impact, however, has taken place not in a Communist country but in Fidel Castro's Cuba. Following his overthrow of the Batista dictatorship in 1958, the fiery young leader made television his primary outlet not only for expressing his ideas but also for imposing his will. Cuba is one of the most highly developed TV countries overseas; almost forty percent of the country's homes are equipped with sets. In 1960 the regime completed its control over Cuba's four networks by nationalizing the last privately owned station. When the Castro regime came into power, Cuba's television screens were devoted largely to light entertainment. There were 62 American television serials on Cuban stations at the time. Much of this was replaced with regimented government programs designed, according to one Castro announcement, to keep the Cuban people "alert and vigilant against the international conspiracy which faces the nation."

The star performer in this new type of television was Fidel Castro himself. Immediately after his militia troops seized Havana, Castro headed for a television station to establish what a 1959 International Press Institute report has called "government by television." This it defines as "a new form of government that is just as original and will prove no less significant in its historic effects than the Greek invention of the ballot, better known under the name of Democracy. For six million Cubans, the sole expression of their government's will is the television speech delivered twice weekly by its chief. . . . Thanks to TV, Fidel Castro has succeeded in preserving the dynamic force of his revolution to the present day."

The television studio at Station CMAB-TV in Havana literally became a seat of government. In one of his appearances Castro announced his land-reform program, the most sweeping change in the Cuban economy since the country's independence. In another emotion filled session, he turned publicly upon the nation's President and succeeded in forcing his resignation before the end of the program. But the common theme of the Castro television appearance during the early years of the regime was hatred of the United States. Television added a new, powerful dimension to the Castro campaign.

The Cuban experience is an outsize example of television's political impact. In lesser ways TV is demonstrating its influence to lull or excite public opinion in scores of countries. Already it is showing its power as a strategic propaganda weapon. Is has strong personal appeal, it is ubiquitous and it can be controlled from a central source. It is, above all, a mass medium that reaches every social and economic class. Despite the generally high cost of TV receivers, television spreads quickly among all classes abroad in much the same way it did in the United States in the late 1940s. In Japan almost 70% of television set owners polled in 1959 made less than $1000 a year; 15% earned only $500 dollars annually. Community viewing is popular overseas, as it was in American bars and taverns a dozen years ago. A survey in Portugal, where three-quarters of the sets are in public places, has shown a viewing audience of 25 persons per set. In Tehran, coffee-house business has enjoyed a new boom since the introduction of TV sets perched high above the customers' heads. Within a decade television may reach over half the world's population with its uncanny power to persuade and convince, to tell the truth or to lie.

From our own strategic viewpoint, what is said and shown about the United States on the world TV screens is a new and compelling fact of life for us during the 1960's. Our ability to influence this electronic image of America is limited by the fact that over two-thirds of free world television stations overseas are under some form of government control. This, of course, follows the pattern of radio stations abroad, most of which are government owned. American films, books, newspapers and magazines circulate with comparative freedom in most free world countries. Our television products, on the other hand, must be approved by a politically conscious government bureau in most cities abroad. Most government controlled TV stations overseas already have regulations limiting the amount of 'foreign' programs that can be presented. This trend can be expected, in the glacial tradition of most bureaucratic regulations, to increase rather than decrease in the coming years.

In spite of these restrictions, American influence in international television is extensive—and it is growing. The field has already been carefully surveyed by our three major networks—the National Broadcasting Company (NBC), the Columbia Broadcasting System (CBS) and the American Broadcasting Company (ABC). In a few instances, the networks have bought controlling interests in foreign stations. ABC made a significant move in this direction in 1960 when it announced plans for a five nation network in Central America known as CATVN. The network, in which ABC has a 51% controlling interest, will eventually link Guatemala, El Salvador, Honduras, Nicaragua and Costa Rica. The other two major networks are also deeply involved in Latin American television. CBS has invested in an Argentine firm making cathode tubes and NBC has a "management-technical association" with the country's first commercial station in Buenos Aires. Both firms are reportedly pressing for similar arrangements in Europe and the Far East. NBC is active in Great Britain and Japan; CBS is assisting a West German firm to develop a second network in that country. American TV-equipment manufacturers also have an eye out for the international market. They face stiff competition from European and Japanese firms which are able to quote lower prices than their American competitors in many cases. Nevertheless, U. S. manufacturers have a good share of the market; television systems in such diverse countries as Iran, Mexico and India were installed by American companies.

The most direct influence that the U.S. commercial television has overseas is in providing TV programs to foreign stations. As early as 1954, American producers were marketing their filmed serials abroad. Overseas favorites then, as now, were situation comedies and cowboys. The Cisco Kid, Hopalong Cassidy and the Lone Ranger have thundered across the TV screens of the world from London to Manila speaking dubbed-in Spanish, Italian, Japanese and German. The market for American serials is big and booming. Costa Rican viewers have a diet of fifteen U.S. shows every week, ranging from *I Love Lucy* to *Sheena, the Jungle Girl.* In Australia there were an incredible 163 American serials being televised in 1959. The rage in Japan is for our 'situation comedies' such as *Father Knows Best, People's Choice* and *How to Marry a Millionaire.* Ninety percent of these American imports are expertly dubbed in the Japanese language. Not all American shows are popular with Japanese viewers. *Dragnet,* together with several other American detective series, proved to be duds. As one Japanese film buyer explained, "our audiences don't go for foreign realism."

Great Britain is an important market for our TV serials. In recent years, American programs have been consistent audience favorites on both the state-supervised BBC and commercial television. The popularity of American television features coincided with the inauguration of commercial television in 1955; earlier the BBC provided a relatively small number of American serials. The commercial stations, eager for mass audiences to win advertising revenue, opened the floodgates to American shows and, once again, it was the hard-riding cowboys who led the way. There are also such TV reliables as the *Perry Como Show, Mickey Mouse, OSS, Lassie, M Squad* and *Sergeant Bilko.*

The heavy schedule of American programs has caused sometimes heated debate in Britain rising up even to the halls of Parliament. The London Evening Standard summarized the arguments of the antis when it declared: "Not only are there too many imported programmes on the home screen, but our homebred programmes are becoming more and more influenced by America." There has been serious talk, particularly in Labor Party circles, of stricter quota restrictions but Britons, aware of the commercial and legal implications of such a move, have been slow to react to such proposals. There would certainly be heavy opposition from the directors of British commercial television stations in as much as an American import such as *Wagon Train* draws up to 75% of the total British television audience when it is showing.

The success of American features on British, Japanese and other foreign television systems has prompted American TV-film producers to give more consideration to expanding their overseas markets. Their decision has been hastened by developments in the domestic industry. With television audiences and stations nearing their peak in the United States the program suppliers are facing constricted markets at a time when the price of their product is rising. The only direction to expand in is abroad. In many respects the television industry is beginning to feel the same pinch between domestic demand and rising production costs that forced the motion picture industry into full-scale exploitation of overseas markets after World War II. However, the comparison is imperfect; unlike television, the motion picture industry had a full-fledged commercial distribution system overseas upon which to build. Television overseas, unlike motion pictures, is controlled largely by local governments many of which will be reluctant to accept a large quota of American film programs.

The television industry has already had its share of difficulties in getting a hold on overseas markets because of local restrictions. A British limit on the number of foreign programs on local stations is an important restriction in a market that could readily absorb more American films. Japan restricts imported television shows to nine 30-minute shows a week on stations in Tokyo and Osaka and, more important from the American producers' viewpoint, sets a price maximum of $300 for a half-hour show and $600 for hour shows. Canada has a generous 55% quota for foreign shows in its television schedules. In some countries currency restrictions are a major problem. According to *Broadcasting Magazine,* American producers have reported difficulty in expatriating local currencies in the Philippines, Brazil, Argentina and other countries in recent years.

Another factor that complicates the placement of American commercial TV programs on foreign stations is the fragmentation of the domestic industry. Whereas American motion pictures are distributed overseas by only a half-dozen large distributors, the television industry consists of over a hundred producing companies of which only a few are strong enough to risk their capital in the uncertain overseas market. So far only the networks and the larger package producers such as Screen Gems and Ziv Productions have been able to consider it. They, in turn, often have had to move slowly in the face of quota and exchange barriers and the other uncertainties of TV program distribution abroad.

The increasingly attractive profit allurements of the overseas market have led to a number of proposals in the TV industry to set up an industry-wide organization to ease the problems involved in foreign distribution. Most of these proposals are variations on the film industry's Johnston Office. Known more formally as the Motion Picture Association of America, Eric Johnston's organization devotes most of its time to promoting foreign distribution of American films. In a deceptively quiet way it has been a major factor in expanding the overseas market for the film industry. The TV people would like to emulate its success.

In 1958 a group of film distributors and the CBS-TV network set up a committe to study the possibilities of a TV version of the Johnston Office. According to industry circles, the Johnston Office proposed to the committee that it handle the overseas affairs of the television industry as well as the film industry. The proposal was rejected, however, and the committee continued its exploration of what has come to be known in the trade as the "TV Johnston Office" proposal. It was given added impetus in 1959 when ABC announced it was in favor of an organization similar to that envisaged by CBS.

Although the proposed TV Johnston Office may step up the volume of American commercial TV programming on foreign stations, it is questionable whether TV distribution overseas will reach the proportions attained by the motion picture industry. As TV distributor Paul Talbot of Fremantle, Inc., points out: "Television is a much more intimate medium than motion pictures and foreigners are going to expect to see more of their own products, reflecting their own customs and culture." Over and above the question of audience appeal is the fact that most overseas stations are controlled, completely or in part, by government agencies. As we have seen, there is already marked resistance to foreign material on these stations. There is no reason to believe that this resistance will become less in future years. Very few governments would be prepared to resist opposition-party objections that the local TV network is becoming "Americanized" by a deluge of our television products.

Despite these difficulties the volume of American commercial TV material can be expected to increase substantially during the next decade. Foreign TV stations will be hard put to maintain full schedules for a long time. American filmed series are a relatively inexpensive way to fill time. Since American TV producers rely primarily on domestic markets for their profit, they can afford to lease their films overseas at reduced rates; the price of a thirteen-week cowboy series to an Italian TV station is less than two thousand dollars. The Italians could not produce a similar series for that price; the series is actually cheaper than anything they could put on the air. On top of this is the demonstrated fact that certain kinds of American TV material are almost universally popular. Most foreign station directors use American material to balance out the heavy-handed programs they are required to show in the interests of "national enlightenment".

Expansion of American television markets overseas does not in itself guarantee that the image of the United States abroad will be enhanced Although Hollywood has been a potent and successful source of American ideas and ideals for people abroad, thoughtful observers question whether the commercial television industry is capable of a similar impact. Unless there is a change in its distribution plans, the TV industry can be expected to continue to export a product that is almost uniformly bland and even mediocre. They will be sending the stock-in-trade of the majority of domestic TV producers—the private-eye series, the shoot-'em-up Westerns and the lightweight domestic comedies where the pratfall reigns supreme. About the only argument that can be marshaled in favor of these films as reflections of America is that there is really nothing wrong with them. There is almost no provision in most of the planning for commercial foreign distribution of TV programs for the export of programs that present anything but the most narrow view of American life. A comparable situation would be having Hollywood ship overseas nothing but cowboy, gangster and musical films. Actually, Hollywood sends everything—from the very worst to the very best—and the balance is in favor of a positive projection of the United States.

The television industry cannot hope to meet its responsibilities in this regard unless it makes a special effort to do so. There are formidable difficulties involved in placing our better television programs on overseas stations. The placement of filmed versions of top entertainment shows—*Perry Como, Dinah Shore,* et. al.—is complicated by what the networks consider prohibitive restrictions on "second release" showings by the talent and craft unions, particularly with regard to the fee schedule requirements for such showings. This is less of a problem with some of the excellent public affairs programs that the television networks present; with some modifications, these would make excellent material for overseas television.

The popularity of good public affairs shows was amply demonstrated in the 1950's when the British Broadcasting Corporation presented the now-defunct *See It Now* news-documentary shows produced by Edward R. Murrow and Fred Friendly and the excellent NBC *Victory at Sea* series. *See It Now* was the first and most successful proof so far of television's capability to report the issues of the day. It was sometimes controversial, sometimes a bit portentious, but it was always interesting and to the point. In terms of overseas audience, it was quiet evidence of the American ability to define our own problems—and those of the rest of the world—with objectivity and understanding. The program had tremendous impact in Great Britain during its run on the BBC. It would have been equally effective on stations in a score of other countries. Although the language barrier would be a problem in many countries for *See It Now* and similar public affairs programs, this could probably be overcome by dubbing the voices. The problem is not dubbing; it is money. There is relatively little profit for the trouble involved in preparing most first-rate American TV programs for foreign distribution. The profits are in the "quickie" cowboy and detective series which can be produced cheaply and distributed without fuss since they are a standardized product that can be used over and over. Until the economics of the industry are modified the bulk of American TV productions sent abroad will be limited mainly to second-grade programs.

There are hopeful signs of a change for the better. One of these is a growing awareness in the television industry of its responsibilities in the matter of good programming. Says distributor Charles Michelson: "Our quality network programs and specials must be sold to foreign countries so that they will see some of the wonderful productions we have on U.S. television". Amen, Mr. Michelson. Another hopeful portent is the development of trans-Atlantic and other international television relays. American networks will want to display their best products on the new international transmissions; they will undoubtedly want to put forth our best-known entertainers and our most important news events. At the current technological pace, there is no reason why the Presidential inauguration in January 1965 should not be televised at least to Europe and Latin America.

For the present, the most significant work in presenting a broad range of Americana on foreign television stations is being done by the USIS television services. Our information service has been in the television business for almost a decade, although its activities were given low priority for years both within the information agency and in the annual Congressional hearings on Agency activities. Until 1958 television activities were handled at the second administrative echelon in the Voice of America radio operation in much the same manner as U.S. commercial radio stations adopted television as an orphan-child. In September 1958 the television service was separated from the Voice of America and given equal status with it. An aggressive new chief, former NBC executive Romney Wheeler, was put in charge of the operation and its staff was expanded.

The most significant result of this change was to give television a new priority in the Agency budgeting process. Television is the only information medium that is being expanded under the current program. Its expansion is being monitored closely by the hawk-eyed group of Democrats and Republicans on the House and Senate Appropriations Committees who have made it their business to keep tabs on the Agency. Their concern for the television operation is legitimate. For years they listened to a procession of witnesses tell them with rhetorical flourishes that television was the propaganda wave of the future. The Congressmen were prepared to accept this thesis but they were unimpressed with Agency plans for exploiting the new medium; they proceeded to go the way of all unimpressed Appropriations Committee Congressmen: they cut the budget.

Where the early TV planners in the Agency made their mistake was not in underestimating possibilities of TV but in lacking a clear-cut idea of precisely what should be done to exploit them. The tendency was to think that we should produce complete television programs in much the same way as we produce films or Voice of America radio programs. In the early days, most of the television advisors in the Agency were film or radio men as was the case in commercial television before it developed its own specialists. When the early USIA television planners were talking about making TV programs for foreign consumption they were really talking about making special TV kinescope films that would be shipped overseas to be shown on foreign television stations. Some excellent films were made in fact. One of them, a series on American life called *Report from America*, narrated by newsman Joseph C. Harsch, had a successful run on BBC television in 1955 and 1956.

However, even good films do not always satisfy the essential quality of television, which is immediacy and intimacy. A film of a hundred girls in a chorus line is not nearly as effective on television as one pretty, cleavaged blonde, telling you to call Bigelow 6-1212 to get your $1.98 soup strainer before the supply runs out. Television is at its best when it is most personal. It is relatively easy for an American producer preparing a program for his own station to exploit these factors. It becomes somewhat more complex when, as is the case for our information services, the problem is one of preparing programs to be televised on hundreds of stations around the world.

How can intimacy and immediacy be achieved under the circumstances? The answer is that, in many cases, they cannot. Nevertheless, the Agency has developed a working pattern for its overseas television operations that provides a surprisingly high percentage of programs with strong local impact. The key to this success is the locally-produced "live" program that incorporates material provided by our information service. The technique has been so successful that it has become, in a few short years, the cornerstone of USIS television operations. It has marked advantages over the previous method of concentrating on the production of filmed shows in the United States. It is obviously cheaper to produce only part of a program than a complete show. Film shows have a "canned" look and, psychologically, they are often looked upon as propaganda by many foreign television station directors because they cannot easily be changed or adapted.

By concentrating on supplying material for local live shows, these pitfalls are avoided. Our local posts overseas thus gain flexibility in providing programs to local television stations. The pattern varies from country to country but it always involves close collaboration between USIS and the local station in developing programs that serve the interests of both. For us, the criterion is a program which effectively supports American political and cultural objectives in the country. For the television station, the criterion is a program that is informative and entertaining. Since most foreign stations are hard-pressed to maintain even part-time schedules each day, our assistance is usually welcomed. In the fifty countries where we provide services to local television stations, several thousand different programs—most of them "local and live"—were produced with USIS assistance in 1960.

The range of these programs is extensive. In Korea our information post collaborates with local TV stations on a program to teach conversational English. In Caracas, USIS originated a live series entitled "Venezuela Looks Toward Her Future", which highlighted Venezuelan progress in various fields and underscored the role of the United States in furthering these developments.

In Guatemala City, USIS produces a weekly show entitled *Guatemala Forges Its Future* featuring the process of American-financed technical assistance projects in Guatemala. In Tokyo, the Nippon Television Network Corporation has been telecasting a USIS-produced program featuring English language lessons every weekday for several years. Hundreds of other television stations around the world have run a fifteen-minute series on American industry entitled *Industry On Parade* produced by the National Association of Manufacturers. An AFL-CIO series on industrial and craft workers, *Americans at Work*, has also been provided by our local information posts to many stations in foreign countries.

It has been found profitable in many countries to offer newsreel material for televised news programs. In Thailand USIS supplies the local TV stations with newsreel sequences showing American-Thai cooperation in military and economic development programs. Our overseas posts do not provide spot news items from the United States. American news and newsreel agencies provide such services to many foreign TV stations. These firms are showing increased interest in foreign television as profitable outlets. They face formidable competition from foreign sources, particularly the newly-organized British company, Visnews, which was formed for the specific purpose of marketing television newsreel material. Visnews is a joint venture of British, Canadian and Australian newsreel and television organizations, a factor that gives it a strong lead in covering international events.

However, the traditionally aggressive American newsfilm organizations, notably United Press International and Telenews, have established themselves strongly in international television especially in Latin America. Their spot-news coverage is supplemented on dozens of foreign stations by USIS news features which are usually produced to the specific requirements of each station. The visit of the Brazilian Minister of Education to Washington is not an event that would normally be covered by the commercial news companies. It is a good story for USIA, which will make a TV report on his activities for Brazilian stations. These special news-feature stories are usually produced in its Washington studios. Early in 1960 these studios were equipped with video-tape facilities capable of producing program material virtually indistinguishable from "live" television. This will strengthen USIS opportunities for placing additional material on foreign stations, most of which will be equipped for video-tape operations in the next few years.

In addition to supplementing live programs on foreign stations, the Agency provides its overseas posts with complete shows on film. These are produced in Washington or acquired from commercial sources. One of the most popular shows during the fifties, the *Firestone Hour* musical show, was made available to local information posts for foreign showings. The program, with its mélange of popular and classical songs, was placed on over a hundred foreign stations.

USIS posts are also interested in educational television—or ETV, as it is known in this rapidly expanding sector of the U.S. television industry. Most government-controlled foreign stations have plans for educational TV without having much idea of how to go about it. The American experience in ETV, although it dates only from 1953, is an important source of information for many of them. The Federal Communications Commission has set up 250 channels for educational TV throughout the country. In 1960 there were over 50 ETV stations in operation in addition to more than 150 closed-circuit installations in school systems and colleges. Direct instruction by television as a regular rather than an occasional teaching aid has been carried on for several years in a group of schools in the Hagerstown, Maryland, area in an experiment financed by the Ford Foundation. USIS has sent many foreign television managers and educators to observe the

Hagerstown experiment. As a result the American experience in ETV has become the standard for comparison and emulation around the world. Kinescoped versions of films produced by American ETV stations have been supplied to foreign education systems by USIS to demonstrate the effectiveness of this new teaching technique.

Despite all this activity, the debate continues inside and outside the American government as to whether the United States is underestimating television's present and potential importance as a strategic propaganda medium overseas. The argument revolves around the question of using American economic aid funds for the construction of television stations in free world countries, particularly in Asia and Africa. The proponents of such aid base their argument on the need for insuring the strongest possible American identification with television developments in these countries. They point out that the Soviet bloc has already built television facilities in a number of countries.

At a different level, the United States also faces competition from its allies; the British and French governments have been particularly alert in extending special facilities to countries that have requested assistance in the television field. The United States on the other hand has adopted an official hands-off policy. The only exception to this has been in the United Arab Republic where, in December 1959, the American government agreed to a loan of over twelve million dollars from a special "counterpart fund" account to assist in the development of a UAR television system. Requests from a number of other countries for similar assistance have been turned down.

There is a basic weakness in the argument of the proponents of direct American aid for foreign television. It is the fallacy that American money and machinery will insure American influence. This is a risky assumption as proved by the fact that a number of wartime radio transmitters built by the Office of War Information have been used by the governments now operating them to peddle an anti-American line. There is no guarantee of political immunity for ourselves or any other nation that undertakes to build up television facilities abroad. By staying out of the business we can at least avoid the onus of alleged "pressure" implied in any subsidy to foreign-government news and entertainment media. Our long-range interests are best served by providing advice and technical assistance when we are asked for it. Rather than to provide television equipment, our best policy is to encourage private industry to participate in the increasing number of bids for television equipment in the international market. American firms have shown enviable resourcefulness in winning contracts for television installations abroad.

Whatever American influence we can legitimately bring to bear in international TV during these formative years will bring important dividends later on. Already television is demonstrating that it will be *the* strategic propaganda medium overseas. Never before has such a propaganda weapon been put into the hands of small groups of people. The American experience already has shown the degree to which television can be used both as a means of truthful information and as a means of mass deception.

Just as many areas of the world, particularly in Asia, have jumped in one leap from the age of the ox cart to that of the airplane, so may they jump from the era of the village story teller to that of television without going through an intermediate period where newspapers, radio or films have a predominant influence. Even in more sophisticated areas, television is already supplanting some of the traditional opinion-making powers of the press and radio. Within a decade, television may reach over half the world's population.

The Russians and their satellite nations have demonstrated their awareness of television's power to persuade in the cold war. They are encouraging television where they think it will best advance the cause of Communism at home and abroad. The Communists have also shown an interest in placing their program material on free world stations. although they have met with more resistance there than we have. The resistance is often based on political grounds, sometimes simply on the dullness of their material. Both of their favorite subjects, happy peasants and stately ballets, are best taken in small doses on TV.

The Russians are shooting for high stakes in international television. They are particularly interested in free world plans to link nations and continents with television networks. The Soviet network has been built with a watchful eye toward facilitating hook-ups from the Communist bloc to the European area and other countries of the free world. The Russians are talking about connecting their network with the European continental network, which now includes fifteen countries. The Soviet link became technically possible in 1960 with the completion of the TV link between Moscow and Warsaw. The language problem of a network covering so many different linguistic areas is formidable, but a fairly successful type of solution has been developed by the European network. Live commentary is sent in the language of the originating point and is translated simultaneously as it is received by the relay studios in other countries. The relay-station translator may lag a little behind the action on the screen but the delay is usually not noticeable or distracting. European television has successfully covered such varied events of wide popular interest as Wimbledon tennis and the funeral of Pope Pius XII; member stations would welcome an opportunity to cover Iron Curtain events. The Russians and their satellites will welcome it, too, since the events they select for coverage will be picked for maximum propaganda effect on the seventy million viewers who compose a typical audience of the European network. The Russians will show only their best whether it is soccer players, circus clowns or military displays.

The participating European countries will also be sending some of their best programs into the Soviet bloc since they will undoubtedly require strict reciprocity from the Russians if they agree to form a link with them. Such western programs will have an important impact on viewers within the Soviet bloc. The Communists will find it difficult to discourage viewing within the bloc without jeopardizing their exchange arrangements. Tactics such as have been used in East Germany to discourage the viewing of western TV programs would certainly not be tolerated under any reciprocal agreement. At present it is a punishable offense in East Germany to view western programs; in August 1959 two East Germans were given prison terms for picking up stations from acress the Iron Curtain.

Our geographic location puts us at an initial disadvantage in relaying live television to any foreign countries except Canada and Mexico. Nevertheless, we are an associate member of the European Broadcasting Union. USIS has prepared a number of special programs for other member stations of the EBU on American scientific developments, together with a children's newsreel and an agricultural series. American television is also well represented on European stations through programs distributed by USIS and by commercial distributors. American and European stations are beginning to prepare for the opening of direct-relay facilities between the two continents sometime in 1963 or 1964. A primitive form of relay was inaugurated in 1959 when the National Broadcasting Company successfully transmitted a portion of a London television interview between President Eisenhower and Prime Minister Harold Macmillan. The picture was sent by cable, frame by frame. The one-minute segment of the interview took over an hour and a half to be transmitted.

American links with international television may depend largely upon the success of our scientists in developing earth satellites designed to relay television and telephone signals. Test facilities for such relays have been built at Holmdel, New Jersey, by the Bell Telephone Laboratories with active testing scheduled for 1961. Sixty-foot dish-shaped antennas will aim a beam of microwave signals at a passing balloon satellite. This will "illuminate" the balloon so that signals can be picked up by directional radio antenna on other parts of the earth. The eventual result of these experiments will be global television coverage. Since there is no reason to doubt that the Russians are as aware as we are of the implications of such coverage, we can expect to see competing systems of television satellites circling the globe unless international agreement on a single system is agreed to in the meantime.

It is unfortunate for us that international television, like international shortwave radio, is being developed primarily in terms of power for political persuasion. The United States would benefit if at least part of the proposed new international network could be organized on a commercial or public service basis. Our domestic system is almost completely commercial and it is not fanciful to imagine American advertisers interested in the commercial advantages of subsidizing programs beamed to rich consumer markets in Europe and Latin America. There is little hope for such a development, however, as long as government ownership and regulation of television is the rule rather than the exception in other countries. If a unified global network is developed the Communist bloc can be expected to take violent exception to any proposal for commercial programming.

All indications are that international television is going to develop primarily as a propaganda influence on others. For the United States this will mean the development of close cooperation between commerical TV and the government to assure that we put our best television foot forward in the new high-stakes game of international TV we have entered.

9

POWER OF THE PRESS

Michael Hadelis, editor of the newspaper *Imerissios Kyrix* in the Greek market town of Larissa, is a gentle wrinkled man who goes to his office every evening and proceeds to write the entire newspaper himself. He has three assistants—a printer who also sets type, a boy who listens to the radio for late bulletins and another boy who brings him coffee and takes the newscopy down to the print shop. At two o'clock in the morning *Imerissios Kyrix* goes to press on a cantankerous old flatbed that just manages to print the five hundred copies which represent an optimistic view of the paper's daily sales. *Imerissios Kyrix* and its views are small thunder in the stormy cross-currents of international opinion but, taken together with thousands of similar foreign newspapers, it is the loudest voice of political persuasion abroad.

While American newspapers are contracting in actual number and in relative influence, newspapers abroad are experiencing a boom. Larissa (population: ninety thousand) has three competitive daily newspapers; only a dozen American cities can match this. In addition to the pro-government *Imerissios Kyrix,* Larissa townsmen read *Eleftheria,* an opposition paper, and *Thessalia,* which supports the political views of a one-man party, its owner. Whether or not these papers are inefficient, badly edited and subsidized, they are influential.

Newspapers in most overseas areas are growing in number and in power to influence public opinion. A recent UNESCO report estimates that there are about thirty thousand daily newspapers now published regularly throughout the world and at least twenty-two thousand magazines with total circulations of about five hundred and fifty million copies an issue. In some countries the number of newspapers has doubled since the end of World War II. This growth is mainly due to the rise in worldwide literacy and also to the movement towards independence of former colonies. Over 35 nations have been created since 1945 and this autonomy has brought with it a new journalism. Under colonial administrations the press was either suppressed or acquiescent. Nationalist firebrand editors wound up in jail or in exile. Independence has brought a blossoming of a great variety of newspapers and magazines, many of them published in languages and dialects which, a few short years ago, had no written literature. They are being sold to people who until recently could not read.

Before World War II there were no regular newspapers in Swahili, one of the major African languages. Another leading language in Africa, Hausa, was represented before the war by one Nigerian publication, *Truth Is Worth A Penny*. Today the African vernacular press is lively and growing. The most influential African publication is probably *Drum*, an English-language magazine. Distributed throughout the continent, *Drum* beats out a crusading message of racial equality and political freedom. Many of its "readers" are illiterates who have the magazine read to them by its quarter-million buyers. Over and above its eye-catching potpourri of cheesecake photographs, gambling tips and sports features, *Drum* attracts its native audience with an editorial emphasis on nationalism, economic betterment and racial developments.

Thus *Drum* has one point in common with most foreign newspapers: they are intensely political. The American concept of a newspaper as a community service is dismissed as impractical by most foreign publishers. They will not waste valuable space with a campaign to get better street lighting at the local equivalent of Elm Street and Main unless it gives them a chance to take an editorial swipe at the opposition political party. There are significant exceptions to this widespread personal journalism among the better British and European newspapers as well as such journalistic towers of integrity as *La Prensa* in Buenos Aires and *The Times of India*. Around the world, however, partisan politics is the bread-and-butter subject of the average newspaper. Inevitably the United States is involved in this editorial partisanship because of the nature and scope of our involvement overseas. Criticism of American policies can be read in editorial columns in almost any foreign city every day. These attacks may be smug and uninformed at times but they are often effective. Offsetting the influence of these attacks is an important problem in our effort to persuade public opinion overseas.

Tactical resistance to editorial criticisms is not simple. The only sure way to control a newspaper is to own it or to buy off its editors or publishers. For moral if not for practical reasons, the United States government does not subsidize foreign newspapers. The number of these papers for sale to the highest political bidder is depressingly great; many papers abroad live on the handouts of one vested interest or another. The Soviet government is continually donating newsprint, machinery or plain cold cash to foreign newspapers. Nor is the practice unknown to some of our best allies. In moments of misguided enthusiasm American officials have been known in the past to attempt such influence over foreign newspapers usually with disastrous results. More than most sins in the propaganda business, this one boomerangs.

What does work, in the long run, is the simple persuasion of facts. Providing the world's press with a clear, straightforward account of American policy is an increasingly imperative requirement for the success of our policies. Although the radio, films and TV have made inroads on the traditional opinion-making supremacy of the press, they have by no means displaced it. The world press is the single most important target for our informational efforts to strengthen understanding of our policies abroad.

Adequate contact between policy-making officials and the press is a recent development. The Presidential press conference itself dates back only to Franklin Roosevelt. (Earlier Presidential meetings with the press lacked the give and take to qualify as press conferences.) State Department press arrangements were haphazard until they were strengthened by Dean Acheson and John Foster Dulles during their administrations. Department press operations were conducted by a third-echelon bureau until 1953 when Secretary Dulles gave the Assistant Secretary for Public Affairs greater status as official spokesman for himself and his Department. He installed a long-time confidant, Washington correspondent Carl McCardle, in the job. Secretary Dulles had a lively awareness of the power of the press; he used it as a sounding board for his thinking both in his private contacts with reporters and in his public press conferences. He also gave new status to the Department's press relations at the many international conferences and other meetings he attended.

This new concern for good press relations extends to American diplomatic establishments overseas. Before World War II no American embassies had officers specifically assigned to handle the press. The idea was to say as little as possible to as few as possible. Today American embassies are important news sources for journalists overseas. The main channel for embassy news is USIS.

USIS representation on embassy "country teams" assures a coordinated presentation of the American viewpoint to the foreign press.[1] The country team keeps our information service in close touch with the details of American policy while the information service, in turn,

---

1. See p. 52 for discussion of the "country team".

reports regularly to the team on current and anticipated press reactions to our policies. This exchange is invaluable to our press officers, who are expected to say the right thing to the press at the right time—even at three A.M. when an officer may be routed out of bed by a local editor asking for clarification of some point of American policy.

A formidable asset of ours in dealing with the free world press is the unrivalled reputation of American commercial news agencies. The two biggest agencies, Associated Press and United Press International, have clients all over the world although UPI is particularly strong in Latin America. Both have heavy foreign competition — notably Reuters, Agence France-Presse and the rapidly expanding West German Deutsche Press Agentur — but none of these can outmatch the high regard most foreign editors have for the American agencies. Other agencies may sometimes provide editors with a story more quickly and more fully, but not more objectively.

Despite their reputations and their worldwide facilities, AP and UPI are somewhat limited in their coverage. The Associated Press serves 2,400 newspapers overseas while UPI serves 1,400. Fortunately these papers include most of the leading foreign journals; but not all. Over two-thirds of the newspapers published overseas have no American commercial source for their news. In a few countries AP and UPI are prevented from introducing or expanding their services because of local censorship restrictions. The main deterrent to an expansion of their services is, however, economic. With its shoestring budget the average small foreign newspaper cannot afford to subscribe to an American or European news service. Its editors must catch their news as they can.

Among other things this means that they do not receive detailed descriptions of U.S. policy decisions from American commercial sources. The same editors often do get free bulletins from Tass, the Soviet news agency. The American government supplements news-agency reports with an overseas news network operated by USIS to provide editors with a day-to-day exposition of American policy and opinion. It is the most extensive non-commercial news distribution facility in the free world. Its radio-teletype circuits provide press material to over twenty-five thousand periodicals in seventy countries. Every day the USIA newsroom in Washington sends six to ten thousand words of newscopy to USIS posts where it is translated and relayed to local newspapers the same day. There are regional editions of this "Wireless File", one each for Europe, Africa, the Middle East, the Far East and Latin America. (The Latin American file is sent from Washington in Spanish.) Each regional edition includes some special material suited to the particular interests of editors and other opinion makers in its particular area. Otherwise the bulletin sent from Washington is the same for all areas.

In addition to serving foreign editors the Wireless File has an important secondary purpose. This is to provide our ambassadors and other officials overseas with a daily account of important policy statements issued in Washington. Sometimes a foreign government will be upset by inaccurate press reports of an alleged statement by the American government which seems to be against its interests. In such instances our ambassador is often able to dispel or to modify the fears of local government officials by providing them with the unadorned full text of the statement in question from the Wireless File.

Providing the full texts of policy statements is the main purpose of the USIA press file. Over half of the file that is sent daily to overseas posts consists of such texts, ranging from Presidential messages to the latest government statement on American bicycle tariff policy. The latter subject may be dull for most of us but it will make headlines in Great Britain, Japan and other countries that want to sell us more bicycles. If a story is important enough and local interest in the subject high enough it will be on the desk of local editors translated into the local language the day it is received by USIS.

The Wireless File is assembled in Washington by a central newsdesk. It is staffed by professionals—many of them USIS press officers serving a Washington tour—who know how to handle a fast-breaking story for a foreign clientele. Let us say that this morning the State Department sends a note to the Soviet Union on the disarmament problem with several proposals designed to break a deadlock on this issue. Agency pressroom editors have been alerted for the story and are ready to give it major play in the coming day's file. They first transmit the complete text of the note in the file to our overseas posts. This is followed up by related stories: one is a "backgrounder" on fifteen years of American efforts to bring about an agreement on disarmament; another is a roundup of initial American editorial comment on the new State Department proposal; a third is a story, datelined New York, giving reactions of the United Nations to the note. Later the Wireless File will provide local posts with a roundup of comments on the proposals from the foreign press based on reports telegraphed to Washington by the posts. If the new disarmament proposals are technical in nature a journalistic description of these technicalities will be prepared. For days—and for as long as the story is important to American policy objectives—similar material will be sent in the file to our overseas posts.

Not all of this material will be relayed to local newspapers by every USIS post. What portions may be locally useful is a decision left to the judgement of USIS and other embassy officers. There are no "must" stories although statements by the President and the Secretary of State are generally translated and distributed to the press and to the local Foreign Office as a matter of course. This and other Wireless File material is provided to editors primarily as "background" material to clarify and supplement the spot news stories they receive from local press agencies, the radio or from the international press services. Our purpose is to provide them with a full account of the American position on key issues to minimize the possibility of distortions of our policy. Very often this does not work.

If an editor sits down to write an anti-American blast because he has been ordered to do so or because he feels like it, no amount of USIS material, however factual or objective, will stop him. However, if he writes with a reasonably open mind, our press release may provide him with useful material to make his own evaluation of our policy on a given issue. He may still disagree with us but he will at least state our position fairly and he may even concede that on this or that aspect of the subject, our policy is correct. If he agrees with our position, our informational material will provide him with additional editorial ammunition for defending his viewpoint.

Many editors run USIS releases in their news columns and credit them the way they do an Associated Press or Reuters story. Our information services have a good reputation for accuracy among foreign editors; in ten years of press work I have never had a kickback on the accuracy of one of our stories. As a result the percentage of placement of our stories in the foreign press is often very high. By virtue of their role as "spokesman" for the American embassy, our local posts are often a good source of local stories in addition to stories from Washington.

Where we have economic and military aid programs USIS keeps the local press informed on these activities. In countries like India and Korea where our aid programs are extensive, a press officer is assigned exclusively to preparing material about them for the local press and other media. Whether our news releases involve news about large aid programs or merely an announcement of a record concert at the USIS library they usually receive a good "play" in the press.

In 1959 I issued over 400 of these stories to the Greek press and only fifteen failed to make the local papers—a fair batting average for any press office.

Feature story material is also made available through our information offices. This is taken from American magazines and newspapers or prepared by the Agency press office in Washington. Most American publications are liberal in granting copyright clearance on their stories for distribution to newspapers and magazines overseas. Tens of thousands of articles and photographs are placed by the information service in foreign magazines and newspapers every year as a result. For small provincial papers, USIA has developed a low-cost plastic photographic plate that can be easily fitted into a flatbed press form and provide a photo reproduction without the complex (and often non-existent) process of making a metal plate. Provincial editors like this service because it "dresses up" their front pages which would otherwise be given over entirely to columns of solid print. The plastic plates usually feature photographs of American scientific or technological achievements.

Photographs and press handouts have their function but they cannot take the place of personal contact. Most of our press officers have a regular routine for visits to working-level editors. A leisurely chat over a cup of coffee or tea helps create the mutual trust and friendliness that is essential to a good working relationship. My experience has been that these meetings with local journalists are best used to let them know that the ears of the embassy and of USIS are available to them. As P. T. Barnum once said: "I can outtalk any man on earth but a printer. The man who can stick type and the next morning talk to a thousand people while I am talking to one is the man I am afraid of. I want him for a friend." It is out of respect for the power of the press rather than fear of it that most USIS posts regard their work with the press as their most important day-to-day activity.

It is easy to underestimate this power and misjudge its potentials. Once early in my USIS career I took it upon myself to visit the editor of a reactionary newspaper in a Middle Eastern city who had made a below-the-belt attack on the treatment of Negroes in the United States. I went in breathing fire, armed with all the facts and figures I could gather to indicate the progress being made in race relations in the United States. The editor sat at his desk, drumming his fingers, while I gave my recitation. The next day his regular column began:

"Yesterday afternoon a bright young man from USIS came down

to my office to tell me how nicely colored people are treated in his country. . . ."

The column went on for ten paragraphs repeating every lie and half-truth of his previous article on the subject. Not only had I failed to convince him but I was the cause of another article on the subject.

The editor does have the last word and, in the case of those who are going to attack the United States come hell or high water, there is not much to be done about it. The lengths to which a hostile editor can go out of his way to twist a simple American gesture of friendliness to his own purpose is illustrated by an incident that took place in Athens during the early days of the American economic aid program in Greece. The director of the aid program made a speech to a Greek organization which was released to the local press by USIS. In his prefatory remarks he established a note of friendliness by saying: "You Greeks and we Americans have very much in common. We like to eat, we like to drink and we like to sit around and talk." The next day, the Communist-line newspaper in Athens summarized this sentence as follows: "Mr. Porter said that we were just like the Americans—gluttons, drunkards and gossips."

The best way to have our story told in print overseas is through the pen of a foreign editor or writer, if he is willing to write it honestly. The second-best way to get our story told is to issue our own publications. In special cases our posts do just that; in all, they publish 57 magazines and 22 weekly or bi-weekly newspapers. The first experiment that our government made in issuing a foreign-language newspaper overseas came as a result of our occupation of Germany after World War II.

The Nazi-controlled press in Germany was ordered closed down and the United States and other western occupying powers issued licenses to anti-Nazi editors in an effort to revive the German press on a democratic basis. We made loans to assist the new papers during their formative years. To supplement them, American occupation authorities started their own paper, *Die Neue Zeitung*, in Frankfurt. By the early 1950's the paper was regarded by many Germans as the best in the country. It was being supported by our information service at a cost of over three million dollars a year, of which about one million was returned in sales revenues. American control of the paper, together with the loan program to other German publications, was ended by 1955. (American occupation authorities and USIS also sponsored the leading post-war German intellectual magazine *Der Monat* in its formative years.) In Austria a similar venture was undertaken when we published the daily *Wiener Kurier* in Vienna. The paper is now published under private auspices.

USIS no longer publishes any daily newspapers overseas. The best known of our current publications are the two magazines we distribute in the Soviet Union and Poland under the terms of recent agreements on the interchange of informational and cultural material. The Russian language magazine *America* is one of the oldest USIS magazines, having been started during the short Era-of-Good-Feelings days of 1946 when the Soviet leadership was still making gestures toward Allied unity. Our original agreement with the Russians provided for the distribution of our magazine in the Soviet Union in exchange for an equal distribution of the Soviet Embassy's publication in this country. *America* quickly became one of the hottest bootleg items in the Soviet Union; printed in the United States, it was a slick-paper magazine which drew upon the best editorial and photographic material from commercial publications and other sources. The going black-market price for the magazine in Moscow in the late Forties was five dollars an issue. Each copy had a readership of dozens of people. It became apparent, however, by 1951 that Soviet authorities were restricting the number of copies in circulation to the point where it was uneconomical for us to continue producing the magazine. Publication was suspended until 1956 when, as a result of the exchange-of-information discussions started at the 1955 Eisenhower-Khrushchev summit meeting in Geneva, the magazine was revived with much the same format and purpose as its predecessor. The 1956 agreement is also reciprocal; the Russians have a magazine, *USSR*, which is distributed on American newsstands.

In the 1946 agreement the Russians had the right of pre-censorship. They examined the contents of the magazine before it was printed and rejected what they considered to be undesirable. The new agreement omits this censorship feature although both parties have agreed to limit the subject matter of their respective publications generally to cultural information.

The USIS editors of *America* in Washington (and Soviet officials in Moscow) are well aware that almost anything put into the magazine is "provocative" in terms of upsetting concepts of America which Soviet domestic propaganda has tried to drill into the Russian people for four decades. The primary purpose of *America* is not to show American prosperity although this factor is not ignored. It is rather to point up the vitality of American life with particular stress on the themes of democratic freedom and inventiveness. This is done largely through pictures; the magazine resembles a combination of *Life* and *Look* in its editorial make-up. The titles of articles in a typical recent issue are indicative of the magazine's contents: *Push-button Hospital Care, New Future for Farm Crops, The Role of the Drama Critic, Test-tube Textiles, Highlights of US-USSR Track Meet* and *Facts About the U.S.: The Clothing Industries.*

A question raised periodically by Congress and other groups is whether the *America* project is worth the money it costs. Production costs in 1960 were about $1.40 a copy. The magazine is relatively expensive to produce because its print run is only about fifty thousand copies. The problem is not whether the magazine has an effect; there is no doubt that it is avidly read by the Russians who see it. The question is whether it receives a wide enough distribution in the Soviet Union. Distribution is handled by the Soviet government since there are no private distributors of newspapers or magazines. Is the magazine distributed outside of a few kiosks in Moscow? The Soviet government claims that it is but there is some suspicion that distribution arrangements are not always fulfilled. The Soviets have raised the point that *their* magazine is not being adequately distributed or sold in the United States. They probably are right about the magazine's selling power; it is well distributed throughout this country but sales are not spectacular.

In the balance, *America* is worth the money spent on it even though there are no iron-clad guarantees that it receives full distribution throughout the Soviet Union. The distribution it does receive is significant particularly in view of the well-documented fact that each copy of the magazine is seen by many people. The total readership of the magazine is minuscule compared with the population of the Soviet Union or even Moscow but in a totalitarian society ideas introduced by relatively few people into the ever-present rumor system travel far and wide. The distribution situation seems to be somewhat more favorable in Poland where USIA has made available a Polish language magazine similar to *America* since 1959. The magazine *Ameryka* circulates freely in Polish cities and, like its Russian counterpart, has a large number of readers-per-copy for its thirty thousand monthly circulation.

Another USIS magazine published in a Communist state is *SAD*, which derives its startling name from the fact that these letters spell "USA" in Serbo-Croat, the language of Yugoslavia. *SAD* is an alertly-edited publication that performs a useful task in keeping Yugoslav opinion leaders, from Cabinet ministers to village mayors, aware of American developments without getting directly involved in the delicate political relationship we have with the Communist regime in their country. Both *SAD* and the Polish language *Ameryka* tailor some of their editorial material to the fact that many of their readers have connections with the United States through relatives who have emigrated. Reports on activities of Serb, Croat and other Yugoslav ethnic groups here help to convey the American story in a sympathetic manner to *SAD*'s readers.

One reason why our publications in Communist countries are so avidly sought and read is that they represent an editorial change of diet from the one-party press. In free world countries, by contrast, our publications face competition from a wide variety of newspapers and magazines. In the early days of the Campaign of Truth there was an almost compulsive desire on the part of our information posts overseas to publish magazines and newspapers of all kinds. In the prosey rhetoric of the Campaign, the idea was to "go straight to the people with the message". Newspapers and other publications sprouted all over the world. Undoubtedly they did some good, but in spending our energy on producing our publications we tended to forget that the best way to get "the message" across is through unattributed local sources. The hard review of the program made in the early 1950's ended many of these publications. Each of the 57 magazines and 22 weekly or bi-weekly newspapers now published by various posts overseas has a clearly definable political reason for existence.

The largest of our newspapers is *American Reporter*, issued every two weeks by our posts in India. *Reporter* is one of the most complex publishing ventures of its kind in the world: it is published in nine languages in four Indian cities. It has a circulation of three hundred thousand distributed among government officials, professional workers, students and other opinion leaders. Since 1951 it has made a major contribution to our program of providing Indians with accurate information about the United States and, in particular, about Indian-American relations.

Reporter goes about its task in a low-key manner, using factual material to highlight American concern for India as a major democratic state in Asia. The paper is especially careful in reporting on American economic assistance to India. It probably has given better and more extensive coverage to the Indian government's community development program—in which American private and public agencies cooperate—than has any Indian paper. In doing this *Reporter* is counteracting the day-and-night propaganda attacks of the Indian Communist Party against the United States. The Party can marshall the services of 168 Party and "front" newspapers and magazines throughout India in its campaign to convince Indians that the Soviet Union is the new world leader and India's greatest benefactor.

The format established by the *American Reporter* in India has been used successfully in USIS newspapers in two other Asian countries, Ceylon and Pakistan, as well as in Ghana in West Africa. Other posts have found magazines an effective way of reaching local opinion leaders. The subject matter of these publications ranges from the scholarly comments of *Atlantico*, a small circulation "little magazine" published by USIS in Spain, to the topical stories and pictures of *Informaciones* which is distributed regularly to 40,000 leading Argentinians. The largest of our overseas publishing projects is the six hundred thousand circulation *Free World* series of magazines which are published in eleven editions in nine languages for USIS posts throughout the Far East.[2] *Free World* editions are produced at a USIA printing plant in Manila which prints and ships an average of eight tons of publication materials every day to posts in Far Eastern countries. (There is a similar plant in Beirut serving Middle East points.) Each edition of *Free World* is edited for a specific audience. The Chinese language edition is intended in part for the many "Overseas Chinese" living in Malaya, Burma, Indonesia and other Southeast Asian countries. Not only are the Overseas Chinese an important political and economic factor in many of the countries where they have settled but they are also a basic element in Red Chinese aspirations in the area. Through *Free World* and other publications USIS provides them with a review of events on the Chinese mainland designed to take the bloom off the rosy picture painted by Communist propaganda.

The Arabic language *USA News Review* published in Beirut is also distributed over a wide area. It influences Arab opinion in a dozen countries where the local press often tends toward editorial excesses about American affairs. In Paris, *Informations et Documents* has provided a bi-weekly view of American life for French opinion leaders that is both comprehensive and factual. *Informations* has one of the toughest audiences in the world; the French are notoriously prone to

---

[2] The languages in which *Free World* is published are Cambodian, Chinese, Korean, Lao, Malay, Thai, Sinhalese, Vietnamese as well as Chinese editions,

disregard any explanation of the United States which is at variance with their own, often baroque image. The editors of *Informations* have met their French readers half way by editing the magazine with a Gallic flair. They seem to say: "Well, yes, the Americans may seem a little incomprehensible at times and almost always un-French in their ways but they do have their points." *Informations* then proceeds to document these points, charmingly and clearly.

Informations achieved some Stateside notice several years ago when it printed a profile story about Richard M. Nixon, indicating in phrases that any journalist might have used about the then-Vice President that he was an energetic up-and-coming statesman. The story was brought to the attention of a group of Congressmen who charged USIA with disseminating Republican propaganda. The flurry soon blew over but not before USIS officers around the world could take some ironic satisfaction in being charged with Republicanism instead of the New Dealer or Communist stigma of the McCarthy days. The incident was taken as a sign in the organization that times had indeed changed.

The Agency publishes only one magazine for world-wide distribution: a scholarly periodical issued six times a year called *Problems of Communism*. It is a sobersided chronicle of current events in the Communist world written by experts in the field. Not all of the contributors are American. Very often they are members of the small, astute group of scholars at Oxford and Cambridge Universities in England who are doing some of the best thinking on the subject today. Total circulation of the magazine is very small but the readership is select and attentive. This is the only USIS English-language publication available by subscription to the American public.[3]

Pamphlets and brochures are standard items in the output of most USIS press offices. These provide general information about the United States or about some specific American activity. The most popular such publication is *Atomic Power for Peace*, an illustrated description of the American "atoms-for-peace" program. Over nine million copies of the pamphlet in 38 languages have been distributed since it was first issued in 1954. Another perennial "best seller" is *Facts About the USA*, an almanac-styled compendium of facts and figures which are most commonly sought by foreigners. *Facts About the USA* is revised by Agency headquarters in Washington periodically; to

---

3. *Problems of Communism* can be ordered from the Superintendent of Documents, Washington 25, D. C., for $1.50 a year.

date it has been distributed overseas in eight and a half million copies in 39 languages. Agency cartoon strips have a larger readership in foreign newspapers than any commercial strips.

Some American newspaper leaders have questioned whether USIS should be in the press and publications business at all. They have expressed the fear that such activities may lead to the establishment of an official government news agency. They are also apprehensive about possible competition between USIS and American commercial news agencies. The latter question has been raised by officials of the United Press International in the past although the other major news agency, the Associated Press, has gone on record stating that it does not regard USIS press output as competitive. The information agency's position on the matter was outlined by Director George Allen in these words:

"Keeping the record straight has become an accepted practice of this government and is essential to our foreign relations. We must make our position clear, and we cannot let distortions about this nation go unchallenged. But we in USIA have a specialized and limited function. The major job of sending news abroad is done, and should continue to be done, by private news agencies and correspondents under our free system. . . . Our government makes extensive use of the printed and broadcast word in its overseas informational activities in eighty countries, but at most we seek only to supplement the work carried on by the American press. There is no effort to compete; we try instead to provide editors abroad with the type of background materials which the American services cannot handle because their wires are pre-empted by the necessity of carrying quickly fast-breaking news of prime importance. Ours might be called a file of secondary news about America, plus official announcements, texts and other material which normally is crowded off the press service wires by spot developments."[4]

In order to meet any further criticisms of the information program on this score Congress has prohibited USIA since 1957 from extending its press services where they "would prevent private U.S. concerns from selling corresponding services." In practice our overseas posts have good working relationships with the local correspondents of American news agencies. The purpose of the USIS press services is to fill a vacuum in printed information about the United States abroad.

---

4. Speech before Nevada Press Association, April, 1959.

American journalism is the weakest of our major commercial media abroad. In most cities of the world you can buy an American book, see an American movie or a television program but it is often difficult to find an American newspaper or magazine.

There are only two American newspapers with a substantial overseas circulation. Fortunately they are among our best—the *New York Times* and the *New York Herald-Tribune*. There are several smaller American papers available abroad: the Rome *Daily American* is widely read in the Mediterranean area and the *Bangkok Post* is a well-known journalistic fixture in Southeast Asia.

The *New York Herald-Tribune's* overseas edition is published in Paris and has a seventy-year tradition of authoritative reporting throughout the Continent. Shortly after World War II a Soviet diplomat asked General Charles de Gaulle what newspaper was essential reading for diplomats and statesmen. De Gaulle replied: "As a Frenchman, I don't like to say it but there's only one. It's an American paper called the *Herald-Tribune*." The Paris *Trib* is a mélange of first-rate news and political commentary plus light features and travel articles to support its extensive tourist advertising.

The *New York Times* publishes an international edition in Europe which is a tightly edited version of the New York edition. Although it is delivered from two to four days late in many parts of the world, it has won an attentive audience among statesmen and other leaders through its authoritative news reports and sound editorial comment. Normally it consists of from 10 to 12 pages but its size is expanded when a major story breaks, in accordance with the *Times* tradition of full coverage. Copies of the *Times'* international edition are purchased by USIS posts in Europe, Africa and Asia for presentation to political leaders and other opinion makers.

Among American magazines the *Readers Digest* leads by a good length in global sales. Its famed format of information-and-uplift, human-interest-and-humor circulated around the world in 22 language editions is read by over 15 million subscribers and newsstand customers every month. These foreign editions usually include special articles of local interest but the bulk of the overseas *Digests'* editorial material is the same as in the American edition.

Both *Time* and *Newsweek* magazines have international editions with an important readership among English-speaking opinion leaders overseas. *Time* prints five editions for distribution outside the United States; their total sales are 590,000 copies of which 240,000 represent sales in Canada. *Newsweek,* with two foreign editions, has an overseas circulation of 105,000 copies.

Since they are selling "perishable" news, a large part of the success of these two magazines is dependent on quick distribution to all parts of the world within a day or two of their Stateside publication dates. Both magazines rely on the international airlines for this distribution although sometimes difficulties arise that have little to do with disrupted airline schedules. Both magazines have been banned at one time or another in over a score of countries usually because they have allegedly insulted the local government or its ruler. In Formosa the magazines have to submit to an unusual form of local censorship involving the photographs of the Red Chinese leader, Mao Tse Tung. Any photos of Mao have to be stamped over with the Chinese word for "bandit" before the publication can be distributed in Nationalist Chinese territory. Other important American publications distributed abroad are *Life,* which has a Spanish edition for Latin America and a fortnightly English language edition for the rest of the world, and *U.S. News and World Report,* which prints a thin-paper airmail edition for foreign distribution.

Despite these relatively important gains in the distribution of American newspapers and magazines overseas our commercial press and publications are still poorly represented in broad areas overseas. In the coming decade there will undoubtedly be a greater interest in the overseas market on the part of the American newspaper and magazine industry as well as an increased use of American commercial news services by foreign editors. Until then the burden of providing the press in many areas overseas with an accurate account of American policies rests with the USIS press services.

9

BOOKS AS WEAPONS

It has been called "the silent revolution" and it may well be the most profound change taking place among all the heady changes that mark our age. It is the revolution in literacy. We are living in the first generation in which most of the world's population will be able to read and write. Perhaps we have reached this goal already; no one has yet developed an acceptable formula for measuring world literacy. The United Nations recently estimated in a UNESCO report that 44% of the world's population could be classified as literate. The range of achievement among countries is broad. According to UNESCO, 98% is the literacy rate in Sweden and the illiteracy rate in Mozambique. While variations continue, the overall mean of literacy is being raised every year. Its evidence can be seen in the flood of books, the number of new schools and the circulation figures of newspapers and magazines that serve the hundreds of millions of people who have broken the bonds of illiteracy that enslaved their ancestors.

This burgeoning new development concerns the United States directly in carrying out its strategy of truth. What the new literates read and what they write—what they *do* with their new power—will affect our own destinies as they come to judge more accurately the American impact on their own destiny. We either meet this challenge of the new literacy forcefully or we lose by default all the advantages that can accrue to us from the fact that more people are making up their own minds about their political and social affairs.

Most people abroad have a seemingly unquenchable thirst for reading material of all kinds. It is not unusual during school time in many countries to see students standing in line to use inadequate library facilities. Although the current increase in book production overseas is phenomenal, many students in Asian and African schools still do not have a single classroom book. They will have books eventually and what they read and understand about us will be a vital factor in the equation of American influence on the new generation of Asian and African leadership.

Until recently the amount of available reading material on American life and ideas has been pitifully small overseas. Moreover this lack has been greatest in the newly-independent nations of Asia and Africa where an inexperienced leadership is looking for solutions to a whole range of problems from how to draft a Constitution to how to run agricultural cooperatives. A decade ago it was often impossible for a reader abroad to find an American book he wanted either in English or in his own language. Except in a few of the larger national libraries in Western European countries there were no significant collections of American books in foreign libraries. Those that did exist were kept under lock and key, following the now-crumbling foreign tradition of libraries as preservers rather than dispensers of books.

American books were seldom used in foreign schools, nor were they stocked in quantity in foreign bookstores outside of a few large cities. When he was Ambassador in India in 1952 Chester Bowles walked into a large bookstore and discovered that the only American book on its shelves was an Uncle Wiggly children's book. He was discovering for himself what was a normal situation in most Asian bookstores. It was also difficult to buy an American newspaper or magazine at most foreign newsstands. In short, the primary sources of American ideas—whether it was a book on Abraham Lincoln or the most recent issue of *The Atlantic Monthly*—were not available.

This situation has changed swiftly in the past decade, largely as a result of USIS efforts in the library and the book publication and distribution fields. USIS now operates the most extensive chain of libraries in the world and is the largest originator of foreign-language books with the significant exception of the Soviet government Foreign Languages Publishing House. Millions of American books and periodicals, in English and in translation, have been placed in overseas libraries through USIS efforts. More foreign school systems are adapting their curricula to American standards with American books. The world's bookstores and kiosks are carrying quantities of American books of all kinds, from encyclopedias to pocket-book novels. There are still gaps in the supply of U.S. books and periodicals overseas but it is safe to say that there is no longer a city of any size in the free world without a useful source of American publications either in a library or a bookstore.

Primarily responsible for this accomplishment is the worldwide system of USIS libraries. They are, in my opinion, the most effective single part of our entire information operation. There are libraries in 161 cities in 65 countries throughout the world, from the sedate precincts of London's Grosvenor Square to the bazaars of Peshawar. They have 26 million patrons annually who come to find out about something American. The motives of these readers are as varied as their callings. Many of them are students who pore over technical publications, making notes in crabbed handwriting. Others are businessmen consulting the large variety of commercial publications in the magazine racks and the reference shelves. There are also the old-crone dressmakers who come to copy the latest fashions from *Vogue* and *Harper's Bazaar.*

Day in and day out hundreds of thousands of people pass through our libraries to enrich their personal and professional lives, to relish the simple pleasure of browsing or just to gaze at the pictures in *Life* or in an illustrated edition of *Tom Sawyer.* Thousands of others receive USIS books by mail; one such subscriber, a teacher who lives in the Gerhwal hills of northern India, is two days' walk from the end of the mail route.

Over eight million books were borrowed from our libraries in 1959. Of all the innovations USIS has introduced overseas this one has been especially popular. Most foreign libraries do not permit their books to circulate among the general public. There are, of course, exceptions: British libraries have a long tradition of book circulation as have those in Scandinavian countries. But the typical library abroad is still a reliquary for books with a "Do Not Disturb" sign on the front door. This situation is changing rapidly, due in large part to the liberating example set by the USIS libraries. Our collections average four circulations a year for each of their books. This is well above the rate for public libraries in the United States. The rate of loss in USIS libraries is well under American standards, even in countries where the custom of borrowing books is new.

More of a problem than loss or theft is the sheer wear and tear on our books and magazines because of constant handling. Magazines as popular as the *Saturday Evening Post* or the *Ladies Home Journal* are often worn through in a few weeks; reference books like the World Almanac and the encyclopedias also have a short life expectancy. The information post in Paris reported an unusual example of enthusiasm several years ago when a patron informed the library that he could not return the book he had borrowed—Dr. Spock's famous book on infant care — because part of the book had been eaten by his baby. USIS donated the rest of the book to him but the librarian could not resist including in her report Sir Francis Bacon's famous maxim: "Some books are to be tasted, others to be swallowed, and some few to be chewed and digested."

Collections in our larger libraries usually total between ten and fifteen thousand volumes, or about as many as a suburban library in the United States. USIS collections are more heavily weighted in favor of non-fiction—technical works, history, economics, etc.—and reference books than the average American library. However, they also include representative American fiction. Children's books are usually small in number although they are well-patronized not only by children but also by adults who borrow them to study English. Although most books catalogued in our overseas libraries are in English, the libraries in Latin America include sizeable collections of books in Spanish on American subjects. Thirty percent of the books in our Latin American libraries are in the local languages. Libraries in other parts of the world also have books in local languages but on a more limited scale. Works about the United States in languages such as Gujarati, Persian or Hausa are still hard to find.[1] Occasionally a third language is also represented. The library in Cairo has 24,000 books in English, 2,500 in Arabic and a smaller number in French for the small but influential group of Egyptians who can also speak and read that language.

American books by American authors predominate in our libraries but there is always shelfroom for a good book on an American subject by a foreign author such as Lord Charnwood's classic study of Lincoln. Books by foreign authors are also purchased if their works are useful in promoting Western democratic ideals or in exposing Communism. Among these authors are such noted British specialists on Soviet affairs as Edward Crankshaw and H. R. Trevor-Roper. Our periodical collections include such foreign publications as the magazine of the local American Chamber of Commerce or a cultural review featuring American arts.

Selection of books and periodicals is usually made by the American library officer on the scene. They have considerable leeway in ordering what they think the patrons want. The United States government is under no obligation to provide every variety of book. It serves its own interests, however, as well as those of the library patrons when it hews to the American tradition of liberality in supplying the broadest range of titles that it reasonably can.

This tradition and the integrity of the USIS library system came under severe attack during the McCarthy investigations in 1953. Before the investigations, the government followed a liberal book-selec-

---

[1] Hausa is an African language that may not be known to most Americans, but it is the native tongue of more people than is Italian. There are no books in Hausa about the United States.

tion policy. The State Department's Advisory Committee on Books Abroad declared in May 1952: "The Committee is positive and unanimous in its decision to recommend . . . that authorship should not be a criterion for determining whether a book is available for USIS libraries abroad." The criterion, the Committee declared, was subject matter and its appropriateness to a library specializing in American subjects. This policy was among the first to be questioned by the McCarthy investigators in January, 1953. The presence of books by alleged Communists and other undesirables was hammered at during the entire investigation.

In an effort to redefine the policy on works by such authors, the State Department issued an order in February, 1953, prohibiting the use of material by "controversial persons, Communists, fellow-travellers, etc." This vague directive, which could be interpreted to cover almost every book written, was followed up by a number of clarifying directives which eliminated the all-embracing "etc." but which made clear that authorship—or, more particularly, the politics of an author—would be a dominant factor in determining the suitability of a book. This still did not entirely end the confusion. Who was a "controversial person"? Or a "fellow traveller"? Or even the most definable word in the directive—"Communist"? Book procurement ground to a halt while information-program officials pondered the formidable problems of applying a security clearance to each of the tens of thousands of authors represented in our library collections. The monthly flow of books to our overseas libraries was cut down from a normal fifty thousand to three hundred by May.

Even more confused than Washington officials were the USIS officers abroad charged with interpreting the vague prohibitions against books and periodicals already on the shelves. Most of them sat tight, backed by their ambassadors, waiting for a clarification of terms. They were fully aware of the damage that could be done to our information programs and to American prestige in their countries of duty by a wholesale removal of books from the libraries.

In a few cases there were indiscretions in removing books from the shelves; the resultant furor was as much responsible as any single event for bringing the entire problem back to reality. One librarian removed the works of Thomas Paine. Another eliminated books by such eminent anti-Communists as Walter White, then director of the National Association for the Advancement of Colored People, and Bert Andrews, Washington correspondent for the *New York Herald-Tribune*. In most cases the books were stored while the librarians waited for further instructions. At several posts, unfortunately, this procedure was not followed: some books were put to the match and the redolent phrase "book burning" hit the headlines. The phrase was a sobering one for the American public. The book-burning incidents (involving only eleven books) pointed up the dangers inherent in capricious censorship.

There were a few unsuitable books on our shelves at the time the controversy started but in a frenzy of overzealousness the problem was blown up out of all proportion to its actual dimensions. Some libraries had books by Communists and fellow-travelling authors. Most of these volumes had been turned over to them by the 35 foreign libraries of the Office of War Information when they were transferred to the State Department in 1945. The books in dispute were mostly out-of-date, inaccurate descriptions of American-Soviet relations as seen in the rosy light of our wartime political honeymoon with the Russians. The actual number of these books on USIS shelves in February 1953 was 39 copies representing 25 titles by eight authors who were known or avowed Communists. This was a minuscule portion of the three million volumes by 85,000 authors represented in our libraries at the time. These 39 books did not, of course, belong on our shelves purely on the ground of unsuitable subject matter, over and above the question of the politics of the author. Once the error was discovered they could have been removed quietly and effectively.

Sharp public reaction to the book-burning incidents meanwhile had created a better atmosphere for the resolution of the entire problem. On July 8 the State Department announced a new policy that was both definitive and reasonable. The directive, which is still in effect, reaffirmed the basic integrity of purpose of the overseas library program. Books are chosen on their merits and more particularly for their usefulness to the information program. Generally writings by Communists or by persons who have pleaded the Fifth Amendment when questioned about Communist affiliations are proscribed. Plans for making full-fledged security checks of authors represented in our libraries were quietly dropped. Within a few months the Great Book Scare of 1953 was a forgotten issue.

Any decision other than a reaffirmation of traditional American liberality in book selection would have been disastrous. The success of USIS libraries depends upon accessibility of a wide range of subject material, including so-called "controversial" subjects. Any attempt to limit books to a sanitized list of "official literature" would negate the entire purpose of the overseas library system. The victory for common sense which was scored in 1953 over some bitter and powerful opposition is reflected today in any free world city where there is both a USIS and a Soviet library. The difference between the two is immediate and striking; the USIS library is invariably filled with readers and the Soviet library, with its guarded collection of official books and magazines, is almost always empty. The moral need not be labored. Students and others who have a choice between American and Soviet libraries vote with their library cards in favor of full and free access to information.

The popularity of USIS libraries is also a credit to the skill of the American librarians who operate them. Not only do they show professional skill but also a flair for taking such unprofessional situations as riots, earthquakes and language barriers in stride. Our libraries, as we have seen, are favorite targets for anti-American political demonstrations abroad. More than one serious incident has been averted by the cool manner in which a lady librarian has faced a group of rowdies. Even on non-riot days, running one of our libraries is a somewhat different experience from any our librarians had expected when they graduated from library school back in the States. "If someone had told me that I would be operating a library that included a delivery route manned by donkeys, I would have laughed out loud," one of our librarians told me once. And, she added, she loved it.

In Rangoon the librarian for thousands of students and officials is Mrs. Zelma Graham. A former Baptist missionary who is also a trained librarian, Mrs. Graham has operated the USIS library in the Burmese capital since the country won its independence in 1948. The Burmese are sensitive to foreign influence, real or alleged. They were somewhat suspicious of the new American library when it opened. Their suspicions were soon dissolved when they found it to be almost the only ready source of reliable technical information on the knotty problems they faced in setting up a government. The gaily-painted, light-filled room on the ground floor of a British bank in the middle of town has become as much a part of Rangoon's life as its temples and canals. In a report on Mrs. Graham's library, the *New York Times* once said: "Without fuss or fanfare, it has made thousands of friends for the United States in a part of the world where people automatically suspect and distrust the motives of the West and where the Communists' chief propaganda line is anti-Americanism. . . . It exemplifies the kind of aid which Asian countries really welcome."

Male librarians also serve with great success at some posts. Maurice Leach of the University of Kentucky operated our library facilities in Cairo during the difficult years after 1956 when American relations with the United Arab Republic were strained. Even under the strain of political tensions the library was continually patronized by students and intellectuals. It was one of the few American installations that was permitted to operate without difficulty during those years. At my present post in East Pakistan, the librarian is personable Tennesseean James Hulbert, who operates a 12,000-volume library in the provincial capital, Dacca, and supervises smaller reading rooms in six other cities. The reading rooms are serviced by jeeps and by boats plying the Bengal rivers. Book shipments receive special handling from the Pakistani river captains and their crews, many of whom are cardholders in our libraries. When he is not moving up and down the rivers himself on visits to the reading rooms Jim Hulbert is in the central library supervising the staff and meeting with the Pakistani students who come in to ask him all kinds of questions about his country. For several years he has also been busy teaching the first course in library science ever given at Dacca University.

Answering questions is an essential service of any USIS library. Some of the questions are vague. ("Please give me some informations about your country?") Others are hopeful. ("What is the American cure for cancer?") Some are intended to bait us. ("Why do the Americans always mistreat the Negro people of South Carolina?") All of them are given careful consideration. Antonios Karavias, a Greek employee of USIS who operates our library in the provincial town of Kavalla, once made a listing for me of some of the questions he was asked during a typical day. In part, he wrote:

"Mr. Costa Doranis, lawyer, wanted to know about marriage and divorce rates in the U.S.

"University student Thanos Papadopoulos was supplied with names of early explorers and dates of explorations.

"Miss Pappas, graduate of a commercial school and planning on studies in the United States, was given information on all colleges in Indiana.

"Mr. Argyropoulos, owner of an olive press, was given addresses of American factories making hydraulic presses.

"Amateur fisherman Spyros Bettos, planning to build a boat, found interesting models in the book, *Boating is Fun.*

"Circulation figures on American publications were supplied for Mr. Panos, a journalist.

"Messrs. Herman and Dubonnet, United Nations officials assigned to make a motion picture of technical-assistance accomplishments in our area, asked for our cooperation in finding them an interpreter and a rented automobile. Both were secured at reasonable rates."

Mr. Karavias' library in Kavalla is one of more than a hundred small "reading rooms" we maintain in provincial cities throughout the world. They are operated by local employees under the supervision of American library officers, who are usually stationed in capital cities. The work of these provincial libraries is often supplemented by bookmobiles, a USIS innovation in some countries. Other large provincial audiences are reached by mail through the distribution of "book boxes" circulated among small towns, usually under the auspices of a local cultural society. Originally these "book boxes" consisted primarily of hard-cover books but in recent years there has been a shift toward paperback books which are more compact and also more expendable. A typical "book box" is the one called "Classics of American Literature" featuring twenty inexpensive paperback editions of such works as *Moby Dick, Leaves of Grass* and Franklin's *Autobiography.*

In addition to maintaining their own high professional standard, USIS libraries have often helped improve other library services in the countries where they are located. The information services have assisted in the development of modern library systems in over a score of countries including Turkey, Egypt, Thailand and Vietnam. Frequently local librarians come for training in American methods. In Turkey, where books in the national library were classified by size until USIS helped Turkish librarians introduce the Dewey Decimal System of classification, the country's first library school was recently established with the help of USIS and the Ford Foundation. Other library training schools in Burma, Malaya, Iran and Egypt owe their development to the cooperation of USIS. Our libraries have also helped foreign universities and other institutions build up their collections of American scientific and technical periodicals and books as well as their general collections on American subjects. Most of our libraries also make presentations of American books, magazines and newspapers to influential individuals. The presentation program is especially liberal in countries where foreign exchange restrictions limit the import of American publications.

Another special service is to provide American music scores for interested groups. The emphasis is on serious music including our best jazz and folk music. There is not much need to provide the works of

Tin Pan Alley which can be heard everywhere on radios and phonographs, thanks to the effective arrangements American record companies have with their foreign affiliates. Many of the latest American popular tunes are translated and recorded abroad within a few weeks after they are introduced here. Even the staid British Broadcasting Corporation uses a substantial amount of American popular music on its programs; the British Songwriters Guild passed a resolution in 1958 censuring the BBC for its American tastes. According to the Guild only one third of the popular music played on the BBC was British; the rest was American. The BBC replied that it could not resist the persistent demands of listeners for American records. The requests received by the BBC are echoed in hundreds of other radio stations around the world.

More serious forms of American music are less well known. Until recently the amount of serious American music available abroad either on records or in printed scores was limited in both range and quantity. As a result our music was not well represented in the repertoires of symphonic orchestras and other musical groups in foreign countries. This disadvantage is being gradually overcome by the establishment of collections of American music scores at USIS libraries in sixty foreign cities. In addition almost all our libraries overseas now have record libraries featuring both American compositions and standard repertoire works performed by American orchestras and soloists.

Since the purpose of these collections is to have American music played by local musical organizations, the problem of copyrights arises. Most American composers are members of the American Society of Composers, Artists and Performers (ASCAP) or Broadcast Music Inc. (BMI) which have representatives overseas who monitor local concerts for possible copyright violations. Many foreign musical groups do not have the dollar funds to meet these copyright costs. In such cases, USIA helps its posts abroad in arranging for the rental of scores and also in obtaining performance rights to American works.

American music is thus gaining recognition in the repertoires of musical organizations abroad and audiences are being introduced to the lively experimentation that is the keynote of contemporary American music. At first foreign groups played only occasional short works by American composers. Now their interest—and that of their audiences—has been built up to the point where they are performing American symphonies and operas.

Several years ago the director of the opera company in Athens came to our office to discuss his plans for the coming season. His plans involved another round of the standard repertoire — *Aida, Barber of Seville, Carmen* and the other Italian and French worthies.

"Why don't you try an American work?" I suggested.

His initial reaction was to look at me as if I had proposed that he fly around the ceiling. "Is there an American opera we could do?" he asked. I assured him that there was and that we could probably obtain the score of at least one.

A few weeks later I turned over to him the score of Gian Carlo Menotti's *The Medium* which he accepted with graciously concealed skepticism. Two days later he was back in the office, this time all excited.

"Magnificent! We'll do it," he shouted. "But there is something missing."

"What is that?"

"Menotti! He must conduct it."

Somehow or other Mr. Menotti was persuaded to come to Athens during one of his trips to Italy to conduct the first American opera ever presented in Greece. It was such a creditable performance that no one in Greek musical circles will ever again give a fly-around-the-ceiling look at the mention of American opera.

In some countries music can be one of the most important aspects of our information program. This is true in Austria where (to quote Joseph Wechsberg) music is "always a necessity, never a luxury . . . To be an Opernarr (literally an 'opera fool'), who thinks, talks, dreams opera, is a great distinction." The USIS office in Vienna publishes a first-rate magazine about U.S. musical life. It has also assisted Austrian orchestras to increase the range of American works in their repertoires.

Complementing efforts in the library field is our program for encouraging the sale of American books in foreign bookstores. These stores range from the erudite sophistication of Foyle's of London, with its tradition of providing any book ever published, to the hole-in-the-wall stalls of the Tehran bazaar, where used books are spread on the dirt floor for a browser's inspection. The setting is different but the problem is the same for USIS: making sure that American books, in English or in translation, are available to foreign book buyers.

Here is a field where we face a direct challenge from the Communists and where until very recently we were soundly outmatched. The Russians have done a first-class job of distributing low-priced books in politically sensitive areas around the world. Their resources for this endeavor are strong: the Foreign Languages Publishing House in Moscow has facilities for publishing books in 50 foreign languages and dialects. It printed and distributed 30 million books in foreign translations in 1958. Until the early 1950's distribution of Soviet books in most countries was generally small. In the past ten years, however, the Russians have launched a major campaign in the low-priced book field.

India is a prime example of the extent and the effectiveness of their techniques. In 1955 the Russians offered only two new titles in India, totalling 17,000 copies. In two years this figure jumped to almost three million books and at the present time it is over four million a year. These books are printed in English and in local Indian languages and are almost always sold at prices below production costs. A multi-volume set of the works of Lenin can be bought for less than a dollar. Children's books printed on heavy paper with colorful illustrations sell for the equivalent of five cents. They are available everywhere—on kiosks, in bookstores and through the local network of the Indian Communist Party. In their early efforts the Russians concentrated on straight Marxist tracts and on an excellent series of translations of Russian classics. In recent years their offerings have been more varied. Now the typical Russian work on Indian bookstalls is a popularized science book describing how Russians invented rockets in the tenth century, how Peter the Great discovered the law of gravity with a slight assist from Isaac Newton, how the airplane was invented without benefit of the Wright brothers and concluding, inevitably, with Sputnik.

The Russian pattern of book distribution in India is being repeated with local variations in almost every country in Asia, Africa and Latin America. A similar but less subtle pattern is being followed by the Chinese Communists who tailor their books and magazines to a key audience—the large colonies of "Overseas Chinese" who are politically and economically influential in Malaya, Indonesia and other Southeast Asian countries. The theme of their publications is the wave-of-the-future role of Communism in Asia, reinforced with quotations from Mao Tse Tung and other Red leaders.

The USIS effort to reach Asian, African and Latin American opinion through books is necessarily governed by different and more difficult rules than those of the Communists. Book publishing in Communist countries is a state enterprise conducted without regard for author's rights, distribution agreements, profit margins or other commercial considerations. Publishers' budgets are part of the state budget and the usefulness of their activities is measured primarily in terms of Communist propaganda aims at home and abroad.

For USIS, on the other hand, the pattern is to work with American commercial publishers to get appropriate books into foreign channels. In the past decade a series of arrangements has been developed by U.S. publishers resulting in a significant increase in American books available abroad both in English and in foreign translations. Before this time, most American publishers were inactive in the foreign market. Those who did sell abroad usually handled their business through European publishers who sold their books on a commission basis with "exclusive territory" privileges. This system offered little incentive to increase distribution; the foreign demand for their products was relatively small and therefore a nuisance to American publishers.

"It *is* troublesome to receive an ambiguous order on a queer letterhead, written in picturesque English by someone you never heard of and whose credit rating is completely unknown," says New York publisher Datus Smith. "The easiest disposition of it seems to be in the wastebasket, and I fear that has been the destination of many foreign orders in the past."

Currency exchange problems also harass American publishers when their customers pay in pesos, rupees, francs and pounds. Despite recent liberalization measures most countries still keep their dollar reserves bound tight in red tape. In the book business, where individual transactions often involve small sums, the rewards are hardly worth the bookkeeping troubles involved. To ease these difficulties and to stimulate foreign sales the American government introduced in 1949 special currency arrangements for American publishers.

Known as the Informational Media Guaranty Program (IMG, for short), the arrangement provides dollar reimbursement to American publishers who sell books and periodicals abroad in thirteen dollar-short countries. In order to qualify for reimbursement the publisher applies to USIA in Washington for certification before shipping his books or magazines. When his shipment has been approved the publications are delivered by him to a foreign distributor who pays his bill in local currency at the local USIS office. The amount is then credited to an IMG dollar account in Washington and the American publisher is paid in dollars. The local currencies which are collected by USIS overseas are used to finance the operations of our embassies and other government installations abroad.

By alerting publishers over a decade ago to the strong demand for

American books in countries where it operates, IMG has aroused their interest in expanding other foreign markets. It has stimulated many publishing houses to set up export departments which in turn directed attention to non-IMG countries as well. In addition to facilitating the distribution of over $50 million worth of books and periodicals since 1949, IMG has also helped foreign publishers who want to issue translations of American books. Several years ago when Soviet books were flooding bookstores and kiosks in Israel, IMG made it possible to offer Israeli publishers the newsprint they needed to put out American books in Hebrew. Hard pressed for paper stocks, the publishers eagerly accepted the offer. Within a few months large printings of over a hundred American titles ranging from the works of Mark Twain to those of Robert Penn Warren poured on to Israeli book stalls.

Since few American publishers have yet ventured into the field of foreign translations of their books, most IMG support goes to books in English. This has automatically limited their use to a small though significant portion of students, technicians and professional people abroad who can read such books. Because they cannot read English, the majority need books translated in their own tongues. This constitutes a difficult problem for our publishers. Many of them have unhappy memories of their books being pirated by foreign publishers. Ignoring international copyrights is regarded as a venial sin at worst by many publishers in Asia, Africa and Latin America. Another factor inhibiting American publishers has been their belief that their books in translation—pirated or not—will harm the steady business they have built up for their own English editions overseas. Against these objections is the hard fact of the heavy foreign demand for American books in translation, particularly technical works. The reluctance of our publishers to do business only encourages foreign publishers to continue pirating American editions or rewriting them under thinly-veiled local sponsorship. The result usually is a poorly produced and often inaccurate book which does no credit to American scholarship or to foreign needs.

In recent years USIS has helped bridge the gap of misunderstanding between American commercial publishers and their foreign colleagues. To help create new markets overseas, American publishers have set up two non-profit ventures, Franklin Publications and Overseas Editions, to handle translation problems for all publishers in Asian and African markets. Franklin Publications began operations in 1955 with agents in Tehran, Cairo and other Middle Eastern and Asian cities. It offered foreign publishers first-rate translations of American books, plus a reasonable business deal. As a result, Franklin has arranged for the translation of over a thousand books in eight languages since it was formed. At the end of 1960 the total print run for Franklin books stands at 10.5 million copies. One reason for Franklin's success—over and above its financial arrangements—has been its ingenuity in persuading American publishers and authors to adapt their books to foreign needs. An edition of the Edward R. Murrow book *This I Believe* was a sell-out success in Cairo several years ago because it had been adapted to include statements by leading Arabs.

Overseas Editions, Inc., is a newer venture which promises to match the Franklin Publications success. It concentrates on that postwar publishing phenomenon—the low-priced pocketbook. American-style pocketbooks with their attractive glossy covers are now a common sight on Asian kiosks. Their main selling attraction is price: Overseas Editions' pocketboks sell for under twenty-five cents in most Asian and African countries. The company has arranged for the production of over 150 pocketbook editions of American works totalling ten million copies since it was founded in 1956. And this is without benefit of Mickey Spillane! The redoubtable Mickey has not yet crashed the Overseas Editions lists which favor best-seller novels, current-events books and anthologies. However the private eyes will have their day, as was proved in Greece where the local Overseas Books publisher, pleased with his initial success, independently added a supplementary series of books by Agatha Christie, Erle Stanley Gardner and, inevitably, Mr. Spillane.

To meet the special needs of students and other foreigners whose knowledge of English is weak, Overseas Books has marketed editions of standard American works in simplified English. These books sell for the equivalent of a dime in most Asian and African countries. Franklin Publications and Overseas Editions may justly claim credit for setting a significant trend toward breaking down the barriers against foreign circulation of American books. They have done this by capitalizing on the profit motive in encouraging American publishers to take a new interest in the overseas market. USIS pump-priming efforts and the initial achievements of American publishers in expanding foreign markets have already resulted in a startling increase in commercial sales. American publishers are currently exporting books at a rate of $65 million annually. The market is strongest in hardcover technical books and reference books, textbooks and other scholarly publications. However, paperback books are rapidly increasing their share of the overseas book trade as they have in the domestic market.

Roger H. Smith, news editor of the authoritative trade journal *Publishers' Weekly,* has estimated that 15% of American book exports are now paperbacks. Discussing our export "book bag" he says: "Paperbacks have not pushed hard-cover exports out of the bag but rather have stretched the bag. Even approximate counts of the number of copies sold abroad are impossible . . . but some glimmer of the high overseas sales may be seen by one estimate: India will soon be buying 10 million United States paperbacks annually."

USIS has operated its own book translation projects to supplement these commercial programs. Its projects involve some form of assistance to local publishers who are willing to undertake the production of American books in local languages. The mode of assistance may be to provide a good translation or to supply paper stocks or to commit USIS to buy a certain number of books. The most useful means of sharing costs is to provide the publisher with a competent translation. This assures a better-than-average translation since we can usually afford to pay a higher rate for the translation than the average publisher, in the interests of a better job.

Most of the books translated for the information program are the American classics such as the works of Jefferson, Emerson, Thoreau and Whitman. Sometimes other types of books are chosen to meet a particular local need. Our library in Ankara had an overwhelming demand for Robert's *Rules of Order* in 1951 shortly after the ruling Republican People's party was overturned in Turkey's first free elections. USIS decided to issue the book in Turkish and the book was an instant success. For the first time Turks enjoyed the privilege of going to meetings conducted by a book of democratic rules. The translation program has also produced a series of useful books on the subject of Communism. Especially effective have been the translations made of *The God That Failed,* an anthology of statements made by such distinguished former Communists as Arthur Koestler, Ignazio Silone and Richard Wright describing their experiences in the movement. Over 3,000 separate editions of American works have been translated into 46 languages under the translation program. The number of copies produced is well over 28 million. The most popular book ever translated was one that had been only a temporary best-seller in the United States—*The Big Change,* a popularized history of the evolution of the American economic system by the late Frederick Lewis

Allen. It has sold almost a quarter million copies in twenty languages overseas.

In the immediate years ahead American publishers and USIS will need to make available more titles at lower cost and in greater volume overseas. Despite the rapid development of English as an international language the trend will be towards more translations of American books as the demand for them spreads more widely among the world's readers. "Easy reader" English books will also be increasingly useful as a teaching aid to millions of students studying English. Since 1958 American publishers have produced a series of such books for overseas distribution. Some of them have a "high frequency" vocabulary of only a thousand words; others have vocabulary ranges up to 5,000 words. USIS has helped distribute over a half million of these easy-reader books abroad.

High priority must be given to translations of school textbooks. Here is a challenge. Half a billion school children abroad could benefit from American curriculum advancements through textbooks adapted to their special cultural and social needs. Only a few American publishers have so far successfully marketed translated books overseas. For the present USIS is taking the greater share of responsibility in breaking ground in this field—a task which can pay ideological dividends for generations to come. Foreign educators are sensitive, as they should be, to any taint of "cultural imperialism" in textbooks from other countries. Respecting this sentiment, USIS is laying a foundation of trust for the introduction of American textbooks and other curriculum aids into foreign classrooms. Officials in over thirty countries are currently working with our information posts on the placement of American textbooks in their curricula. Use of American textbooks is often combined with the activities of Point Four educational experts who have been invited by local governments to advise on school problems. In an increasing number of countries, however, USIS is directly involved in textbook programs as a result of a Congressional action allowing foreign currencies made available by the sale of our government-owned agricultural products overseas to be used for the translation and production of American textbooks.

During the past decade an important beginning has been made by commercial publishers and USIS toward meeting the worldwide demand for publications about America. But it is only a beginning. Our ideological requirements call for a greater effort in this field. We have an obligation to present ourselves to the new tide of literate humanity, and books have pride of place in this task. Our zest for wanting to communicate with one another in split seconds may result in a world wired for sight and sound but all this effort cannot match the lasting influence of books as carriers of ideas.

11

THE EXCHANGE OF IDEAS

"What is the new man, this American?"

Hector St. John de Crevecoeur posed this question in 1783 and then proceeded to write his famous book, *Letters from an American Farmer*, to answer it. De Crevecoeur was one of the earliest and best known of a long line of observers who have written about American life. His shrewd observations had a tremendous influence on eighteenth-century Europe. Today the same kind of influence is spread in the written and spoken reports brought from America by the hundreds of thousands of foreigners who come here for study, business or pleasure every year.

Before World War II attempts to bring foreigners here to study or to see what we were doing were haphazard and scattered. With our traditional mixture of self-confidence and naiveté our attitude was that anyone who could get here was lucky and the rest were not.

Today the attitude toward foreign visitors is not nearly so casual or cavalier. Since 1948 the American government has, as a matter of national policy, encouraged the exchange of students and other key individuals from all over the world. Official concern for foreign visitors also extends to tourists for the first time. In 1960 the government and the domestic tourist industry cooperated in a campaign to invite foreigners to visit the United States as tourists. The project had a commercial motive since foreign visitors are now spending close to a billion dollars annually here. But it also had propaganda overtones. After 150 years of taking foreign visitors for granted, Uncle Sam has decided that it is time to encourage them to come over to see us.

Exchange activities by private organizations are also on the rise. They range from the large program of scholarships and other grants maintained by the Ford Foundation to the Rufus B. Wheeler memorial scholarship awarded yearly by Gettysburg College in Pennsylvania to a deserving student. These private grants are an important factor in the increase in foreign students in American schools from 10,000 in 1939 to 50,000 in 1960.

It is, however, the Federal Government that dominates the broad field of sponsored foreign visitors. The largest single program for bringing foreigners here is operated by the Defense Department; it has trained over 75,000 military officers and enlisted men from free world armed forces in recent years. Non-military exchanges are administered with some exceptions by the State Department. The Department first became involved in exchange activities during World War II when a program for inviting Latin Americans here was begun. The program was extended and given permanent status in the Smith-Mundt Act of 1948 which authorized the Department to set up programs for the exchange of Americans and foreigners in all parts of the world. The pattern for student exchanges was similar to that of the Fulbright scholarship program approved by Congress a year earlier. More significant was the Smith-Mundt innovation of authorizing the invitation of foreign leaders from all over the world to the United States on an all-expenses-paid tour to give them a full view of American life.

The leader program, as it is known, has been the most successful experiment in our exchange operations. No other country—not even that alleged past master of propaganda, the Soviet Union—has developed such a consistent program for showing itself off to the leadership of other countries. Every year in over 90 countries political, cultural and economic leaders are invited by the American ambassador to make a tour of the United States as a guest of the State Department. Since the program was set up on a world-wide basis in 1948, over 12,000 foreign leaders have taken part in these tours; currently about a thousand invitations are issued every year. These invitations and other details of their visits are handled overseas by USIS posts.

The program is successful largely because the foreign leaders decide their own itineraries and activities. Although USIS and the State Department provide advice on these matters, every effort is made to avoid anything smacking of the guided tour. Most of the leaders prefer to make a general tour of the country, seeing the things they have read and heard most about. (TVA, New York City and San Francisco are perennial favorites with Disneyland moving up fast.) They see what they want to see, whether it is slums, skyscrapers or dude ranches. Almost all the leader grantees from Asia and Africa are interested in American race relations, a subject on which they usually have an exaggerated picture. They take a good hard look at this aspect of our society during their visit; the result is not always approval of what we are doing. Almost always, however, they come away with a better understanding of the problem and what is being done about it.

The leader program is not intended to provide visits for the top leadership of foreign countries such as prime ministers or presidents.

These visits involve rigid protocol requirements and are usually handled by the State Department's protocol division. The leader program aims for the up-and-coming leadership overseas. The perfect visitor under the program could be described as the man who is going to be prime minister in his country five or ten years from now. He may be a member of the party in power or in the opposition party. In the latter case his selection for a grant by our embassy sometimes ruffles the government in power which interprets his selection as a political act on our part.

The Communist press is often quick to interpret the selection of any non-Communist politician for a grant under the program as a sign that he has "sold out" to the Americans. (In many cases, this may merely be Communist pique at not being able to get him to visit the Soviet Union.) These factors are all weighed by our embassies and information posts before making their selections. In the case of political leaders selection is balanced over the years to include representatives of the major political parties in each country; the program is not a "reward" for pro-American political figures overseas. Its most effective moments often occur when a neutralist or otherwise skeptical foreign leader has his negative opinions of us modified by what he sees and hears on his tour.

The results are often impressive. Predicting future leadership in a foreign country is a chancey business at best but the program has a good record on this score. A dramatic example of good selection occurred in Greece where in 1955 a new government was installed which included a prime minister and three cabinet ministers who had been to America under the leader program. The credit for these selections goes largely to Dr. William Weld, a lean lank up-State New Yorker who served as cultural attache in Greece in 1950-55 and who is now deputy director of USIS operations in Great Britain.

Although selections have been weighted in favor of political leaders, about forty percent of the leaders brought to the United States under the program come from non-political fields. High priority is usually assigned to leaders in the media fields—press, radio, book publishing, the film industry, etc. In the past decade the State Department has arranged tours under the exchange program for almost every major publisher and editor in the free world. As is the case with other leader grantees they are provided with an interpreter if they do not speak English. Among the outstanding foreign intellectuals and other opinion leaders who have visited the United States in recent years under the program have been

Willy Brandt, the Mayor of West Berlin; Eigo Okazaki, the founder of Japan's Liberal Democratic Party; U Maung Maung, editor of the Guardian of Rangoon, Burma; and Jacques Fauvet, chief political analyst for Le Monde of Paris.

Editor Fauvet and hundreds of other foreign leaders came with an open mind and found an America that was, in the balance, a vibrant, healthy civilization. Like many another of his fellow visitors, Mr. Fauvet remains a perceptive critic of specific American policies and attitudes. He and the other participants in the program have seen us as we are and they have interpreted what they have seen to their fellow countrymen. The books and articles written by returned leader grantees are a useful source of foreign insight on American life today.

The leader visits are intended for the foreign elite. At a somewhat more modest level is the program for exchanging American and foreign experts in specialized fields, the so-called "specialist program," which provides foreign professionals with an intensive view of American developments in their own fields. Whereas the foreign leader stays in the United States as a State Department guest for two months at the most, the specialist visitor remains for at least six months and often for a year. In most cases he spends his time in what might be called advanced graduate training although he will probably not register at a university. Thus a leading Japanese cancer specialist will visit the cancer center at the National Institutes of Health near Washington and three or four other cancer research laboratories during a six-month tour to acquaint himself with American research techniques. An average of four hundred foreign specialists are brought to the United States from ninety countries each year under this program.

The success of the specialist program depends upon the cooperative arrangements between the State Department and American professional societies for placing the foreign specialist in contact with his colleagues here. For many years the American Medical Association, the National Association of Broadcasters, the American Library Association and similar groups have done a quietly effective job in assisting foreign specialists referred to them by the State Department. The American newspaper publishers have sponsored a system for placing foreign newsmen as "guest reporters" on their papers for several months. Since 1953 over 130 foreign editors have received a first-hand view of American journalism and of American life in general under this arrangement.

The State Department is experimenting more and more with bringing foreign leaders and professionals here in groups, thus obviating the language barrier which is a formidable obstacle to many otherwise qualified foreign visitors. A non-English-speaking person in a group (which usually has an interpreter assigned to it) will profit more from his tour than he would if he were alone. Another benefit of group travel is that more elaborate programs can be arranged for the group than would be justified for one person. The group-project system has been used successfully with thirteen teams of professional leaders from NATO countries. The NATO tours were begun in 1956 specifically for journalists and other media representatives; they have been extended in recent years to include special tours for economists, parliamentarians and business leaders.

The most significant American experiment in a mass cultural exchange reaching every social level was carried out in our occupation zone in West Germany after the war. Over 10,000 German leaders were brought here in groups that represented all segments of German society. At one time housewives were included in the program as members of so-called "cooperative action teams" made up of representative cross-sections of people from individual German cities. The German exchange program was a conscious effort to influence the development of stronger democratic institutions in that country after fifteen years of Hitler and occupation. The emphasis was placed on the exchange of younger leaders, a group that was psychologically prepared after the bitter defeat of 1945 to reject the more rigid patterns of their elders in favor of something new.

Since 1948 the State Department's leader and specialist programs have provided a unique channel for bringing thousands of foreign opinion makers into contact with the realities of American life. With minor exceptions these programs have had a healthy effect not only in tempering the opinions of the visitors themselves but also in shaving down the threshhold of mythology that separates America from the older civilizations abroad. However, the leader and specialist programs are only a small part of the postwar development in exchange activities. The largest part of the program has been devoted to the exchange of teachers and students.

Profound changes are taking place in education throughout the world from the kindergarten to the university level. These changes are reflected in the burgeoning school enrollments in all countries, particularly in Asia and Africa. The United Arab Republic's educational budget has gone up a hundred percent in recent years. In Indonesia the number of elementary students increased one hundred percent, secondary students eight times over and university students six times over in the first ten years after independence. Saudi Arabia, one of the most educationally underdeveloped countries, has seen an increase in the number of its schools from less than fifty in 1953 to over five hundred in 1958, with the number expected to double in another few years. In western countries the improvement in educational levels has been carried out in more sophisticated ways with the development of advanced technical schools, the improvement of rural school systems and in revised curricula.

The pressure for more educational facilities is as much a chronic problem for governments in Asia, Africa and Latin America as it is for budget-conscious school boards in our own school districts. The pressure for more educational facilities overseas often takes a violent turn. Student riots are a problem. In France there are riots because classroom facilities have not been provided to account for the doubling of the university student population since 1949. In Greece student strikes protest the low number of state scholarships. In India students strike because universities with enrollments of 1.1 million and facilities capable of holding only three-quarters of that number won't admit more students. The pressure for an academic degree is so great in India that dozens of students commit suicide every year after failing their university examinations. Others are more philosophical about their failure: it is not unusual for an Indian to present a calling card which lists after his name the phrase "A.B. (failed)" or "M.A. (failed)". This acknowledgment of failure makes sense in a society where it is a distinction to have reached a status where one has an opportunity to fail a university examination.

This new attention to mass-level education abroad has important implications for the United States bearing on our survival as a world leader. The idea of universal education is profoundly American; we were the first large nation to adopt it as a policy and the first to achieve it as a practical goal. The concept of an educated citizenry is not only a premise of our domestic society, but also for the world order we are trying to build.

We have by no means reached our full potential for educational exchange with people of other nations. During the 1959-60 school year there were about 50,000 foreigners studying and teaching in our schools. This is an impressive figure but it is less so when compared with the records of other countries. The ratio of foreign to native students in our schools is probably lower than in most European countries. Our record is somewhat better than that of the Communists but there is every sign that they intend to catch up with us. The Soviet Union is currently setting up a university for foreign students in Moscow with an eventual enrollment of five thousand. The Russians had 20,000 foreign students studying in their higher schools in 1958. Most of them came from Communist satellite countries. More significantly, about eighteen percent of the free world students in Soviet universities come from the turbulent underdeveloped countries in Asia and Africa.

The United States, with more facilities for higher learning than any country in the world, could take in more foreign students than it does. There are hundreds of thousands of qualified students and professional people throughout the world who would study in American schools if they had the chance. They are restricted primarily by economics. It costs a European student about $3000 a year to study here; for African and Asian students, added transportation costs raise this in some cases to almost $4000. These are prohibitive costs for the average foreign student, as they are getting to be for many American families who intend to send their children to universities. For foreigners these costs are out of line with what they have to pay at home. A student at the Sorbonne can pay his tuition and board for a school year for about $700. An Indian student spends from $300 to $500.

Most foreign students must rely on scholarship help if they plan to study in the United States. Until a decade ago such scholarships generally had to come from universities or other private sources in America. Before World War II there were fewer than 10,000 foreign students studying here each year; probably less than half this number were scholarship students. Considerable scholarship assistance was provided to foreign students by such diverse organizations as the Carnegie Foundation, the China Medical Board, the American-Scandinavian Foundation and the Belgian-American Educational Foundation (BAEF). Set up in 1920 by Herbert Hoover with funds left over from American war relief activities in Belgium, BAEF has financed the exchange of over a thousand Belgian and American scholars. It is a model of the effectiveness of scholarly cooperation: Belgium probably has a greater percentage of American-trained academicians in its higher schools than any country in the world.

In 1946 the American government decided to participate more

extensively in educational exchange—the last large country to do so. (There had been a small exchange program with Latin American countries during the war.) The initiative came from a Senator, J. William Fulbright of Arkansas, whose name is now one of the best-known non-dictionary nouns, adjectives and verbs in the international academic community. (A Fulbrighter is a Fulbright scholarship winner who Fulbrights at a foreign school.)

The idea behind the Fulbright program was as inspired as it was sensible. At the end of the war millions of dollars in American equipment was left idle in warehouses or in open fields all over the world; it consisted primarily of military equipment but it also included hundreds of tons of material useful for peacetime operations. Senator Fulbright proposed to sell these materials to friendly foreign governments for their own currency and use part of the money to finance exchanges between American and foreign schools. The proposal appealed to Congress; in August 1946 it was voted into law and later the Board of Foreign Scholarships was set up to select participants and supervise the program. The Board and the State Department cultural division gave new form and scope to the hitherto scattered relationship between the American academic community and its counterparts abroad. In fifteen years over 29,000 students and teachers have been exchanged with thirty-seven countries under American government grants at a lower cost to U.S. taxpayers than five hours of World War II.

The Fulbright exchange programs vary in size in individual countries. The program is directed in each country by a Fulbright Commission made up of both American and local personalities. By custom the American ambassador is usually an honorary member of the committee with his USIS cultural attache serving as an active member. Competition for grants is so intense that qualifying examinations are given in most countries. In 1959, 4,318 American and foreign students, teachers and professors were exchanged under the Fulbright program. This is a sizable delegation; it is also, on examination, a lopsided one. Because Fulbright scholarship programs are generally restricted to countries where American war surplus equipment was sold, the program has obvious geographical gaps in its effectiveness. Norway has a lively program of Fulbright grants, but Ethiopia has none because it did not buy war surplus from us. In 1960, there were Fulbright programs in only 39 countries. The amount of money available in each country is often disproportionate to its size. Greece, with a population of only eight million, has one of the largest Fulbright programs in the world thanks to the millions of dollars worth of war surplus sold there to finance the program. In neighboring Turkey, whose academic needs are if anything greater than those of Greece, the Fulbright program is only half as large. Other countries where the program is operating under financial handicaps are Burma, Thailand, Sweden, Ceylon and Paraguay.

Considerable study has been given to the problem of maintaining Fulbright programs in countries where it is threatened by shortages of funds and of initiating similar programs in countries which do not have a Fulbright program. An important stimulant to the Fulbright program was provided by the passage of Public Law 480, the Agricultural Trade Development and Assistance Act of 1954. This law authorizes the use of foreign currencies obtained as the result of surplus agricultural commodity sales abroad for educational exchange purposes and has made it possible to initiate Fulbright programs in eight Latin American countries and to continue programs in countries like France, Austria, Japan, India, Iran and Pakistan that were threatened with the termination of their programs because of the exhaustion of war surplus currencies.

Here again, however, the funds available depend upon the vagaries of agricultural commodity trading and not upon the needs of the countries concerned. In rapidly developing countries like Argentina, Chile, the Philippines, and Turkey, the average annual amount of available Fulbright funds is only $200,000. In Japan, Taiwan, France, Germany, Italy, and the United Kingdom, the maximum permissible Fulbright expenditure of one million dollars annually is available and is utilized.

Since Fulbright funds are all in foreign currencies they cannot provide foreign students with money for tuition and maintenance in the United States. They can be used by foreign students only for travel to and from the United States or for studies in American schools overseas. (Fullbright grants have provided considerable scholarship support for students at such famed overseas American schools as Robert College in Turkey, the Wattaya Academy in Bangkok, the American Farm School in Greece, and the American University in Beirut.) A Fulbright grant for study in the United States must be matched with a scholarship awarded by an American college or foundation unless the student can pay his own way. The largest "clearing house" for such scholarships is the Institute for

International Education, a non-profit organization in New York financed largely by Ford Foundation contributions, which matches thousands of American scholarships with thousands of deserving foreign students every year. The demand is always greater than the supply but in 1959 the institute helped 3,343 foreign students with scholarships in American schools.

American students who want to study abroad can get full scholarships under the Fulbright program because of the availability of foreign funds. Since 1947 over nine thousand Americans have studied abroad under Fulbright grants. European universities in particular have adapted parts of their curriculum for American undergraduates. The academic standards for graduate students are as stringent as ever. Ninety percent of the 915 Fulbright scholars studying overseas in 1959-60 were enrolled in European schools. The Fulbright program has been a special boon for American painters and other artists studying in European academies; one of the highlights of the tenth anniversary of the Fulbright program in 1956 was an exhibition in New York of work done by Fulbright painters and sculptors.

Only seven percent of the 50,000 foreign students in American schools are studying under Fulbright or other American government grants. Most of the others are self-supporting or have scholarships from their own governments or from private American schools and other organizations. Asian, African and Latin American countries have had long-standing programs for sending students to American and European universities for advanced training. These scholarships usually involve a commitment by the student to enter government service when he returns home. European universities are often favored in the distribution of these scholarships because of the generally lower tuition, living and transportation costs. However, the superior technical facilities of the leading American schools provide a strong incentive to most governments to continue to send scholarship students here despite the high costs involved. Some foreign governments have concentrated their students in certain American schools in order to provide continuity and to take advantage of special conditions. Chinese students have traditionally concentrated at such West Coast schools as Stanford and UCLA. Utah State College in Provo has always had a large number of Iranians among its overseas students because Utah farming conditions are similar to those in Iran. The quality of foreign students studying under grants from their own governments is relatively high since most countries will withdraw scholarships from those who fail to get acceptable grades.

Occasionally, however, scholarships are awarded to—and not withdrawn from—students whose primary qualification is an uncle or father who is influential in the government back home.

Other foreign students are by and large deadly serious in their studies, perhaps too much so. An American finding himself in the middle of Patagonia has less cause for bewilderment than an Indonesian student standing in the lobby of the Student Union building on his first day at the University of Wisconsin. Emotional adjustments to their new environment are difficult for many foreign students. Over and above its personal aspects the problem has an important impact on their reaction to American life in general. Too often the most brilliant and sensitive students return home from the United States with a sound technical education and a gnawing hatred for what they regard as American hypocrisy and immaturity. The problem has special overtones for African and other colored students who find themselves faced with social rebuffs or—what most of them regard with greater bitterness—thinly-veiled condescension.

The pressures from home are often equally trying for the foreign student. He cannot afford to fail particularly if he is a scholarship student; aside from academic considerations, there is a disapproving family to face back home if he fails. At the University of Michigan one night in 1955 a Chinese student from Singapore, named Chheng Guan Lim, disappeared. He was found four years later living in the rafters of the Ann Arbor First Methodist Church. He had climbed into the attic out of shame because of his poor marks in engineering, a subject which his father insisted he study. During the years he spent in the attic, sustaining himself on the remains of church suppers, his father had died. Lenient police authorities permitted him to re-enter the university to study his own chosen subject, political science. There are hundreds of foreign students in American schools who are living fearfully in mental attics for similar reasons. Fortunately, many schools are providing foreign-student advisors who are aware of the pressures American scholastic life places upon foreigners.

In 1951 the State Department cultural division took official cognizance of the problem by setting up a pilot program of orientation courses for foreign students before they began their academic studies. The following year the program was put on a permanent basis. Now there are seventeen orientation centers which provide general guidance on American customs and manners with special guidance for *homusicku* Japanese students and for Indians who refuse to shower in the nude. ("I shall wear my swim suit," said one.) The experiment has also been extended to other visitors to the United States who can take an orientation course in American life at the State Department-sponsored Washington International Center.

At the other end of the scale are the students whose adjustment to American life is too complete. They are the ones who don't want to go home. Until recently American immigration laws were loose enough to permit many foreign students to remain here as long as they wished. It was often possible for them to go to Canada and get a visa extension at an American Consulate without difficulty. Other "students" managed to stay here for years by taking a few night courses. Others would return home for a few months and then come back with new visas.

In 1956 Congress tightened the exchange-visitor visa regulations primarily by restricting the time-length of exchange visas and by limiting the issuance of immigration visas to students and other former exchange visitors. Despite these measures there are still many students who manage to remain here by one means or another after they finish their studies. In 1960 *Time* magazine reported that of 700 science students who had left Formosa in recent years, only 40 returned. Many foreign students try to assure permanent residence for themselves by marrying an American and thereby becoming eligible for citizenship. Although the great majority of the foreign students who decide to stay here make intelligent useful citizens, their skills are lost to their homelands where they are usually needed more.

Most foreign students in American schools concentrate their studies in the physical sciences. The incomparable research facilities available at hundreds of American universities and colleges remain a potent magnet for young scientists around the world. The recent spate of Soviet successes in the scientific field has done little to undermine American prestige in scientific education. One contributing factor is the universality of English as the new "scientific language" throughout the world. Medical studies, particularly at the graduate level, are an important attraction for foreign students. American hospitals, hard-pressed for adequate medical staff, have been recruiting foreign medical students as interns and residents. This practice has raised a question as to whether hospital standards have not been lowered by employing foreign-trained doctors. In 1957 the American Hospital Association and other professional medical groups established the Educational Council for Foreign Medical Graduates with powers to certify the educational credentials of foreign doctors seeking employment or training in American hospitals. The net result of this professional policing action has been tighter control on foreign interns and residents.

While both American government and privately sponsored foreign scholarship programs have expanded, the amount of assistance available to bright deserving students is still low. In India for instance, there is a university student population of about 1.1 million. The top one percent of this group—11,000 students—might well profit both professionally and personally from an American education. Yet the total number of Indian students holding American scholarships from all sources in 1959 was less than 1800.

Many thoughtful observers of American ideological influence overseas are convinced that the dearth of African and Asian students in our universities and other higher schools is a crucial weakness. The number of students from African countries is less than three thousand. Each of these students will automatically become a member of a small professional elite in his country when he returns. (The Congo Republic, with 14 million inhabitants, began its independence in 1960 with sixteen college graduates.) The real question, however, is whether there will be enough American-oriented Asian and African leaders to counterbalance strong Communist and other totalitarian tendencies which are already threatening their new nations.

The solution lies not only in increasing the number of scholarships available to students from these areas. It also involves the strengthening of relations between American and foreign universities to their mutual scholastic advantage. In our fifteen hundred American universities and colleges we have a wealth of both administrative and scholarship experience that the new national universities of Asia and Africa could well draw upon to develop the professionally-trained citizens they need. American universities in turn would be enriched by closer association with foreign cultures through an affiliation with universities abroad.

The tradition of affiliations between our colleges and universities and foreign schools goes back more than fifty years when a number of affiliations were made with Chinese schools by Harvard, Yale, Cornell and a half-dozen other American institutions. The work of the American schools in China had a profound effect on the development of higher education in the Far East, particularly in the field of medical education. These American-affiliated schools became the target of special attack by the Communists in the 1940's; by 1950, the affiliations were terminated during the Communists' "anti-imperialist" campaign.[1]

More recent ventures in affiliation have been carried out by Johns Hopkins University and the University of Chicago. Johns Hopkins developed an affiliated branch at the University of Rangoon in 1954 and a similar branch at the University of Bologna the following year. Both these projects were small (the Bologna center opened with eleven students and three professors) but they were commendable additions to two important universities—one of them a nine-century-old European intellectual stronghold and the other a young Asian institution. The Johns Hopkins school at Bologna, known officially as the Bologna center of the Johns Hopkins School of Advanced International Studies, is still flourishing as a lively center of American scholarship. The Rangoon experiment was less successful; it closed down in 1959 largely because of inadequate financial support and general difficulties involved in meshing American and Asian methods. Despite its failure the Rangoon experiment was particularly instructive in that it demonstrated some of the potentials as well as the pitfalls involved in exchange between American and Asian schools.

The University of Chicago experienced a similar pattern of scholarly success and administrative difficulties in its affiliation with the University of Frankfurt. The arrangement was begun in 1947 for the avowed purpose of "opening the channels of communication between German and American universities" after the Nazi era. The project has been financed by the two institutions with considerable assistance from American foundations. Exchanges of professors between Chicago and Frankfurt were begun in 1948 and three years later a more permanent program of academic cooperation was approved by the two schools. At the scholarly level the results have been a fruitful exchange of teachers and students under auspices that have strengthened American area studies at Frankfurt and German studies at Chicago.

1. A special example of American educational influence overseas has been the group of schools founded by American missionary groups and others in all parts of the world during the past century. The best known of these are the American Universities of Beirut and Cairo, Robert College in Turkey, Athens, Anatolia and Pierce Colleges in Greece and the Marymount International School in Rome. In addition to their endowments and other private contributions, a number of these schools have received American government assistance in the form of scholarship aid, teachers and funds for the construction of new facilities.

The academic system used by the two schools is the "interdisciplinary seminar" whereby three teachers from one school go to the other institution as a team to participate in a coordinated seminar program. The Chicago-Frankfurt affiliation has been plagued from the start by administrative and financial difficulties. A special Ford Foundation grant in 1956 saved the program from foundering at the time but it was threatened once again in 1959 by lack of funds.

The State Department and USIS have played a small role in both the Johns Hopkins and Chicago affiliation programs although they are both essentially private ventures. A number of attempts have been made in recent years to encourage other American universities to strengthen their institutional affiliations with overseas schools. In a speech at Baylor University in 1956, President Eisenhower solicited more active participation of our universities in international exchanges as part of his "People to People" program:

"Many nations, although their cultures are ancient and rich in human values, do not possess the resources to spread the needed education throughout their populations. But they can wisely use help that respects their traditions and ways. Do we not find here a worthy challenge to America's universities and to their graduates? I firmly believe that if some or all of our great universities, strongly supported by private foundations that exist in number throughout the land, sparked by the zeal and fire of educated Americans, would devote themselves to this task the prospects for a peaceful and prosperous world would be mightily enhanced. In no respect should the purpose of these institutions be to transplant into a new area the attitudes, the forms, the procedures of America. The staffing, the conduct, the curriculum of each school would be the responsibility of the people where the school might be built. Each school would help each nation develop its human and natural resources and also provide a great two-way avenue of communications."

American universities and colleges have not been notably quick to act upon this and similar proposals. The problem, again, is one of costs. Faced with the problem of expanding their facilities to take care of the expected rise in their enrollments during the 1960's, our higher schools are reluctant to take on additional commitments abroad.

In the absence of any large-scale program of affiliations between American and foreign schools the State Department and USIS have concentrated on strengthening American studies in foreign universities through the Fulbright and other exchange programs. Until very recently it was impossible for a student in most foreign universities to do any advanced work on the subject of American civilization. American literature, history, economics and philosophies were ignored or relegated to a minor role in the curriculum. It was not until the late 1940's that any German university accepted American studies as a major field for an advanced degree. Today such degrees are awarded by a half-dozen German higher schools and the number is increasing.

The general rise in interest in American studies in foreign universities is largely the result of careful efforts by our cultural officers to encourage their adoption. During the 1950's USIS and the State Department arranged placement in foreign schools of over twelve hundred American teachers, most of them specializing in American studies. The problem is not to get an American professor placed in a foreign university; many higher schools abroad welcome such academic assistance from us. The difficulty comes in keeping the post of "Visiting Professor of American Civilization" filled every year so that it becomes a permanent part of the school's program. In too many instances an American studies course will be started by a first-rate American scholar only to have the program founder a year or two later when a less effective academician fills the post.

It is almost impossible to determine in advance whether an exchange professor is going to succeed in his assignment; the criteria for success in foreign assignments is usually not the string of academic degrees possessed by the professor but his ability to adjust to local and often frustrating situations. Taking into consideration the difficulties involved, the ratio of successes to failures in these assignments is generally high.

In addition to American-studies programs encouraged by USIS, an extensive program of affiliations between American and foreign schools is conducted under our economic-aid programs. Fifty American universities and colleges have contracts with the International Cooperation Administration to carry out Point-Four type projects in 34 countries throughout the world. The program was set up in 1953 largely through the initiative of Harold Stassen, then director of the overseas aid program. Until that time the Point Four program had been carried out largely by technicians sent out individually or in small groups to assist foreign governments on technical assistance projects. The results were often haphazard: the initial stages of a project were often encouraging but the project would bog down when the American technician who started it left for home leave or, as is often the case in Asian and African countries, was laid low by illness.

Goaded by Congressional criticism, the economic-aid administrators decided to put the management of many of their larger technical-assistance projects into the hands of American universities. The pattern varies but it usually involves a contract between the American and overseas universities to carry out a specific technical project. Preliminary negotiations are initiated jointly by the two governments but once an agreement has been reached operation of the project usually becomes the direct concern of the two schools involved. The whole technical-assistance program has generally gained in stability and accomplishment under this plan.[2]

The range of these university projects is wide. The University of Oregon teaches teachers in Nepal; Purdue has a home-economics project in Brazil; Tuskegee Institute is working in vocational education in Indonesia. These are intended as "pilot projects," designed to show foreign technicians how to carry out an operation rather than to do the operation itself. Educational needs are so great in many of the countries where ICA missions operate that the university "pilot projects" become a major contribution in themselves. In 1954 the University of California agreed to a Point-Four affiliation with the University of Indonesia to improve medical training there. In 1959 the first graduating class under the new system consisted of 97 doctors, representing about a ten percent increase in the number of native doctors in Indonesia. By Indonesian standards, the California medical-school program was much more than a pilot project.

These university affiliations are setting important precedents for our long-range efforts to strengthen American ideological influence in foreign universities. A weakness of the ICA university contract program is its limitation to technical education. We are vulnerable to foreign critics who say we favor allegedly materialistic studies in

---

2. A lively critique of this aspect of the technical-assistance program to be found in the Carnegie Foundation-sponsored study, "Is The World Our Campus?" by Walter Adams and John A. Garraty, Michigan State University Press, 1960. The authors bring considerable documentation to their thesis that the university contract system is not necessarily an effective way to help underdeveloped countries. Professors Adams and Garraty are also the authors of a Carnegie-financed study of American students at European universities in which they stick some pointed pins in the puffed-up balloon of "studying abroad." The study, "From Main Street to the Left Bank," is also published at Michigan.

agriculture and vocational education. There is a large area of academic blindness in their attitude and a certain amount of unreality concerning the real needs of their own societies. But there is also danger for us in appearing on the scene at foreign universities with such a heavy emphasis on technical education. Our universities have undoubtedly a great deal to offer in this field; it is one in which we have done a large share of the pioneering work and the advanced research. However, we have even more to offer in the humanistic studies; we may also have more to learn here.

In terms of our influence on foreign education we are still weak in this area of the humanities. With some significant exceptions the new generation of Asian and African leadership—the lawyers, editors and poets who will influence national destinies in the next thirty years—are being trained without benefit of adequate exchange with scholarly American influences.

It would be well to define our national goal in this regard. We certainly should not rush in with some overblown academic Point Four program for swapping poets and history professors. The new national universities of Asia and the old universities of Europe and Latin America are too proud of their own academic prerogatives to succumb to American crash-program techniques. They are particularly on guard against anything smacking of "briefing the natives." What is needed, first and foremost, is the development of confidence in our motives in making available more American teachers and scholars in the humanities and social sciences. Sensitivities among foreign scholars can be high on this score, higher than our own national self-esteem may be prepared to admit. Some of the reluctance to accept academic assistance stems from general political attitudes towards the United States. Resistance also stems from a condescending attitude towards American educational methods particularly in European-oriented schools. Many foreign schools are set up along German, French or British academic lines with their stress on the traditional "faculties" and a corresponding reluctance to adapt these faculties to accommodate Americans whose specialties are more loosely defined.

The greatest stumbling block, however, is plain academic chauvinism. The area where American ideological influence could be most effective—in the teaching of the humanities and the social sciences—is precisely where such influence is most jealously guarded in most of the new universities of Asia and Africa. It is one thing to offer to teach an Asian how to operate a diesel engine and quite another to imply superior knowledge in politics or economics; we are more or less expected to do the former but we are often suspect when we propose the latter. Such suspicions may seem unreasonable to us but they exist. They will be modified only through patient work in demonstrating both the objectivity of our motives and our scholarship in providing helpful assistance.

In the past decade we have begun to break down some of the academic barriers between our universities and their overseas counterparts through the exchange of students and teachers. An American student or teacher was a rarity at most foreign universities before World War II; today they are becoming increasingly familar. But academic exchange is still spotty. In 1955 there were only eight American teachers in Indian universities. By 1960 this figure has risen to 44, but it is still an inadequate representation for a nation with over fifteen hundred schools of higher learning to send to the largest free nation in Asia.

The relatively modest official expenditures we make on the exchange program—approximately $25 million a year—are usually justified on political grounds. If enough Argentinians, the argument runs, visit the United States we will have fewer political misunderstandings with Argentina. There is a large element of non-sequitur in this type of statement and also an element of short-sightedness. The free movement of visitors in and out of the United States is actually a requirement of our society. It is needed, as George F. Kennan has said, "just as rain is by the desert and needed . . . for our sakes alone, for our development as individuals and as a nation, lest we fall into complacency, sterility and emotional decay; lest we lose our sense of the capabilities of the human spirit, and with it much of our sensitivity to the possible meaning and wonder of life itself. For this reason I would be prepared to say: let us by all means have the maximum cultural exchange, even if America had before it no problem whatsoever of outside opinion; even if we had no need of any sort for other people, if all that was concerned was our own development here at home."

Modern American life was shaped by the impact of successive waves of immigrants who came here during the past two centuries. Each of these immigrants was his own Columbus, come to find his own version of a new world. Most of us are formed from this unprecedented movement of Old World blood and talents. Restrictive legislation has reduced this movement to a cramped shadow of its great days. Whatever the justification of this policy, it means that we have lost some of the force of the alien ideas—in the best sense of that much-maligned word—which gave us foundation strength.

More and more our survival as an open culture—a culture which receives and adapts alien ideas as much as it offers its own ideals to others—will be dependent upon foreign visitors. Considered in these terms the fact that we have 50,000 foreign students in our universities seems less an accomplishment than an indication of our possible cultural poverty. We could take in twice this number of students and the total number of foreigners would still be less than five percent of the enrollment of our higher schools. The total cost per year of this increase would be about $100 million, less than one-tenth of one percent of our national budget and one-hundredth of one percent of our yearly national spending. Using these funds to bring a new generation of Asian, African, and Latin American leadership to America for part of their education could be the strategic and political bargain of the 1960's.

The alternative to the influx of alien ideas on a scale to match our world role is a new age of cultural isolation and the eventual withering away that is the fate of any civilization that does not keep its borders open to new ideas.

12

THE DELICATE ART OF EXPORTING CULTURE

"In the four quarters of the globe, who reads an American book? Goes to an American play? Or looks at an American picture or statue? What does the world yet owe to American physicians or surgeons? What new substance have their chemists discovered?"

Posed in 1820 by the English critic Sidney Smith, these questions have long since been answered in the centrifugal explosion of American influence in every field throughout the world. No one, not even among our detractors, denies this influence and nowhere is the debate over it more marked than in the amorphous field known as culture. The debate takes many forms but it almost always includes the charge that the United States is a land that has been eluded by the bright butterfly of culture. Too often the American rebuttal is statistical. We reply that we have more symphony orchestras, art galleries and hi-fi set owners than any other nation on earth. Our recitation leaves most foreign observers unimpressed.

The problem is largely semantic; we are usually talking about two different things. What most of our foreign critics have been arguing about is not culture in the sense of the total expression of a society but rather the smaller area of an accepted body of ideas and arts. They see in American life, with its free-for-all attitude toward the older values, a threat to their own ways. "If France allows itself to be influenced by the whole of American culture," Jean-Paul Sartre has written, "a living and livable situation there will come here and shatter our cultural traditions. . . . " The fear reflects a sense of the potency of American cultural influence with which even we are reluctant to credit it. It also reflects a sense of the inadequacy of more traditional cultures in the face of twentieth century problems.

To clarify our achievements and our purposes as a national culture, we must first recognize the differences between ourselves and our foreign critics—the characteristics that make us unique. The United States does not have an officially-inspired culture but it provides the framework for cultural expression. Of all the world's major societies, ours has been the most resistant to the idea of cultural mandarins who set the standards. The anti-mandarins in these mandarin-dominated societies may object to the standards set by the artistic and ideological dynasty in power but their only recourse is to overthrow the dynasty and become mandarins themselves.

There are, of course, mandarin groups in America—thousands of them. Therein lies the rub; none of them has the final say. Nothing confuses foreign intellectuals so much about the condition of the American intellectual community as its lack of coterie. Although our intellectuals have their favorite cultural watering holes, they are usually widely dispersed and self-sufficient. "Even in New York," says British writer C. P. Snow, "distinguished literary figures show a cheerful unawareness of each other's existence." The independence and diversity of our artists goes far to explain why, despite the attempts of the salon cataloguers, there are no "American schools" of painters, poets, philosophers or musicians. And yet there is in each of these fields an informed American spirit that sets our culture apart from the many traditions from which it has drawn its influences.

Our unity-in-cultural-diversity is an essential part of our character; we must make this feature understood as we present ourselves to world opinion. In the face of the Communist threat the political segment of our message seems most pressing. However, if we are to give a heart and mind to our age, we must first clarify our entire national meaning and experience. We must be able to share the latest ideas of our poets and sculptors as well as the newest development in our political policy. The task of self-expression is complicated by the continuing domestic debate on the form and function of our cultural life. At one extreme are those who echo the foreign critics of our "mass mind" culture. They are able to bring documentation to the argument that our cultural expression is second rate, geared to a common denominator of taste and of education. At the other extreme is an equally myopic group for whom American culture can do no wrong. These are, to use John Kouwenhoven's characterization, members of the Neo-Pollyanna school who cast their cultural nets wide and shallow. The latest Rock 'n Roll singer, the newest TV comedy show or an Iowa needlework fair are all lifted by the Neo-Pollyannas from the realm of inadequacy or bad taste and endowed with their blessing as "cultural vigor" and "popular American art". In our vast pluralistic society the Native-Born Deplorers and the Neo-Pollyannas are both right and wrong. Neither has a copyrighted definition of American culture, and foreigners are entitled to wonder just what we do believe sometimes.

The debate over what people abroad think of our cultural life has taken on new urgency since the end of World War II. Soviet propagandists have been riding hard to catch and brand us as a barbarian culture-starved society. This is the cold-war aspect of the problem of making our true identity known. Another aspect of our need for world recognition is that a general understanding of American life is necessary to the successful projection of our overall policies. Unfortunately, we often seem bent on reinforcing misunderstandings in the minds of many Europeans and Asians through our stress on technical and financial assistance together with declamations that we have no intention of interfering in cultural affairs. This attitude is based on a genuine respect for cultural freedom and diversity; but it is often a little too pious, a little too naïve and perhaps even a little phoney.

The fact is that many of us feel a little Americanization wouldn't hurt the rest of the world. "No one ever puts it quite this baldly," William H. Whyte points out, "but there lurks deep in some American breasts the feeling that there is a mystically beneficent quality in certain of our folkways and that if only they could be exported the chasm in understanding would be bridged." Our Heavens-to-Betsy protestations about not wanting to impose our ideas on the rest of the world may convince us but our foreign critics know better. No one ships $100 billion, thousands of technicians, hundreds of Hollywood films overseas without leaving a cultural impression, whether they want to or not. Our fault is not that we have not been exerting an influence but that it has been a lopsided one. Too often the dominant picture of America overseas is that of a technologically-advanced civilization which expresses itself in terms of techniques and machines. The impression is an unfair one. Faced with cold-war pressures to develop a better understanding of our society we are at last taking steps to promote our cultural achievements abroad through government action. Self promotion was implicit in the development of the USIS library system and its cultural centers during World War II. It was given added impetus after the war when Congress authorized the first student exchange programs. These represented an important break with the traditional hands-off attitude of the government in cultural matters. The misgivings which many Congressmen and government administrators had about the new policy at the time was shared by many American intellectuals.

They were aware of the manner in which many European governments have subsidized the arts at home and abroad, apparently without applying the thwarting hand of censorship. Britain's post-war experience in subsidizing the arts through its Arts Council has an excellent record in providing financial underpinnings for ballet, theater and other artistic endeavors. The French and Italian traditions of state subsidies have been established for generations. The only significant American experience in this field was the New Deal project for providing support for unemployed artists under the Works Progress Administration. Although the WPA program was an incubator for some significant artistic talents it was often poorly managed; it produced enough second-rate and even ridiculous art to give its critics the ammunition they needed to finish it off.

The fears of American intellectuals about government activities in the cultural field seemed justified in 1946 when the State Department came under attack for its sponsorship of an exhibit of modern art in Europe. In a campaign sparked by the Hearst newspaper chain the Department was ridiculed about the modern paintings that had been selected for the show. Congressmen and newspaper editorialists condemned the show as "un-American" and "pro-Communist". The latter charge was bolstered by the allegation that a number of the artists represented in the show had connections with the Communist Party or its front organizations. The State Department decided to withdraw the exhibit. The incident seemed to confirm the proposition that the government should stay out of the business of promoting our culture abroad.

The necessity of strengthening cultural relations overseas was too imperative to be put off for long, however, and by 1950, the State Department was taking a new interest in the subject. Action was forced in part by Communist activity in the field and in part by a European post-war phenomenon—the development of cultural festivals as a means of attracting tourists and of advertising national artistic wares. In early years of the new festivals American artistic representation was pitifully small, only because of a lack of private or government support for the expensive business of participation. USIS posts in Europe pressed the State Department to develop some means for American participation in the festivals.

The first big break came in 1951. The Department decided that participation in the new Berlin festival was indicated for policy reasons. Arrangements were made with the American National Theater and Academy (ANTA) to stage the musical *Oklahoma*! It was followed the next year by the Robinson Jeffers version of *Medea* with Judith Anderson in the title role. Both performances were critical and popular successes thanks to the high quality of the artists involved and to ANTA's efficient management of the enterprise. ANTA was a natural choice for the assignment. It is a privately-sponsored, non-profit organization operating under a Congressional charter to strengthen the American theater. Its Berlin successes in 1951 and 1952 were important first steps in bringing our "live" cultural presentations to a wider world audience.

The credit for breaking through all remaining barriers goes to *Porgy and Bess*. In 1952 New York producer Robert Breen mounted a new version of the Gershwin folk opera with a brilliant cast, new sets and an unabashed violence and sexuality in its staging that won critical applause when it opened in New York. Breen was interested in putting the show on tour in Europe but he had difficulty in finding financial support for his plan. An appeal was made to the State Department for assistance.

I happened to be stationed in the Department at the time and to witness the looks of holy horror on an assembled throng of Department officials as a group of fellow-conspirators and I recommended support for Mr. Breen. The initial attitude of staid officialdom was that we were out of our collective minds to propose that a play about Negro slums in Charlestown, one that includes a murder and a rape, should be the beneficiary of the Department's small cultural fund. "It's all very well for New York or Chicago," their argument ran, "but overseas. . . . " We forebore the temptation to point out that the year before the U.S. government had sponsored *Medea,* a drama about a faded belle who kills her two children because her lover is bored with her. *Medea* is set in antiquity while the Charlestown slums are an unpleasantly current reality. After weeks of pleading and with some helpful support from the highest levels of the Department the *Porgy and Bess* project won the necessary approval. Those of us who were enthusiastic kept our fingers crossed for *Porgy's* success in Europe. If the play failed not only would the new cultural-presentations program be in danger but we might wind up in the Department's equivalent of Outer Mongolia for picking the wrong cultural horse.

The tour was a resounding success. From Belgrade to Athens to

Cairo and then back to Italy, *Porgy and Bess* exploded before its audiences. In Athens' venerable Royal Theater, where *Porgy* was the first play ever presented by a foreign troupe, the audience stood for a half hour after the curtain calls. "They were stunned, literally stunned," reported one observer. But the most warming of all the reactions to *Porgy's* tour was that of a Yugoslav government official. Taken aback by the frankness and the forcefulness with which the play described a seamier side of American life, he said: "Only a psychologically mature people could have placed this on the stage". It was as good a reason as could be given for showing *Porgy and Bess* and other examples of the vitality of American arts.

The Gershwin play went on to a successful Latin American tour and later to Moscow at the invitation of the Soviet Ministry of Culture. The State Department meanwhile pressed its plans for expanding the cultural presentations program. In 1954 Congress agreed to an Administration proposal for subsidizing commercial overseas tours by American artists. The American National Theater and Academy was given the responsibility for selecting the artists and administering the program under State Department supervision. (The Amateur Athletic Union does a similar service for a small number of athletes who have been sent overseas under the program in recent years.) USIS posts were designated to handle details of the program overseas. The selection of ANTA gave the program weight and influence in American artistic circles. It also relieved the State Department of some of the political pressures involved in the selection of artists. The number of artists who have recommended themselves or who have had their Congressman do it for them would fill a dozen Chautauqua circuits.

Overall, ANTA has been able to maintain a generally high standard in its selection process. It has sent abroad 160 artistic groups to 105 countries since 1955 including an American Indian dancer named Tom Two Arrows to Pakistan and Marian Anderson to the Far East. All four of America's permanent ballet companies have travelled abroad under ANTA sponsorship as has the Martha Graham dance troupe which created a major sensation in its 1955 tour of the Far East. In 1959, the Jerome Robbins dance group had a similar experience when its jazz-oriented dancing drew critical praise in Europe and the Middle East. For the first time millions of people overseas have had an opportunity to see top-flight American artists and to re-examine the mythology of our cultural poverty. We are now assured of good representation in artistic festivals abroad.

Our contribution is sometimes a full symphony orchestra. Each year the State Department has underwritten the tour of at least one symphony orchestra, scheduling its performances to coincide with one or more festivals. European and Latin American festival-goers have learned a new appreciation of our musical skills through the appearance of the symphony orchestras of Boston, Philadelphia, Minneapolis, Cleveland, Washington and New York.

A spectacular tour was that made by the New York Philharmonic in 1959. After an extensive tour of Europe and the Middle East the Philharmonic went to the Soviet Union where it pleased music lovers and outraged Cultural Ministry officials by playing two works of Russian-born Igor Stravinsky, the pioneer in modern music whose compositions have been banned in the Soviet Union. As an added fillip Conductor Leonard Bernstein then led the Philharmonic through the Fifth Symphony of Dimitri Shostakovich, an approved Soviet artist, in a performance that was hailed by Moscow musicologists as the finest interpretation of the work they had ever heard.

Jazz artists from Wilbur de Paris to Dizzy Gillespie have toured the world under ANTA auspices bringing lively interpretations of this American art form to audiences from Bombay to Oslo. When Benny Goodman and his orchestra visited Thailand they added a new dimension to Thai-American relations by including four popular Thai ballads in their repertoire, one of which was sung in Thai by vocalist Dottie Reid. The band also played four unscheduled jam sessions at the royal palace for the country's jazz-enthusiast monarch, King Phumiphol Aduldet. Less spectacular and less publicized than the overseas tours of large orchestras and ballets have been the barnstorming tours made by lesser-known American artists. The ANTA program has acquainted hundreds of thousands of music lovers in smaller cities throughout the world with American talent. The tour made by violinist Joseph Fuchs in South and Central America brought together a talented musician and an eager audience.

The ANTA program has demonstrated to American artists and their managers that there is a large responsive audience in areas of the world they would not have considered touring a few years ago. Many of the professional amenities are lacking and the concert halls often leave something to be desired but the audience is waiting. In many parts of Asia and Africa USIS serves as stand-in impresario for visiting artists, providing them with everything from advance publicity to hotel reservations. More and more American artists are following the tour trail blazed by ANTA. Subsidies will be necessary for some time to come, particularly for large organizations such as orchestras and theater companies, but the day of the unsubsidized world tour for individual American artists is also here.

The most stickling problem in our overseas cultural relations is that of stating our case in terms that are comprehensible to foreigners. Inevitably we express ourselves in our own terms and we are not always understood. What is needed is not a soap box from which we can declaim but a cultural meeting ground on which we can hold a mutual discussion.

Such a meeting ground is provided by the USIS world-wide system of cultural institutes. The first institute was started under private auspices in Buenos Aires in 1927. Actively encouraged by our government on a full-scale only since World War II, there are now 97 such organizations around the world. A majority of them are in Latin America where they are a familiar part of the local cultural scene in every large town. Throughout the world, the pattern for our bi-national cultural institutes is similar. They are usually operated by a board of directors composed half of local citizens and half of resident Americans; the leading officers are elected from the board. The director of the institute is often an American whose salary is paid by USIA. In addition, USIA may pay the salary costs of other American personnel such as the director of English-teaching and related academic activities. Most of the centers are self-supporting but when they are not, USIA provides a partial subsidy. The Latin American centers generally support themselves on membership dues and English-teaching fees. The newer organizations in the Middle East and Asia still depend upon USIA support.

Whenever USIS posts have worked with local groups to form a center, they have become a primary arm of American cultural activities in the area. Most of the centers have extensive libraries; many of them also have auditorium facilities for their lecture and concert programs. The centers offer an opportunity for Americans overseas to meet with intellectually alert citizens of their host countries and to share in local cultural activities; the centers are often used as meeting-places by local bi-national organizations. When the Turkish-American Association in Ankara sponsors a concert featuring Turkish folk songs, it is demonstrating American interest in Turkish culture. The centers are not one-way transmission belts for "selling" American culture. All of the centers have extensive English teaching programs.

The rise of English as the most widely-spoken world language is a valuable asset to us in promoting intellectual and social exchange. In addition to the work being done by the cultural centers, USIS posts cooperate directly with over forty governments to strengthen the quality and scope of English teaching in their school systems.

In Paris hundreds of students and intellectually curious others crowd the *Centre Culturel Américain* building in the St-Germain-des-Près quarter every day. They come to use its library, a smaller but more academically oriented one than the large USIS Benjamin Franklin Library a few blocks away. They come to see American documentary films or an exhibit or to sample the center's extensive collection of phonograph records. The center is a pleasant oasis where students may meet and refresh themselves on the cultural waters of Americana. "They go," says the *New Yorker's* Janet Flanner, "because it is free, because they are interested in the United States, and because they think that what comes from the States is bound to be stimulating, new, valuable and different from what comes from the rest of the world". The success of our center in Paris may be largely attributed to the efforts of its first director, a young USIS officer named Rudolph Aggrey who surmounted his bureaucratically-bestowed title of Youth Affairs Officer to become a familiar and welcome sight to thousands of Parisian students.

In Germany cultural activities were carried on through a chain of 47 Amerika Haus centers and 115 reading rooms which were founded by occupation authorities in the late Forties. Through their services, German intellectuals were re-introduced to American life and ideas after the war. Today only 16 of the original Amerika Haus and 10 of the reading rooms remain; many of the others are now operated by Germans. One of the busiest of our centers is in Berlin close to the East Berlin border. Day after day hundreds of East Berliners drop in to read newspapers or books or to hear lectures that keep them in touch with western ideas.

Another avenue for conveying our ideas to large audiences overseas is through trade fairs. The trade fair is an old, lively tradition in Europe and Latin America; it is also taking hold in Asia and Africa where independent nations are beginning to seek world markets for their products. The fairs are not only used as commercial market places; they are also used to promote prestige for both the sponsoring nation and for other exhibiting countries. Their propaganda value has been widely exploited by the Communist bloc at home and abroad. The United States rarely took part in trade fairs officially until 1954 when Congress authorized a program for such participation. (American commercial firms have participated in foreign fairs on their own initiative for many years.)

The trade fair program is managed by the Department of Commerce with the assistance of the State Department and USIA. In 1960 the United States participated officially in 14 such fairs around the world ranging from the Milan Fair where American business puts its best merchandising foot forward to meet European competition to the Poznan Fair where the United States has had a unique opportunity in recent years to display the products of its economy to millions of Poles. We have also taken part in such outstanding prestige events as the 1958 Brussels World's Fair and the 1959 World Agricultural Fair in New Delhi, where three and a third million persons toured the American exhibit.

The information agency maintains its own exhibits program on a continuing basis, providing its overseas posts with a wide variety of shows such as the prize-winning photographs of the annual Eastman Kodak camera contest for high school students and the pavilion-sized exhibits of original American paintings and sculpture loaned to the Agency by leading museums. The Museum of Modern Art's famed photographic show, Family of Man, was exhibited by USIS posts in all parts of the world.

Although our exhibits program concentrates on cultural matters, it also serves broad political objectives. Local posts have used exhibits to dramatize our progress in developing peaceful uses of atomic energy and in exploring the mysteries of space. Possibilities for the peaceful use of nuclear power have been highlighted in exhibits in almost every free world country during the past six years. These exhibits have usually enjoyed high-level local sponsorship; the atomic energy commissions of such diverse countries as India, Spain and Greece sponsored our Atoms for Peace exhibit in their respective countries. The Soviet achievement in launching the first earth satellite in 1957 was a propaganda setback for the United States. Since that time USIS posts have dramatized more recent American accomplishments in their exhibits in an effort to modify the initial Soviet propaganda coup in the field of space exploration and other sciences.

Almost every aspect of American life has been visualized through exhibits, including our love of sports. When the post in Madras, India, received the sports exhibit, it decided to supplement the show's photographs and texts with a "live" demonstration of an

American baseball game. A field was procured and a team was formed among the American employees of USIS and the Consulate. Since there were not enough Americans for two full teams, some Indian students from the local YMCA college were persuaded to form a team so that the game could be properly demonstrated. The experiment showed admirable vitality with only one unforeseen result: the Indian team won the game 21 to 16.

The biggest of all U.S. exhibits was the famous American National Exhibition in Moscow in 1959. Under the terms of a 1957 cultural agreement, the United States and the Soviet Union presented exhibits in Moscow and New York respectively. The Eisenhower administration decided to take full advantage of the opportunity to present America directly to the Russian people and $3.6 million was allocated for the show. Although we had less than seven months to plan and ready the exhibit from the time the Russians gave their final permission for it in December, 1958 until it was opened in Moscow's Sokolniki Park, ten acres of the park were transformed into a panorama of science, technology and other major arts of the American people. By and large the USIA planners correctly gauged their audience who showed a heartening enthusiasm for learning about everything American. From the ranch-style house with interiors by Macy's to the free Pepsi-Colas, the audience reaction was overwhelming.

The surprise hit of the exhibit were the seventy-five young Russian-speaking American guides. They were hired to explain the individual exhibits but they found themselves instead answering questions on all aspects of American life. *Are American slums underground? Is it true you publish Anna Karenina as a twelve-page comic book? Are Marx and Engels banned or published only with critical annotations? What is your family's budget?* The direct good-natured replies given by the guides were effective enough to elicit a propaganda barrage in Soviet newspapers in which the guides were variously accused of giving misleading answers to questions, of offending the Soviet people and once even of pinching a hotel maid. These allegations, together with the rest of the Soviet government's attempts to dismiss the exhibition as an exercise in deception, seemed to have no effect on the enthusiasm shown by the 2.7 million people who saw the show during the six weeks it was open.

There were inevitable criticisms by some Americans who saw the Moscow exhibition that it was "incomplete" in its portrayal of

American life. It was. Who can compress the American story into ten acres? The exhibition emphasized our material gains because these are the most tangible products of our civilization and its activities. There is no reason to assume that we are automatically branded as people without a soul when we exhibit them. The question of whether material riches and spiritual vigor can be reconciled has been answered affirmatively over the centuries by the men of Athens, Rome, Peiping, Florence and Paris. In our own way we can also re-affirm this truth as it applies to our own popular culture. We should not flaunt our riches before the world but we have a legitimate interest in demonstrating the material benefits that we have derived from the political and economic system we have developed. It is part of what we are and it is an achievement that most of the rest of the world wants to emulate.

Our cultural life will not be measured overseas by technological advance alone, nor by the statistics of student-exchange programs, nor by number of square feet of paintings USIA sends abroad every year. We must beware the hot-house smell of "official culture" no matter how extensive or well intended it is. Our national achievements are either alive and kicking all by themselves or they are not worth showing. USIA has taken the position that they are worth showing even at government expense. The day is past when American professors and oboe players are a novelty overseas. We must continue to seek new ways to show depth as well as variety in what we say and do culturally. Above all we need to be more imaginative in showing how our civilization can offer a net gain in the lives of all men everywhere. That is the gain by which thinking men will measure the quality of our national culture.

The Americans who helped unlock the secret of nuclear fission made such a net gain for all of us; so did those who developed the polio vaccine. There will be others in the coming years who will make other permanent gains across the whole gamut of human problems. These men and the society that nurtures them can give a heart and mind to our age. Not in the cold war struggle, but ultimately here is where we will receive our most lasting judgment from the rest of mankind.

12

BALANCE SHEET

How effective is our overseas information program? It is a legitimate question if only because the American people are asked to provide $100 million a year to maintain its operations. Even more important than the question of its dollar value is whether the program is playing its proper role in the international challenge we face in the 1960's. Unless there is a suicidal nuclear war the balance of power between ourselves and the Communists will be largely determined in the arena of world opinion. Are we equipped to match the Communists in this fight? Can we steadily outmatch them? Can we transcend strategic needs and give a heart and mind to our age?

The effectiveness of propaganda operations is extremely difficult to measure. Propagandists themselves have an inherent tendency to exaggerate their ability to persuade. They are something like Chanticleer, the rooster of French fable, who thought the sun rose every morning because he crowed. The complexity and geographically widespread nature of USIS operations make them particularly elusive to analysis. The organization has been bedevilled over the years by the insistence of both its friends and critics to "prove" its effectiveness. In the past, some USIS officials attempted to meet these demands by citing specific "evidences of effectiveness" in the organization's work. Occasionally the "evidence" was a bit stretched in the recounting; a little French girl's thank-you letter to the USIS library in Paris might be cited as a proof that European youth was showing a greater understanding of our cultural achievements. One of the signs of USIS maturity as an organization has been its giving up of such bumptious efforts to justify its existence.

Elusive or not, a continuing estimate of effectiveness of the information program is needed. We must have some measure of its current operations in order to determine future information policies. For such appraisals and recommendations, the Information Agency relies largely on its own research and evaluation unit. In addition to analyzing reports from USIS posts overseas, the unit also receives intelligence data from other government sources such as the State Department, Central Intelligence Agency and the military intelligence bureaus. Universities and private research organizations are called upon to make studies of specific public-opinion attitudes overseas as they relate to our national policy.

In the past decade USIS posts have pioneered in the extension of public-opinion polling techniques in Asian and African countries. In many of these areas polls are still a novelty and their results are often unreliable in consequence. Since many of the questions are political in nature, people are liable to suspect that the poll is a government device to check on their personal opinions. In one Near Eastern country a survey made after a national election recently showed that only five percent of the voters said they voted for the Communist-front ticket. In fact the Communists had won almost 25 percent of the vote in the area where the poll was taken. From all these evaluation efforts comes a general pattern of just where USIS can be effective—and where it cannot.

The measure of its effectiveness is the degree to which the program advances the strategic policies of the United States. This relationship between policy and propaganda was succinctly outlined by USIA director George V. Allen in a talk to Agency employees when he became head of the organization in 1957:

"I have long been convinced that ninety percent of the impression which the United States makes abroad depends on our policies and that not more than ten percent, to make a rough estimate, is how we explain it—whether we say it softly, or loudly, or strongly, or belligerently, or with dulcet tones. We can work our hearts out for years building up goodwill for the United States in a given country when suddenly one little policy action is taken which does more to destroy our position than the USIA can rebuild in a very long time. I want to make it absolutely clear that I am not writing down the importance of the U.S. Information Agency. I am writing up the importance of having the public relations aspects of policy taken into consideration when policy is made. . . . There may be other reasons why policy cannot always follow our recommendations. I perfectly well recognize that. A lot of policy decisions are going to be taken which will make your job and mine more difficult. And many times we can't help it. Other considerations may overweigh ours. But if we can continue to make available to those who have to make policy the tremendous importance of the public relations aspects of whatever is done, we will gradually, I hope, achieve an appropriate and proper role for our activity in the formulation of policy."

The integration of information program activities into the foreign policy machinery has made considerable strides in recent years. The turning point in this development was the transfer of the program from its second-echelon status inside the State Department in 1953 to the independent U.S. Information Agency. The move was regarded by some observers at the time as an unfortunate one because it separated information activities from diplomatic control. In fact, however, it gave the program a stronger status in the foreign-policy area without loosening State Department control.

The new agency was assigned a role in National Security Council planning operations that gave it an opportunity to highlight the importance of overseas public opinion factors in NSC's strategic decisions. Although this has been an important gain, many experts feel that the information program can be even more closely integrated into the top level of foreign policy planning. They point out that USIA's role in the National Security Council has been more as observer than full-fledged participant, although its Director sits in on Council deliberations and other offices discuss before the group matters which are directly related to Agency programming. These advocates of fuller participation by USIA in the decision-making process argue only that the Agency should be a consultant in the process; they do not propose that USIA should be a policy maker. Any move to weaken the State Department's traditional control over the formulation of foreign affairs in the interests of policies dominated by propaganda considerations would be untenable.

The information program's gradual integration into the Washington policy-making machinery during the past decade is also reflected in the changing position of USIS operations in embassies overseas. During the 1940's most information posts were regarded with varying degrees of suspicion by embassy officers, including many ambassadors. Their suspicions were based on intangible doubts about the value of the information program together with tangible examples of operational ineptness in certain USIS posts. Today most of these doubts have disappeared as the information services have become an integral part of embassy operations. Public affairs officers (directors of USIS posts) are members of embassy "country teams"—the top-level committee which helps each ambassador carry out American policy in the country he is assigned to. In larger embassies such as London, Karachi and Tokyo the public affairs officers hold the rank of counselor of embassy, one of the highest ranks. Almost all policy recommendations transmitted back to Washington now are reviewed by USIS as well as other elements of each embassy.

The improved status of the information program in the policy planning field affects its day-to-day media operations. In its early days the program was plagued by the amateurish quality of some of its output. This was due in large part to some second-rate personnel and in part to a lack of guidance from the top on what to say and how to say it. By and large, the USIA media divisions have weeded these faults out of their organizational gardens. Policy coordination between the various media and the USIA and State Department policy planners is close and continuing.

The Voice of America radio operation in particular has sharpened its effectiveness in this regard in recent years. This is the result of a studied attempt to eliminate any elements of high-pressure salesmanship in its broadcasts in favor of authoritative news and feature output. Political commentaries are generally restricted to low-key expositions of American policy and opinion. In another development, VOA is reaching out for a relatively small but specialized audience of opinion leaders in Asia, Africa and Latin America through programs designed to attract doctors, scientists and government officials. The primary mission of the Voice will continue to be broadcasting to audiences behind the Iron and Bamboo Curtain. Shortwave broadcasting remains our main channel to hundreds of millions of people under Communist rule; numerous reports attest to the fact that VOA is an important free world voice for them. In other areas of the world, the Voice still lags behind in its ability to match Communist and other radio services. Since 1959 it has been in fourth place behind the Russians, Red Chinese and Egyptians (United Arab Republic) in the amount of program hours broadcast.

The USIS press services provide our chief means of daily communication with free world opinion leaders, particularly in underdeveloped areas, on factual information about current American policy. Through its daily news file transmission to local posts from Agency headquarters in Washington, the press service sends out the texts of official policy statements along with supplementary material to all parts of the world. A statement by the President tonight will be put into the hands of hundreds of thousands of editors and other opinion leaders, translated into their respective languages, by tomorrow night. Most of our posts can provide the translated statement to local newspapers within a few hours after they receive it from Washington. Although its activities are strictly limited in Communist areas, the press service produces two influential magazines distributed behind the Iron Curtain—the Polish-language *Ameryka* and the Russian-language *America Illustrated.*

Television services of the information program are just beginning to hit their operational stride. After a slow build-up during the 1950's, television is now the most rapidly-expanding media service in the Agency. The TV service is currently placing its news and feature materials on over 200 stations overseas; this number can be expected to double within the next five years. International television networks will soon extend around the world, perhaps through the use of American and Soviet communications earth satellites. The United States will have to come forward with a definite plan for making the best of its commercial and public-service telecasts available to overseas network audiences. USIA has already made a start in this field through its cooperative arrangements with the Eurovision television network in Europe. The day may soon come when television will become *the* strategic propaganda medium; any planning that we can do now to further insure American representation in international television will pay big dividends then.

Motion pictures will continue to hold their own as a major propaganda asset for the United States with hundreds of millions of foreigners continuing to get their most indelible image of America from Hollywood productions and other American films. The Agency film service provides a documentary picture of America to a half billion people every year around the world in an effort to supplement and correct the dramatized image of America that Hollywood presents. Our image abroad is further elaborated by the USIS exhibits program.

Our worldwide system of libraries and cultural centers presents more than an image; they communicate directly and personally by mind and heart. In many Asian and African cities, these libraries and centers provide the only book-lending services available although this situation is changing rapidly as other libraries follow the USIS example. An increasing number of American books is also appearing on the world's bookstalls as a result of the Agency's programs for book translations and for encouraging foreign distribution by commercial publishers here. American-styled pocket books are now a common sight in the bookstores and on the kiosks of foreign cities. A new and promising field for USIS is in encouraging the world's school systems to adapt American textbooks for their classrooms.

The initial success of this program in South Asia is a significant development in strengthening American influence in universities and primary schools in this and other areas.

The exchange of students and of foreign leaders under the State Department's cultural program is our closest and most personal tie with cultural developments in other nations. The exchange of students might well be accelerated in future years. Foreign students now account for less than two percent of our university student population. The present number of 50,000 foreign students could well be doubled within the next five years in order to strengthen our influence among the young professional groups of Asia, Africa and Latin America. Many observers feel that we should also step up our assistance to the new universities of Asia and Africa for the same reason. Educator Harold Taylor, former president of Sarah Lawrence College, came to this conclusion following a 1960 survey tour of Asian universities:

"For most students the conditions of education are almost impossibly difficult. Improving these conditions offers the United States one of its greatest opportunities to redirect our foreign policy towards positive social action. . . . Yet we have not even begun to think in the larger concepts demanded by the size of the problem. Our foreign policy has concentrated on winning military and political allies rather than making common cause with those in Asia who have broken free from foreign domination and are now creating new societies. As a result, our cultural policy, with meager funds and an underdeveloped philosophy, has been conceived in the spirit of our foreign aid—as an aspect of an American defense posture. This must be changed. We must have a bold national program of educational aid to Asian students. They are the ones on whom will depend the future relations of Asia with the rest of the world, including the United States, and they are determining that future right now."

Anyone who has dealt with the problems of Asian education will look sympathetically on Dr. Taylor's plea for American support to its schools. We have expanded our activities in this field in recent years, particularly in providing educational materials for libraries and for individual teachers and students, together with exchange scholarships. Private organizations such as the Ford Foundation are also doing significant work in this field.

In summary, the U.S. Information Agency has a full range of informational and cultural activities in its 200 posts in over 80 countries around the world. After years of trial and error, it has learned how to identify public opinion problems overseas and has developed programs to cope with them. Its corps of information and cultural officers, together with specialized technicians, have acquired considerable experience in judging what they can and cannot reasonably expect to achieve through their operations toward strengthening U.S. influence overseas.

They have learned that propaganda showmanship can never substitute for good policies. It cannot bail us out of unpleasant consequences that result from unpalatable policies. The time to win a propaganda advantage is during the formulation of policies: either by adapting them to the requirements of world opinion or by preparing to meet a sharp public-opinion reaction against them overseas. As a free world leader we are sometimes required to pursue decisive policies of action whether or not they will be unpopular. The landing of our Marines in Lebanon in 1957 to forestall a possible collapse of the government there was such a case. When the move met severe criticism in Asia and Africa, USIS posts in those areas were prepared to explain why the action was imperative to our own vital interests as well as to those of the free world in general. Many opinion leaders were persuaded by our explanations, especially after the United States showed its respect for Lebanese independenc by pulling out its troops on schedule. The moral is: the straight story, backed by straight actions, pays off.

The most important contribution our overseas information program can make is to provide public opinion overseas with a precise statement of what the American purpose is and why it is what it is. If our government information operation were to be voted out of existence tomorrow by Congress there would still be American voices overseas; the voices of our tourists, of Hollywood and of the press associations would still speak for us abroad. What the information program does which none of these can do is to provide the world with a clear statement of American purpose. It is most useful precisely because there are so many competing private voices of America. Whatever the validity of our many other voices, none of them individually expresses the general consensus of our nation or the specific policies of the government.

Providing these facts about ourselves is important; but facts are neutral and they have a meaning for us only to the extent that they have some emotional content. If we were engaged in a war of facts, we would have won a long time ago. Long before anyone ever thought of a U.S. Information Service the problem has been how to influence the way people feel about the facts and the way they intend to act upon them. The value of our overseas information program is that it gives meaning to both the facts about ourselves and also to the ideas we represent. Most influential people overseas are prepared to accept our USIS output as an expression of the American viewpoint. This may not seem to be a spectacular achievement but it is the all-important beginning of the way toward understanding. There are no shortcuts on the long rocky road to a better understanding of the United States by foreign peoples. Nor is there any point at which we will "win" world opinion to our side. The struggle goes on every day with no time out and no silver trophies for the winners. Our information program has to be flexible enough to change as conditions change but steady enough in purpose to sustain the confidence of our old friends and win the confidence of new ones.

In recent years there has been a steady diminution in the practice of publicly re-examining our information program to see if it "works". The program has no special claim for exemption from investigation by Congress or other official groups but it should not be pawed over continually. As Dean Acheson once pointed out during a period of clamor for investigation of our foreign policies, you can't keep pulling flowers up by the roots to see if they are growing. The horticultural metaphor carries over to the information program and its attempts to develop the equally delicate growth of a favorable public opinion overseas. One way to reconcile the needs of uninterrupted long-range planning in the information program with the Congressional function of investigation would be to have a permanent Congressional committee on information-program activities which would conduct a low-key continuing review of what the program is doing and make its recommendations and estimates accordingly.

Another area in which the information program has been hampered in its efforts at long-range planning is the Federal government's budget process. Along with other government agencies, USIA goes to Congress every spring for the annual ritual of budget hearings and an eventual appropriation. Congress holds the purse strings and, with few exceptions, it appropriates money only one year at a time. This automatically places some realistic limitations on the ability of USIA to do any meaningful long-range planning beyond the one-year fiscal framework in which it now operates.

Until quite recently the information program was so controversial and its future so unsure that it did not have the organizational stability to carry out many long-range projects. There were no assurances from one year to the next that it would have enough money to pay for even minimal operations. Many useful long-range projects were actually carried out during these years by officers who whistled their way past each budget like little boys going past a dark graveyard, hoping not to be noticed. The organization is considerably more mature now both in its operations and its sense of purpose. Congress has recognized this in the general approval it has given the program in recent years.

The problem of adjusting the year-to-year budget process to long-range planning requirements has not yet been entirely solved. It should, however, be possible to develop a solution which would make possible such planning within the present annual budget process. Congress could authorize USIA to set aside, say, ten percent of its appropriation for long-range projects. The money for these projects would be voted annually; some form of review of each project could be made by Agency authorities and Congress each year to determine whether they should be continued. The procedure would be somewhat cumbersome but it would provide a sounder basis for planning long-range programs than now exists.

At present USIS offices overseas have no authority to make program commitments beyond the next June 30, the end of the federal government's fiscal year. Let us assume that a scholar in the mythical new kingdom of Ruritania has just been appointed head of the country's leading university. He admires American culture and he decides to set up a special course in American studies. He pays a visit to the USIS information office to find out what help he might expect from our government for the project. He knows that the French and British governments provide support for studies of their cultures and so do the Russians when they get the chance. The Americans, he soon finds out, are more reticent and he cannot understand why. The cultural officer he talks to is enthusiastic about the project and he offers whatever help he can. Why then is his help so limited? Why should the representative of such a prosperous country as the United States be unwilling to make any financial commitment beyond the current year? The American studies project at Ruritania University could be an important means for expanding American influence in the country over the next decade. Why are the Americans apparently so disinterested in offering long-range help?

How much more realistic and effective it would be if our post in Ruritania could make a firm promise actively to support the new American studies program at the university over a five-year period while it was being developed. The USIS officer's dilemma in not being able to advance a project which is so plainly to our advantage arises in our local posts all around the world. When long-term commitments are made, it must always be with the proviso that "it depends on next year's appropriation".

The question of how to give flexibility to appropriations is in fact more crucial than the question of whether funds for USIA activities should be increased in the coming years. The new Soviet propaganda campaign is often cited as justification for a larger program on our part. Such reasoning errs in equating propaganda effectiveness with the amount of money spent on it. It took a long time before many people learned that $20 million added to the information program's budget does not necessarily mean an equal rise in the program's effectiveness. In fact such dramatic increases—usually under the guise of a "crash program"—tended to upset the program structure since they forced administrators to expand too rapidly under the unyielding rule that all appropriations have to be spent (or allocated) by the next June 30. Too often the result was waste and confusion, followed by the inevitable Congressional threat to reduce the program. Fortunately for the program and for the American taxpayer, the "crash program" approach to our information activities has subsided.

There is a case for increasing the present annual level of USIA funds which now hover around the $100 million mark. One reason is to permit an expansion of USIS program activities in the new nations of Africa and Asia over a period of three or four years. Thirteen new countries have been created in Africa in 1960 alone; the Agency has lagged in setting up operations and staffing its posts in these countries because of a shortage of funds. The new posts that have been opened in Africa have been financed partly by closing down program activities in other areas, particularly in Europe. A shift in geographical emphasis may be warranted but the point has been reached where it becomes difficult to build up new posts in Africa without crippling the program elsewhere.

Another reason for a gradual increase in the budget is worldwide fiscal inflation. The cost of everything is going up overseas and our information program has had to pay for most of this inflation by reducing its program activities in recent years. The problem was stated clearly by USIA Director George V. Allen in testimony before the Senate Appropriations Committee which was examining the Agency's 1961 fiscal year budget: "Why shouldn't the Agency be able to carry on a creditable program with the same amount of money and the same staff as it had last year? The answer is twofold: each year the amount of program we can carry on with the given amount of money declines and each year the magnitude of our job increases. Next year mandatory wage increases for our foreign nationals abroad and inflationary price increases of materials purchased overseas will mean that we have to pay $596 thousand more than during the current year. In addition we must expect to pay out another $620 thousands in Federal health insurance contributions and within-grade increases of American employees. In other words, slightly more than $1.2 million of any appropriation granted must be used to pay these inescapable additional costs before program needs can be considered."

If the present trend of holding the annual budgets to about $100 million a year continues we will face the new Soviet propaganda offensive with a program that is becoming progressively smaller. (The Soviets are, by the most conservative estimates, spending a half billion dollars a year on their propaganda operations.) The problem is compounded by the imminent need to allocate tens of millions of dollars in the next few years to finance the replacement of obsolete equipment. Most of the Voice of America radio transmitters are wartime or early post-war models which should be replaced with new and more efficient ones. Such equipment is expensive; the new transmitting station at Greenville, North Carolina, is costing over $25 million.

Sound budgeting as well as intelligent programming will require, first of all, that we have a clear idea of exactly what we are up against in the battle for world opinion during the 1960's. When Nikita Krushchev stomped out of the 1960 summit meeting in Paris he seemed to close the door on western hopes for a general agreement on reducing world tensions for some time to come. Everything he has said and done since then has only confirmed the Soviet intention to wage unremitting political warfare, backed by nuclear strength, against the free world.

The ingredients of the new Soviet offensive in the cold war are much the same as earlier Communist strategy except for one key fact: the growing conviction of the Soviet leadership that they now have the psychological offensive. Their previous wave-of-the-future claims could be dismissed as Stalinist bluster; today their claim has the dark brown taste of reality. The new Soviet industrial resurgence, the success of their space exploration programs and their progress in missiles have given the Communists a heady sense of power. The Marxist-Leninist predications of the inevitability of Communism, a glimmering hope for four decades of Soviet leadership, seem about to burst into fulfillment. Moreover the post-Stalinist leadership can count on greater support from their own people as a result of encouraging popular pride in Soviet technological achievements and by easing up some of the more repressive aspects of their police state. As Arthur Schlesinger, Jr. points out, ruthless coercion has been partially replaced by ruthless popular enthusiasm for the new sense of power that pervades Soviet society. Day in and day out a new surge of power is reflected in Soviet and Chinese Communist propaganda as it trumpets the theme that the future belongs to Communism.

Aside from suicidal nuclear war, the greatest danger we face in the 1960's is the new Communist offensive in the battle for world opinion. The Communists are convinced that they now have the resources to make good their claim of world leadership without risking a general war. Their primary weapon is psychological pressure built up by all the political, economic, military and propaganda power at their disposal. The wrecking of the 1960 summit meeting by Krushchev marked the end of Soviet attempts to present a facade of "peaceful coexistence" with the United States. Within a few weeks after the abortive meeting Communists were stirring up new troubles on every continent.

The danger for us is that the Communists stand a chance to win in the 1960's unless we take specific measures to meet their offensive at every level. Every indicator of world opinion in recent years has shown an increasing awareness of Soviet strength. Even in pre-Sputnik 1958 a majority of Frenchmen, Britons, Belgians and Indians polled by Dr. Gallup named the Soviet Union when asked what country will be strongest in ten years. Around the globe the legend of American technological supremacy is being modified by reports of Soviet moon probes, atomic plant construction and agricultural advances. Such Soviet achievements are given added meaning in Asia and Africa by the Communist ability to identify Russia and mainland China as "newly developing countries" whose problems are similar to those faced by other Asians and by Africans. The moral is there for anyone to see: you can do it, too, if you follow our lead. It is a powerful appeal in an area of the world that is looking for the shortest way to economic and social fulfillment.

The question of our conflicting appeals goes to the very heart of our national strategy. As President Kennedy has pointed out, our prestige overseas is not to be confused with popularity, but involves the issue of our survival and of our leadership of the free world. "If the people of the world once get the idea that the Russians and the Communists represent the strongest power," he has said, "how many of them will stay with us? How many people in Latin America, Africa and Asia will decide that we represent the way of the future?" Here is the crux of the problem confronting the Administration and the American people as we move into the crucial years ahead.

Faced with this challenge, what should we do? We have lost ground in recent years in certain areas but any objective evaluation will show that the balance of world force and prestige is still tipped in our favor. We continue to maintain a network of strong loyal allies who have freely accepted our leadership. Whatever the shortcomings of our policies in the past we have consistently shown that we are prepared to honor our commitments in a showdown with the Soviets. For all its flexing of political muscles the Soviet Union has increased its territories only once since the Second World War: this was in 1946, when it grabbed the southern half of Sakhalin Island in the northern Pacific. Whenever the western democratic peoples and above all the United States have shown a determination to defend freedom against aggressive forces, the Communists have pulled back.

Our greatest asset in the struggle for world loyalties is the fact that the revolution of our age is grounded in American experience. Communism is the counter-revolution that seeks to return the newly-independent nations of Asia and Africa to their colonial status under Soviet and Chinese control. Whatever the faults of omission and commission in our specific policies, the new leadership of Asia and Africa recognizes this vital distinction between the two leading world powers.

An historian looking back on our era may count still another factor as the one which changed the course of American life in these heady years. This is the searching new look we have been taking at ourselves since our traumatic reaction to the first Soviet sputnik. The debate on national purpose, covering every aspect of our life from infant training to graduate sciences, has matured into a serious re-examination of what we can do to improve our personal lives and our collective destinies in an increasingly complex world. The lazy slugs of mediocrity and indifference are still among us but they are diminishing. Part of the current debate can be dismissed as cheap rhetoric, part as a passing twinge of conscience but more of it represents a healthy attempt to find where our future lies. In Aubrey Menen's words, we are no longer looking for a convincing explanation of our own astonishing excellence. We are looking instead for some hard answers to the needs of our age.

In our national life this is reflected in our search for a plan of action that will meet the challenge of the revolutions of Asia and Africa as well as the threat of Communist expansion. Our eventual objective is to reach the Iron Curtain peoples themselves and to gain their support in modifying the Communist blueprint for world conquest. In preparing for this next phase of the cold war during the 1960's we must avoid frenzied plans and headlong action. One danger will come from the advocates of a new ideological crusade. It is an appealing idea which, at first glance, seems to meet our need for a dedicated program to match that of the Communists. Such a course of action, however, could be disastrous to our leadership of the free world. Our strongest political appeal overseas is our willingness not to impose our ideological standards on the rest of mankind. If we approach our differences with the Communists in an aggressively crusading spirit, every small quarrel between East and West becomes a possible fight to the finish. One of the lessons of history is that it is difficult to stop short in an ideological crusade. Unlike the earlier Crusades, any attempt on our part to smote the heathen could end in nuclear pulverization.

We need the strength that our ideas and ideals give us as we face new challenges. We need them not as slogans or propaganda points but as guides to informed actions. Our success in countering Soviet psychological strategy hinges not so much on what we say as on what we do in establishing a new image of America. The problem of our propaganda is actually the problem of our society and its purpose. For a century and a half after our independence our goals were centered around domestic developments as we fashioned a new continent and a new race. Today we have achieved most of the material goals of our early history. We live in the most comfortable society ever known, in the center of what Barbara Ward has called "the golden circle of western wealth". But we are also the heirs to a world-wide struggle for freedom and we cannot escape the consequences of this destiny. "It seems to have been reserved to the people of this country, by their conduct and example, to show the way to political freedom". Thus did the authors of the *Federalist Papers* state the case at the beginning of our own independence.

Are we capable of producing the great innovations that can break down the boundaries now separating freedom and despotism throughout the world? Can we make ourselves heard throughout the world? A most heartening sign was the intense interest shown by people overseas in the debate surrounding our 1960 Presidential election. Although we regarded the contest primarily as a domestic one, uncounted millions of foreigners paid us the tribute of affirming that their lives and fortunes were tied to our debate. They know that these are the years of decision between a despotism that will enslave us all or a world society where everyone will have a chance to "yield that peculiar fruit which each man was created to bear".

Who will speak for America during these years? Not only the American government or its official information services. They are only the instruments of our collective will and can do little more than mirror our strengths and failures. No amount of propaganda can mask a retreat from our responsibilities, if that is the course we take. The true Voice of America is all of us, 180 million individuals, when we act with understanding and skill in giving a heart and mind to our age.

If we rise to this challenge in the coming years, I and my colleagues in the United States Information Service will have the privilege of telling the rest of the world the most exciting story of the century.

BIBLIOGRAPHY

Almond, Gabriel A., *The American People and Foreign Policy,* Harcourt, Brace & Co., New York. 1950

Barrett, Edward A., *Truth Is Our Weapon,* Funk & Wagnalls Co., New York. 1953. A summary of the overseas information program's activities during the early post-war period by a former Assistant Secretary of State who directed the program at the time.

Berelson, Bernard and Janowitz, Morris, *Reader in Public Opinion and Communications,* The Free Press, Glencoe, Illinois. 1950. An anthology on the subject of public opinion theory and practice.

Buchanan, William and Cantril, Hadley, *How Nations See Each Other,* University of Illinois Press, Urbana. 1953.

Cantril, Hadley (editor), *Tensions That Cause Wars,* University of Illinois Press, Urbana. 1950. An anthology of the conclusions reached by a group of American and foreign social scientists who were commissioned by UNESCO in 1947 to study "tensions affecting international understanding." Interesting particularly for the viewpoints expressed by European sociologists on the subject.

Carroll, Wallace, *Persuade or Perish,* Houghton, Mifflin Co., Boston. 1948. An analysis of the importance of world public opinion in achieving our strategic goals.

Creel, George, *How We Advertised America,* Harper & Brothers, New York. 1920. A first-person account by its director of the work of the Committee on Public Information during World War I.

Doob, Leonard W., *Public Opinion and Propaganda,* Henry Holt & Co., New York. 1948

Harter, D. Lincoln and Sullivan, John, *Propaganda Handbook,* 20th Century Publishing Co., Philadelphia. 1953. A popularized account of how to avoid the pitfalls of propaganda.

Harvey, Ian, *The Technique of Persuasion,* The Falcon Press, London. 1951 A series of sprightly-written essays on propaganda theory and technique by a British observer.

Hoffman, Paul G., *Peace Can Be Won,* Doubleday & Co., New York. 1951 A political pamphlet by the director of the Marshall Plan on the need for coordinating political, economic and psychological factors in our strategy. There is a chapter of the role that propaganda played in carrying out the Marshall Plan.

Inkles, Alex, *Public Opinion in Soviet Russia,* Harvard University Press, Cambridge. 1951 Although the pattern of public opinion has changed somewhat since this work was written, it remains an authoritative description of the basic Soviet mechanism for channelling Russian opinion towards Communist goals.

Kissinger, Henry A., *Nuclear Weapons and Foreign Policy,* published for the Council on Foreign Relations by Harper & Brothers, New York. 1957 Although this work is concerned primarily with the politico-military aspects of our strategy, it raises important questions in the field of our overall impact on world opinion. See particularly the last chapter, "The need for doctrine."

Lee, Alfred McClung, *How To Understand Propaganda,* Rinehart & Co., New York. 1952. A popularized account of how propaganda works with the emphasis on its domestic applications.

Lerner, Daniel, *Skyewar,* George W. Stewart Publishers, Inc., New York. 1949. Lively description of how psychological warfare operations were conducted during World War II.

Lerner, Daniel, *Propaganda in War and Crisis,* George W. Stewart Publishers Inc., New York. 1951. This anthology, edited by Mr. Lerner, is particularly useful for its first-person accounts of OWI and War Department psychological warfare operations during World War II by such participants as Elmer Davis, James P. Warburg, Wallace Carroll and Martin Herz.

Linebarger, P. M. A., *Psychological Warfare,* Infantry Journal, Washington, D. C., 1948 Well-rounded account of "sykewar" theory and practise by a veteran observer.

Lippmann, Walter, *Public Opinion,* Harcourt, Brace & Co., New York. 1922. This is the best work ever written on the subject of public opinion and propaganda. The original edition is often hard to find but it has been reprinted recently by the Macmillan Company in its paperback series.

Lumley, Frederic E., *The Propaganda Menace,* The Century Co., New York. An interesting compilation of pre-war American attitudes toward propaganda.

Mackenzie, A. J., *Propaganda Boom,* John Gifford Ltd., London. 1938. The uses to which Hitler, Mussolini and Stalin put their propaganda machines before World War II are documented in this British study.

Markel, Lester and others, *Public Opinion and Foreign Policy,* Harper & Brothers, New York. 1949.

Marshall, Charles Burton, *The Limits of Foreign Policy,* Henry Holt & Co., New York. 1954. A former State Department official, Mr. Marshall writes of the limits within which an effective foreign policy must operate. His wise words on the need for moderate approaches to attainable goals in our overall strategy can also be applied to our propaganda operations.

Martin, L. John, *International Propaganda,* University of Minnesota Press, Minneapolis. 1958. Mr. Martin concentrates on the controls that nations have tried to apply both domestically and internationally in an effort to curb propaganda through legal and diplomatic devices.

Mock, James R. and Larson, Cedric, *Words That Won The War,* Stanford University Press, Stanford. 1939. A history of the activities of the World War I Committee on Public Information, our first organized government propaganda service.

Smith, Chitra M.; Winograd, Berton and Jwaideh, Alice R., *International Communications and Political Warfare: An Annotated Bibliography,* Rand Corporation, Santa Monica, California. 1952. Although somewhat dated, this bibliography is an important source for students of propaganda.

Spaulding, E. Wilder, *Ambassadors Ordinary and Extraordinary,* Public Affairs Press, Washington, D. C. A former State Department official provides enlightening historical perspective.

Stephens, Oren, *Facts To A Candid World,* Stanford University Press, Stanford. 1955. Written by the director of the USIA office of research and analysis, this work provides a scholarly review of the American government's experience in developing an overseas information program coordinated with our overall strategic needs.

Schnapper, M. B., editor, *The Facts of American Life,* Public Affairs Press, Washington,

D. C. 1960. A very useful handbook of information assembled by USIA for reference purposes.

Summers, Robert E. (editor), *America's Weapons of Psychological Warfare,* H. W. Wilson Co., New York. 1951. An anthology of official statements, press stories and other comments on the overseas information program during its "Campaign of Truth" phase.

Thomson, C. A. H., *Overseas Information Services of the United States Government,* Brookings Institute, Washington. 1948. This Brookings report was the first scholarly attempt to define the information program and its purposes. Although it is somewhat dated, it remains a useful introduction to American overseas propaganda.

White, Llewellyn and Leigh, Robert D., *Peoples Speaking to Peoples,* University of Chicago Press. 1946. This study, underwritten by the Commission on Freedom of the Press, includes an historical introduction on the development of international communications facilities.

Whyte, William H., *Is Anybody Listening?*, Simon & Shuster, New York. 1952. Although this work deals primarily with the problems American corporations face in communicating with their workers and the general public, it has an excellent chapter on our overseas propaganda efforts, "Have we any friends?" reprinted from the February 1951 issue of *Fortune* magazine.

INDEX

D

E

I

J

K

L

S